MW01264271

DECEPTION BY DESIGN
The Mormon Story

A study of the history and influences upon Mormon
Church founder Joseph Smith, his unfolding
revelations and doctrine, with helpful approaches to
winning Mormons to faith in the biblical Christ.

Allen F. Harrod

Library of Congress Catalog Card Number: 98-92713
ISBN: 1-57502-764-X

Printed in the USA by

MORRIS PUBLISHING

3212 East Highway 30 • Kearney, NE 68847 • 1-800-650-7888

**JUST
FOR
JOYCE**

CONTENTS

PART THREE
EXAMINING THE PHILOSOPHY OF MORMONS

PART FOUR
EXPOSING THE PROBLEMS OF MORMONS

PART FIVE
ESTABLISHING THE PRESENTATION TO MORMONS

PREFACE

This book has been written with several objectives in mind. First, I have sought to present a discerning brief history of Mormonism, refute their doctrinal teachings, discredit their claim to authority as the restored church and show that Joseph Smith was not a true prophet. Secondly, I have tried to address the issues with limited references to non-Mormon sources, commonly referred to by Mormons "as anti-Mormon." Documentation has been mainly from the works of major Mormon writers, particularly their scholars and historians. While the works of some non-Mormon writers have been cited, there has been a determined attempt to steer clear of sensationalism and exaggerated points.

The third objective is evangelism from a scholarly perspective. Always when a work of this type is produced there will be some Mormons who will read it and, as a result, turn from the errors of Mormonism to true faith in Jesus Christ as presented in the Bible. No doubt some will read a book of this nature, who have already been struggling with some of the major questions facing honest Mormons. Others will read it in order to refute its contents. Such a challenge is welcomed. Obviously, most Mormons will not touch any book challenging the truthfulness of their church.

A fourth objective is to help prepare evangelicals to answer the challenge of Mormons at the door, and those who live in the neighborhood and with whom they work. There are a few skillful and knowledgeable writers presenting various aspects of Mormonism. Some are former Mormons. It is believed this work will help address the claims of Mormonism and equip evangelicals with the proper tools for presenting the true gospel.

This book is an attempt to address as many comprehensive areas as possible in one volume. Most of the published references in this work are now in the author's personal library which has been fervently collected for the last ten years at no little expense. Much of the initial study began in major libraries of America until the books could be acquired. Some of the materials are not on the market at any price and some are far too prohibitive to purchase. These have been photocopied.

ACKNOWLEDGMENTS

Every writer is indebted to institutions and individuals for both helpfulness and information. Any current writer on Mormonism is obliged to the many early writers on the subject, both Mormon and non-Mormon. Some of the important facts would have no doubt been lost, had it not been for the myriad of early writers on the subject.

Currently, some of the most careful and fair research is being done by Jerald and Sandra Tanner of Utah Lighthouse Ministry, right in the shadow of the LDS headquarters. Mormon scholars have cited the research of these two former Latter-day Saints. Sandra is the great-great-granddaughter of Brigham Young. They have been patient and helpful to clarify information over the past several years. The Utah Missions, Inc. in Marlowe, Oklahoma, has been extremely helpful in locating references and obtaining information. Maurice Barnett, who has compiled two very helpful volumes on Mormon materials, lent me thirteen valuable microfilms of early and hard to obtain Mormon materials.

The following libraries were very helpful in my research. In the beginning, the Rare Books Department of the Hamilton County Public Library of Cincinnati, Ohio, furnished some important materials. Mr. Jim Lloyd, Director of the George Mark Elliott Library of the Cincinnati Bible Seminary, continually made available their Mormon related materials. The New York City Public Library has many valuable holdings for the researcher of Mormonism. The Utah Historical Society provided by mail photocopies of references to many rare items. Both the Bancroft

Library of Berkeley, California, and the Harold B. Lee Library of the Brigham Young University in Provo, Utah, were patient to provide copies of materials requested. The Missouri State Archives and the Missouri Historical Society supplied copies of important documents of early Mormon history. From the Special Collections and Archives of the Utah State University and the Kansas City Public Library, I obtained additional photocopies of materials. During a stay in London, the British Library endured the many requests for materials, particularly those pertaining to the British section of the Latter-Day Saints. The Library of the Reorganized Church of Jesus Christ of Latter-Day Saints was always courteous and helpful. Mr. Robert O. Rowe, Town Historian for Palmyra, New York, was an immense help in checking some pertinent facts concerning Joseph Smith that appeared in the newspapers during his early years in Palmyra.

Debra Mathis copied onto the word processor the manuscript and made many helpful suggestions. Harley Sykes proofread the manuscript and noted unclear sentences. Rose Mary Hendrix did a superior job fine tuning the manuscript. Thanks to my staff who have endured countless discussions on the particulars of Mormon history and theology. Loving appreciation goes to my wife Joyce who patiently encouraged me through this long undertaking. In final preparation, David Tarkington edited the manuscript and placed it in proper order for printing. Finally, I offer my gratitude to the only true, eternal, unchanging, and sovereign God, who has redeemed me and sustains me through the Son of God and God the Son - Jesus Christ.

INTRODUCTION

The presence of the Mormon church in the world today demands a clear evangelical witness to the historic teachings of the Christian church. If, as they claim, the church became apostate after the death of the twelve apostles of the New Testament and the true gospel has been restored through Joseph Smith to the Church of Jesus Christ of Latter-day Saints, then mankind needs to heed their doctrine. If they are, as one authority describes them, one of the " . . . unorthodox theological systems that were introduced in the New York hinterland between 1800 and 1850. . .," [1] then we need to confront them with the true gospel of Scripture. Certainly, Milton R. Hunter, Mormon writer and member of the first Council of Seventy, was not likely thinking of his own religion when he wrote about occult mystery religions as being pagan rivals of Christianity[2], but the most casual student of Mormonism will recognize that it has elements of both the occult and the mystery religions.

The Church of Jesus Christ of Latter-day Saints claims to be the restored church. They teach that the first-century church had prophets that received revelations from God and a dual priesthood who experienced authority as elders and bishops. They also teach that the church had apostles who ruled over the membership and had a plan of salvation by works, rather than grace.[3]

They further believe as the apostles died out, divinely appointed authority ceased, and the true doctrine was lost. During the years between the first and nineteenth centuries, the church had no divine authority, no divinely approved ministry, and no living prophet.[4] Then in the early part of the nineteenth century the true gospel was restored to the church through revelations given to Joseph Smith, Jr. The idea of a restored gospel was likely carried over into the Mormon philosophy from the Cambellite movement by Sidney Rigdon.

At the death of Joseph Smith, Jr., June 27, 1844, there was a struggle to gain the presidency by several leaders of Mormonism, with Brigham Young emerging as the victor.[5] In 1846 a large group of Mormons, having been ordered by the State of Illinois to vacate Nauvoo, began their difficult trek across the Southwest to the valley of the great Salt Lake. Later this area would become part of the State of Utah. On July 21-24, 1847, the first group numbering 148 Mormons entered the Salt Lake valley with Young. Ten other groups followed at different times that year totaling approximately 1,700. During the winter of 1847-48, 2,500 followed the trail to Utah.[6] Between 1847 and 1887 it has been estimated that 85,220 persons began the journey to Salt Lake basin. Six thousand of them were buried along the trail.[7]

Members of the group who remained behind in the Midwest settled in Missouri to form the "Reorganized Church of Jesus Christ of Latter-Day Saints" (RLDS) in 1852. They were referred to as "Josephites," whereas the Mormons of Utah (LDS) were referred to as "Brighamites."[8] The Reorganized group is today the second largest body of Mormons still in existence. They reject the doctrines of polygamy, the concept of God as an exalted man, polytheism and the belief that man has the potential to become a god. The Reorganized Church of Jesus Christ of Latter-Day Saints claim to be a continuation of the original church organized by Joseph Smith, April 6, 1830. They emphasize the fact that Joseph, in the *Doctrine and Covenants* (Section 43:2c and 27:4c) gave these revelations providing for Apostolic succession. In an effort to avoid being labeled "Mormons," the RLDS adopted the term "Saints' Church,"[9] a term seldom used today. At a conference in Amboy, Illinois on April 6, 1860, Joseph Smith III was elected president of the Reorganized group.

Emma Smith, wife of the prophet, with her four sons refused to follow Brigham Young to the West. She later married Major Lewis Bidamon, a non-Mormon which some considered as a gesture of contempt for the teachings of her late husband. In 1880 a court decision awarded title of the first temple erected in Kirtland, Ohio, to the RLDS on the basis of these revelations and the fact that Joseph Smith III, son of Joseph Smith, was then president. A second court action in 1894 in Missouri named the RLDS as rightful successor and heir of the original church.

The Reorganized Church claims that before his death in 1844, Joseph Smith Jr. appointed his son to succeed him in office as president of the Church. It was generally understood, they further claim, by all the Saints that Joseph III would be his father's successor.[10] At the age of twenty-eight Joseph Smith III reluctantly accepted the position as president of the church continuing until his death in 1914. Three of his sons, in succession, followed him as president of the RLDS church. In 1978 Wallace B. Smith, son of William Wallace Smith, was elected president. Today, W. Grant McMuray holds the office of president.

Steven L. Shields, former missionary in the Republic of Korea for the Utah based LDS, now serves as a member of the Quorum of Seventy at the RLDS headquarters in Independence, Missouri. He has written on the significant similarities and decisive differences between the two major Mormon groups.

Similarities include the fact that both groups have a large choir. The RLDS has the 290 voice "Messiah Choir" and the LDS has the 325 voice "Mormon Tabernacle Choir." Both Mormon groups have an organizational structure somewhat alike, except the president of the RLDS is elected by democratic action rather than automatic appointment on the basis of seniority in the Utah church. Both branches believe that the canon of Scripture is open for additional revelations from their prophets. The RLDS and the LDS recognize Joseph Smith Jr. as the first Prophet/President of their church and the *Book of Mormon* as an inspired book. The idea of a restored church dominates the warp and woof of

Mormon theology in both camps. Tithing is taught by both groups as a means of supporting their work.

Differences include their view of God. The RLDS believes in God the Father, Christ the Only Begotten Son of the Father and the Holy Spirit. Although they may appear Trinitarian, they are rather modalist. The LDS believe in many gods and that the god of this world has a resurrected human body. Accompanying this heavenly human god is a Mother god who shares in the procreation of spirits that take up their residence in earthly human bodies. Brigham Young once taught that Adam was actually God, a teaching refuted by most present day Utah church officials.[11]

The Independence Mormons teach that Joseph Smith had only one wife and never taught polygamy. They claim they have always been monogamists as testified by Emma Smith, wife of the Prophet, a position difficult to defend in light of the facts of history. The Utah Mormons practiced polygamy until a Declaration, promoted by national pressure, in September 24, 1890, declared it against church teachings. The original church has no secret temple ordinances. Everything is done in open worship. The Mormons that migrated to Utah under Brigham Young practice secret ritual in their temples for the elite and more dedicated Mormons, which they maintain is only sacred teachings, yet no one outside these select temple Mormons is allowed inside the temples once they are dedicated. The main headquarters for the Reorganized Church joins the Auditorium in Independence, Missouri. The Independence Church boasts one of the finest pipe organs in the world with an auditorium that seats 5,800. Annually, the "Messiah Choir" performs the "Handel's Oratorio" which is televised throughout the western United States, Canada and some foreign countries.

Mormon historian, Steven Shields, catalogs 216 splinter groups that formed from the original organization established in 1830.[12] Some of these groups died out with their founders. Others persisted into second and third generations and a few merged with other splinter groups. There are at least twenty of these sects still in existence. They were formed around a follower of Smith who usually received additional revelations or saw a need for reform in the church that had, according to their beliefs, become apostate under Brigham Young. These groups, with some variance, usually accepted Joseph Smith as a prophet and the *Book of Mormon* as sacred.[13]

> A Christian authority on Mormonism has written: *Following the death of the prophet, the succeeding presidents supposedly were qualified to receive revelations, but few of them did. Brigham Young experimented with the 'gift', but his attempts seemed not to emanate from the same supernatural source. So he gave up and relied on his own good judgment and hunches. The presidents and prophets of the past several decades have been much more prone to receive their revelations from the spirit of Dow Jones.*[14]

The Church of Jesus Christ of Latter-day Saints recorded in the year ending 1996 that they have almost 9.7 million (9,694,649) worldwide members. Of that number 3,994,988 are in the United States. The Reorganized Church of Independence, Missouri, numbers a worldwide membership as of September 1997, at 249,053, of which 195,511 are in Canada and United States. This book will deal primarily with the LDS of Utah, with limited attention given to the RLDS in Missouri.

The concern of many evangelicals today who view more than one-half million people each year being drawn into the maze of Mormonism is expressed in an article in *Christianity Today* written more than fifteen years ago. Some provocative answers are offered in this article as to "Why Your Neighbor Joined the Mormon Church."[15] Admittedly, the Mormons appear to care for the needs of their people. They seek to maintain the family unit, provide programs for their youth and believe in divine revelations through the prophets. The writer of this article calls the Mormons a "layman's church." If it was ever true, this organization is now anything but a layman's church. It is ruled by an exalted hierarchy with the laity having little, if any, input into the course of faith.

Individual Mormon wards are not autonomous. They do not enjoy the freedom of complete self rule, nor the license to question any teaching of the church and remain in good standing. While there is more liberty now than in the days of Young, the central headquarters in Utah maintains strict control over its members. Aside from the fact that the Saints have been forced to legally concede their previous positions on polygamy, the place of blacks in their church, and rescind the blood oaths, they affirm their autocratic administration of the Saints. The dramatic presentation of a preacher being in league with Satan in their secret temple ritual has also been deleted. The church today remains as strong in its attempt to present itself as the only true church on earth, thus aggressively proselyting and controlling adherence to their doctrine.[16] Members are discouraged from reading any material critical of the Church or associating with apostates. Those suspected or who reveal their doubts will not likely get a temple recommend, which admits them to the secret temple rituals which they believe will ultimately lead them to godhood.

The Mormons may be respected for their philosophical emphasis upon family life, their advances in missions, and the care of their indigent, yet they are by definition a heretical cult. J.K. Van Baalam succinctly summons us to evangelical witness:

> *Since, however, Christianity is supposed to be a salt-retarding corruption, a leaven that permeates, and a light that shines in darkness, and since only the Christ according to the Scriptures is the Light of the World, Mormonism must stand condemned . . . it is guilty of the two cardinal sins of our time: first, it identifies the Kingdom of God with a here and now social utopia, and secondly, it fosters the essentially pagan idea that salvation is by works rather than by grace.*[17]

PART ONE

INTRODUCING THE PROPHET OF MORMONS

"Mormonism...must stand or fall on the story of Joseph Smith. He was either a prophet of God, divinely called, properly appointed and commissioned, or he is one of the biggest frauds this world has ever seen. There is no middle ground. If Joseph was a deceiver, who willfully attempted to mislead the people, then he should be exposed; his claims should be refuted, and his doctrines shown to be false."

Joseph Fielding Smith
Doctrines of Salvation
Volume 1, page 188

Chapter One
A PROPHET IN PALMYRA

A s the smoke spiraled upward into the cold Vermont sky, a baby's cry could be heard from within the poor and dimly lit Smith home. Joseph Smith, Jr. was born on December 23, 1805 in Sharon, (Windsor County) Vermont,[1] He was the third son and fourth child of Joseph and Lucy Mack Smith. In 1816, when Joseph was twelve, the family settled in an area later to become known as Manchester, near Palmyra, New York.[2] He was reared in a family of limited means, little education, and a climate of superstition, particular to the times.

According to New England genealogical records, Joseph Smith, Jr. had a rather illustrious ancestry. His first paternal ancestor that can be discovered was Robert Smith, his great-great-grandfather. Robert was an English Puritan who arrived in America in 1638. Joseph's great-grandfather was Samuel Smith, a gentleman and a representative of the Massachusetts General Court. Asahel Smith, grandfather to the founder of Mormonism, was a captain of the Minute Men who responded to the Lexington alarm and then went to the siege of Boston.[3] Yet history is replete with facts that an illustrious ancestry does not a gentleman make.

Joseph's maternal grandfather was Solomon Mack, who claimed to have experienced divine visitations from heaven. When he was seventy-eight years of age, the accounts of his visions were published in a little book which he peddled to friends, neighbors and anyone who would buy them.[4] He was an infirm man who had to ride sidesaddle on his treks to sell his book.[5] Solomon

Mack was the grandson of John Mack, born in a line of clergy, from Inverness, Scotland, who settled in Salisbury, Massachusetts. Joseph's grandfather Mack was born in Connecticut in 1732. In his journal, Solomon laments that he was never given religious training and little education as a child. This he claims brought him much difficulty in later life.[6]

Lucy Mack Smith, the mother of Joseph Smith, Jr., was ambitious, though limited in formal education. Her religious background seemed to be a reaction to Puritanism of the day. She was highly mystical and spoke with God as if He were an intimate friend invading dreams and providing an abundance of miracles. She has been described in her thinking as "simply the core of Antinomianism—the inner life is a law unto itself; freedom and integrity of religious experience must at all costs be preserved."[7]

Mother Smith was the most enterprising member of the family. In those early years in Palmyra she opened a "cake and beer" shop. It was largely on her labors that the family was sustained. Gingerbread, root beer, pies, boiled eggs and like items were produced in her impoverished home. Joseph, Sr., often peddled these items in the streets by means of a crude handcart.[8]

If Lucy was ambitious, she was at the same time fallacious. In the houses of the village she did family washes. If clothes remained on the line near midnight, they were frequently snatched away by the "washer who was often the winner," assisted by her shiftless sons. According to a lifelong resident and observer of the Smith family, they also had a notorious name for claiming other items from the farmyard.[9]

Two additional characteristics may be identified with Lucy Smith. These are the twin traits of prevarication and superstition. People who knew her said she would stare a listener straight in the eye and weave the wildest kind of tale. When questioned she would go on undaunted, defending her exaggerated statements without shame. It was a trait that would be handed down to her son Joseph.

Along with this attribute, she passed along to her favorite son, Joseph, an immense endowment for superstition. Given to

4

dreams and visions, she often took up the gift of prophecy while living at Turnbridge before moving to Royalton, Vermont. She returned one night from a Methodist meeting, somewhat depressed, to hear her husband declare that he would not attend again with her because of criticism from his father and brother. That night Lucy dreamed of two trees beside a stream, one of which was vibrant and bright. The other tree was inactive and dull. She immediately interpreted the first tree to be her husband who would come to true faith and the other to be Jesse, her husband's brother, who would die in darkness.[10]

Lucy Mack would be known to have other dreams and visions. These divine revelations would be sold to those gullible souls seeking to know the future. For several years she announced that a seer would be born to her family.[11] She had expected that her eldest son Alvin would be the fulfillment of her dreams but when he died unexpectedly, the mantle fell on Joseph.[12]

Little can be said of Joseph, Sr., for little has been written about him. Limited in educational advantages, he seems to have had little determination to excel at anything except fathering children. Joseph, Sr. was enamored with treasure digging and was jailed on at least one occasion for debts incurred. He has been described by the gifted Mormon historian Dale Morgan—as having "no liking for the axe and little more for the plow, and was not the man to immune himself in a lonesome clearing at the outer reaches of civilization."[13] In an affidavit signed by several prominent citizens of Manchester, New York, on Nov.3, 1833, the Smith men were described as lazy, indolent, intemperate, destitute of moral character and addicted to vicious habits.[14]

There were six boys: Alvin, Hyrum, Joseph Jr., Samuel Harrison, William, Don Carlos, and three girls: Sophronia, Catherine and Lucy in the Smith family. Eight years after arriving in the Palmyra area, Alvin became sick at twenty-seven years old and died suddenly. Very little is known concerning daughters in the family. Other than a listing of their names in the Smith bibliography, they seemed to have never had any interest in the religion of their Prophet brother. Hyrum became the most blindly devoted to his brother Joseph and in many ways possibly the most stable of the family. However, his life was too short to judge completely in the matter. Hyrum was appointed Second Counselor to Joseph along with first counselor Sidney Rigdon while the Mormon Church was still in Kirtland, two years before the first temple was built there.

Early on in the history of the church, Joseph lavished appointments freely upon his family. His father was made a patriarch of the church. Don Carlos, before reaching manhood, was made head of the high priests. He would later oppose Joseph on the matter of polygamy. Samuel Harrison headed up the publishing work. Stormy days in the life of this infant Mormon organization began when William, in a dispute with Joseph, knocked him down and proceeded to give him a thrashing until pulled off by Hyrum. Later he offered a resentful confession and was reinstated to the good graces of his brother.[15]

Next, Samuel Harrison, one of the eight witnesses who claimed to have seen the golden plates from which the *Book of Mormon* was translated, later turned against Joseph under the poisoning influence of William. Don Carlos passively followed his brother faithfully until his untimely death due to an epidemic that struck Nauvoo.

Joseph, the fourth of nine children, and the victim of a family that often moved, acquired little formal training. Born into insecurity, he was, until his death at thirty-nine, an unsettled spirit. His family moved twice before Joseph was ten years of age.

Five years after the Smith family moved from Vermont to Palmyra, New York (young Joseph was fifteen at the time), four members of the family joined the Presbyterian faith: mother Lucy, two brothers, Hyrum and Samuel Harrison and sister, Sophronia. Joseph Jr. remained undecided. Joseph wrote much later that he was so disturbed by the confusion and strife between denominations that he was unable to come to a conclusion as to who was right and who was wrong.[16] It was this mind-set that prepared the stage for Smith's first vision.

Sociologically, there were many influences upon Joseph. The beginning of the 1800's was ripe for revival. Spiritual decline in the churches was evident everywhere. The infidelity of Tom Paine spread like a wildfire across the country. Colleges and universities became the centers of both Theism and infidelity. Infidel clubs sprang up across the nation. Revival broke out in New England, sweeping the colleges of Yale, Princeton and Williams. In 1810, when Smith was five years old, the "haystack prayer meetings" occurred. The American Board of Missions was instituted in the same year. During the 1820's the Second Great Awakening touched the western area of New York. The area was flooded with itinerant preachers, Bibles, tracts, and Christian periodicals.[17] It was in this time of revival (around 1824) that Joseph Smith claimed to have his first divine vision in the woods. At least two different accounts of this incident, written eighteen years later, conflict regarding Smith's age. This will be discussed in more detail under Smith's first vision.

Not only were the 1800's ripe for revival, but these years gave rise to several major cultic movements. In 1817 at the impressionable age of twelve, Smith met Isaac Bullard, an eccentric itinerant preacher who came through Vermont wearing nothing but a bearskin girdle. He viewed bathing as a sin and bragged that he had not changed clothes for seven years.[18] Leading his sixty "Pilgrims," Bullard headed west from New York, through Cincinnati and down to Arkansas where he died leaving his followers scattered.[19]

Thirty miles from the Smith farm in Palmyra, the Shakers would build a community hall. Ann Lee, born in 1736, founder of the Shakers came from Liverpool, England to the state of New York in 1774, just two years before the Continental Congress met in Philadelphia. She became known as "Mother Lee" to her followers and viewed herself as the reincarnated Christ.[20] Her followers believed she spoke seventy-two different tongues which were unintelligible to those who heard them and that she was able to converse with the dead. Many of their songs were written in the form of tongues. Ten years later she gave up her earthly journey at the age of forty-eight. The mantle then fell on two men and a woman as leaders of the "believers." Under their leadership the Shakers moved to Pleasant Hill, near Harrodsburg, Kentucky, and flourished for awhile.[21]

It is possible young Joseph attended some of the Shakers' gatherings. Joseph may have observed the dancing participants falling out in a wild frenzy, and speaking incoherent gibberish, which we know today as "tongues." Certainly, he could have read about this practice as it was described in one of the local papers in Palmyra.[22] Brigham Young (the famous Mormon leader who rose to power after Smith's death) would break out in tongues upon first meeting Joseph Smith, Jr. In order to give credence to his new religion, Smith would encourage this gift as a validating sign of authenticity. The gift of tongues was encouraged in an interesting way. A meeting would be called and Smith or Rigdon would call upon someone to speak in tongues. At a Council meeting in Kirtland, a hymn was "sung in tongues" by W.W. Phelps and interpreted by Lyman Wright.[23] At the Dedication of the Temple at Kirtland, Joseph prayed that the "gift of tongues be poured out upon thy people, even cloven tongues as of fire, and the interpretation thereof."[24] There is no evidence, however, that this prayer was answered in that dedication service. Later, tongues would become a problem in excess. People would begin to fall on the floor, wallow and roll, point to the air imagining they were seeing the saints of heaven, and running out the front door in a swoon. This gave Joseph concern because now the laymen began also to imitate his gift as seer. Therefore, after cautioning them to moderation, he finally condemned their practices as coming from the devil.[25] The teaching of tongues is presently a doctrine in the Mormon Church. Yet today, few members of the Saints either practice or have observed this "gift."[26]

Of interest is the fact that Martin Harris joined the Shakers after becoming a Mormon.[27] Both the Shakers and the Mormons believe in revelations and visions from God. Numerous Shakers occasionally gave testimony to *A Holy Sacred and Divine Roll and Book: From the Lord God of Heaven, to the Inhabitants of*

Earth. Many of them testified to having seen an angel appear with the book. Although this book was never written down and printed as was the *Book of Mormon*, there are strange similarities with the angel and a book of revelations.

There is another teaching of the Shakers that lead us to believe that Smith may have copied some of their views. They observed a prohibition against the use of coffee, tea, tobacco, and liquor.[28] On February 27, 1833, Joseph Smith gave a revelation known as the *Word of Wisdom*, forbidding the use of these same items.[29] Cola drinks are also seen as a "violation of the spirit of the *Word of Wisdom*."[30] These similarities are too obvious to be insignificant in the new religion of Joseph Smith.

Not more than twenty-five miles in another direction, Jemima Wilkinson, a Quaker, also claimed to be Christ—the "Universal Friend." She proclaimed that she would live forever and lead her group by revelations from heaven. After recovering from a thirty-six-hour trance, she announced that she had been infused with a new spirit. This new spirit then took over her body. A humorous legend attends Wilkinson's controversial history. Attired in her flamboyant robes, she stood before a body of water and appealed to the faith of her onlookers. "Do you have faith? Do you believe I can do this thing?" A chorus of voices affirmed their faith in her ability to walk on water. With a fling of her robes, she said departing, "If ye have faith ye need no other evidence."[31] Her community on Seneca Lake, New York was communal and practiced celibacy as did the Shakers under Lee. The trait of communal living and leading by divine revelations can be found among the first Mormons. They did not, however, adopt the idea of celibacy.

Joseph's Uncle Jason, eldest brother of his mother Lucy, joined the "Seekers" which held, as did the Mormons, that the contemporary Church had become corrupt, the Scriptures were defective, and the faithful could be validated through the Apostolic gifts.[32]

During this same period, the Seventh Day Adventists were organized out of the preaching of William Miller, a farmer by trade. Though limited in education, he was a sincere student of the Bible who believed the Lord would come back to earth during his lifetime. Initially he predicted the second coming of Christ in 1844 and later adjusted his forecast date to 1845. Miller himself, became disillusioned after these successive predictions failed. Although he misinterpreted Daniel 8:14 the "two thousand and three hundred evenings and mornings" to refer to the time preceding the coming of Christ rather than the time that follows His coming, he was sincere in his predictions. Although the Adventists must trace their founding to William Miller, he would not, if living today, likely agree with many of their present doctrinal beliefs.[33]

Joseph Smith, Jr. in 1835, during the time that Miller was predicting the coming of Christ for 1844, prophesied the return of the Lord at the ordination service of the twelve apostles in his new church. He declared that the world scene would be completed within fifty-six years.[34]

Previously, in 1832 at Kirtland, Smith had given a revelation of the "gathering of the Saints to stand upon Mt. Zion...in the western boundaries of the state of Missouri...the city of the New Jerusalem...which temple shall be raised in this generation."[35] Not only did the Lord not return to Independence, Missouri but neither was a temple reared by the Saints there in Smith's lifetime.

There is yet another possible influence upon Smith. Although not a contemporary of Smith, Emmanuel Swedenborg may have influenced him through his writings. They certainly held some of the same views. Swedenborg considered himself a seer of new revelations from God, which transcended the revelations given to the early church fathers and the reformers. He claimed conversation with spirit beings, interpreted his dreams and boasted of visions of eternal things. Modesty was not a strong point of his character. Swedenborg, like Smith, could describe the celestial world in minute detail. The billing records of the *Reflector*, a local Palmyra newspaper, reveal that the Smith family was subscribers. The paper carried an article on the beliefs and the man Emmanuel Swedenborg.[36] Anyone familiar with the teachings of the Mormons will quickly recognize some of the same ideas in Swedenborg. Smith was a borrower of many sources in developing his doctrine of Mormonism.

Sometime before 1826 when Joseph was first arrested for treasure hunting, a man known only by the last name of Walters hit Palmyra like a firestorm with his pretended ability to discover buried treasure by use of crystals and other paraphernalia. Pomeroy Tucker describes a "mysterious stranger" who appeared at the Smith home and lists a Luman Walters of Pultneyville, New York, among the original Mormon followers.[37] However, the Palmyra *Reflector* names Walters as being from Sodus, New York. There is a good possibility that this is one and the same person who lived in both towns at different times. The article typed him as "Walters the Magician" and a dealer with "familiar spirits" using such instruments of witchcraft as a "stuffed toad." He was a hard looking man of pronounced ignorance and extreme imprudence even for a charlatan. While Walters was leading charades of discovering lost treasure, he quoted loud and long in Latin from a copy of *Cicero's Orations* combined with some form of garbled words which he claimed to interpret. The translation usually had to do with some prior inhabitants of America who had buried treasure before their death.

All this was done with the aid of a stuffed toad frog, an old sword and some type of seer stone. Occasionally he would sacrifice a barnyard fowl to ward off evil spirits. He claimed these evil spirits hindered his ability to find buried treasure. Needless to say, as the digging crew trudged home, they left the spot of supposed treasure empty-handed. The story continues in a later issue of the Palmyra *Reflector* by concluding that, when Walters moved on, his mantle was passed on to Joseph Smith, Jr.[38] Joseph picked up where Walters left off applying many of the occult gimmicks in his own treasure hunting campaigns. All of these seem strangely familiar to the discerning student of early Mormonism.

Before his untimely death in November of 1990, Rev.

11

Wesley P. Walters, not related to the former Walters, a Presbyterian Minister and respected researcher of early Mormon history, discovered one of the most significant finds in the study of Mormonism. It established the arrest of Joseph Smith for money digging practices, long denied by Mormon scholars. Stored in a musty basement were two bills, among hundreds of others, that documented Joseph's early activity as a treasure hunter by use of a seer stone. The documents discovered among the 1826 Chenango County items named the two arresting officers at Bainbridge, New York and the judge who tried Smith.

Justice Albert Neely's bill defines the charge as "glass looker" thus linking Joseph, prior to founding the Mormon religion, to occult practices. Present at the trial was Dr. William D. Purple, a friend of Justice Neely who took copious notes. Later Dr. Purple committed the story to print in the local newspaper.

The account of Smith's arrest was confirmed by the original court records of Judge Neely which were torn from the docket book by a Miss Emily Pearsall, niece of the Judge. Miss Pearsall carried these records with her to Utah where she served as a Methodist missionary until her death in 1872. The records were subsequently printed in an British magazine by Gordon H. Fraser and in an article of the American encyclopedia-*The New Schaff-Herzog*.[39]

On July 1, 1830, just three months after Joseph organized his new church, he was arrested a second time and tried at Bainbridge under Judge Joseph Chamberlain. Smith's account of the trial in his *History of the Church* deviate from the actual court records.[40] Young Smith had been working for Josiah Stowell and began to tell him of his ability to find buried treasure by the use of a peep stone. In the court testimony Smith admitted that he had pretended to have this ability for three years. Lucy Mack Smith, mother of the seer, confirms with limited facts that Joseph worked for Stowell.[41]

David Whitmer, one of the original six members of the church and a witness to the *Book of Mormon*, refers to Smith's

12

practice of looking into a hat at a stone to translate the golden plates and receiving revelations.[42] That Joseph was a "glass looker" at this time is authenticated by Isaac Hale, in a newspaper article where he states that his son-in-law had given up "glass looking" to pursue an honest living.[43]

In the 1826 case, Smith, due to his youth, was allowed to escape on his own. In the 1830 case, at the age of twenty-five he was charged as "a disorderly person" in relation to his activity as a "glass looker."

Although vigorously denied in this century by Mormon historians and scholars as "spurious and alleged," the evidence speaks for itself. Regardless how energetic the denial and how intensely the embarrassment to Mormon writers, the use of the "seer stone" is closely attached to the occult practice of crystal gazing. The original stone is now in the possession of the LDS Church headquartered in Utah.

Dr. Reed Durham, president of the Mormon History Association, and Professor of Religion at the University of Utah, delivered a lecture to the Mormon History Association on April 20, 1974 that shook the very foundations of Mormonism. Dr. Durham discovered, and subsequently shared with the Association, that a coin-like medallion, about the size of a silver dollar, that had been regarded as a "Masonic jewel" belonging to Joseph Smith, and reported to have been on him at the time of his death, is in reality a "Jupiter talisman." The talisman was purchased by Wilford C. Wood from a descendant of Emma Smith Bidamon, widow of the Prophet who later married non-Mormon Major Lewis Bidamon.

A talisman is an object engraved with astrological signs believed to have possessed power to avert evil and bring good luck. Such pieces are clearly identified with occult magic.

The lecture called down the wrath of then church President Spencer W. Kimball upon Dr. Durham. It became such a heated matter that Dr. Durham was forced to write a letter of apology and ratify his confidence in the Prophet Joseph Smith in order to retain his church membership. Yet, what was discovered by the

13

research of this Utah university professor remains an undisputed fact. He was rebuffed for telling the truth that revealed that Joseph Smith was into occult magic right up until his death.[44]

A Mormon scholar, graduate in history with honors from Yale University, has meticulously documented that Joseph Smith was indeed influenced by his culture, particularly by his immediate family while growing up. Use of such items as "divining rods" used for treasure digging and "seer stones" for interpreting information were known devices in the culture and place where Joseph grew up. Joseph Smith, Sr. was steeped in witchcraft. David Whitmer, emulating the Prophet, also used a "seer stone." So did Hiram Page, both of which claimed to be witnesses of the golden plates from which Joseph Smith is said to have translated the *Book of Mormon*. It has long been known that the "sunstone" used to cap off the temple in Nauvoo, Illinois, now property of the Quincy, Illinois Historical Society, is an occult astrological symbol. Heber C. Kimball, First Counselor to Brigham Young had a cane made from the coffin of Joseph Smith with which he sought to heal the sick.[45] The Bible strictly forbids the use of such items (Deuteronomy 18:9-12; Leviticus 19:26; Jeremiah 27:9).

Chapter Two
INFLUENCES ON JOSEPH SMITH

Historically, one of the burning questions of the early nineteenth century concerned the American Indians arrival to the North American continent. Where did they come from and how did they get here? Smith and his early associates were no doubt influenced by the theory of the day that the American Indians were descendants of the Jewish people who came to North America by water or land. The *Book of Mormon* is based upon a theme of Jewish people who migrated to America on large boats.

The first two migrations are the most notable in the *Book of Mormon.* Sometime before 2000 BC a group of Jews migrated after the failed attempt to build the Tower of Babel.[46] What Smith did in his *Book of Mormon* was to place these Jews, at a time before the Jewish race actually began. The Jewish people trace their beginning to the prophet Abraham. The most conservative estimate for dating Abraham is 2100 BC. According to Smith, a second migratory group came in 600 BC.[47] A little known migration took place shortly after that of the Nephites of 600 BC by Mulek, whom the *Book of Mormon* claims was the son of King Zedekiah of Judah (Helaman 8:21).

Since the early days of the colonists, in the seventeenth century, the idea that the American Indians were descendants of the Lost Tribes of Israel was not only very popular but also highly propagated. By the time of Joseph Smith, Jr., several books supporting this theory were available. It was a very common view held by many people of Smith's time. Smith's mother recounts in her biography how he would break into a lengthy and detailed account of the ancient inhabitants of this continent, keeping them all spellbound around the evening fire.[48] A Prominent novel entitled *View of the Hebrews* written by Ethan Smith of Poultney, Vermont, publicized the thesis that the Indians migrated to this continent from Israel. Joseph Smith, until around ten years old, lived in Windsor, the adjoining county to Poultney. Oliver Cowdery, a cousin to Joseph Smith who later lived in the Smith home at Palmyra, grew up in Poultney.

B.H. Roberts, prominent Church Historian and General Authority of the LDS toward the end of his life made a scholarly study of the comparison between the *Book of Mormon* and *View of the Hebrews*, concluding that the first source of Mormonism had an earthly author rather than an angelic one. He also concluded that it was very likely that the Smith family obtained a later copy of *View of the Hebrews*. While they lived in Wayne County, New York, he believed the contents were read and discussed in their home, several years before the publication of the *Book of Mormon*.[49]

The theory of the novelist became the revealed truth in the Mormon Bible. As Smith was so apt to do, he borrowed a popular speculation and wove it into his book. Alexander Campbell, with whom Sidney Rigdon was associated in the beginning of the Disciples of Christ Church, was one of the earliest reviewers of the Smith publication. He declared in his critique that Smith had rehearsed part and parcel of almost every philosophy en vogue on the contemporary scene during the early 1800's.[50] Obviously, the American Indians would have to be Semites in order to be descendants of the Jews, which they are not. The most plausible suggestion from contemporary anthropologists today is that the ancient Indians came across the Bering Strait to America. The American Indian is Mongoloid, has the physical type much like the people of Asia,[51] which remains an embarrassing problem in the first source of Mormonism. Mormon writers have tried to accommodate this fact by suggesting that

16

there were other peoples who migrated to this continent along with Lehi and his Jewish family.

Psychologically, an understanding of Joseph Smith's personality is limited since psychology was a relatively unknown field during his lifetime. Sigmund Freud was not born until 1856. To impose clinical definitions of today on a man that lived more than 150 years ago is of little advantage. Yet, a review of his actions may reveal something of the personality of the man.

Smith was without question a complex personality. His inability to handle opposition is easy to examine since he left numerous accounts in his revelations and history. Once he had become drunk with power, he issued numerous excommunications from the church upon those that criticized or disagreed with him. The writings of Joseph carried repeated condemnation of his enemies especially during the Kirtland years.[52] Is it not true that the way one handles opposition reflects something of his own self-confidence? Although occasionally bolstered by intermittent success, he seemed to be haunted by self-doubt until his death. An examination of his actions and words as recorded in his own writings and his peers, reveal certain clear personality traits unbecoming anyone claiming to be a man of God. One trait that can be traced from his youth is that of egotism. He seemed always to have been marked by conceit. He bragged on his appearance noting that people perceived him as handsome. He boasted of his ability as a leader. In an address against the dissenters of Nauvoo, while aboard the steamer "Maid of Iowa," he unabashedly stated that he had "more to boast of than ever any man had. I am the only man that has ever been able to keep a whole church together since the days of Adam . . . Neither Paul, John, Peter, nor Jesus ever did it. I boast that no man ever did such a work as I. The followers of Jesus ran away from Him; but the Latter-day Saints never ran away from me yet.[53]"

A letter written from Charlotte Haven, a resident of Nauvoo, described Smith further:

He is evidently a great egotist and boaster, for he

frequently remarked that at every place he
stopped going to and from Springfield people
crowded around him, and expressed surprise that
he was so 'handsome and good looking'.[54]

Another character trait found in Smith is that of violence. Among the qualifications given in the Bible for a minister of God is that he must not be a "striker" nor a "brawler" (1 Timothy 3:3). Two of the many incidents recorded in *The History of the Church* may illustrate the point. Smith proudly claims he "kicked" Josiah Butterfield out of his "house, across the yard, and into the street." In another incident Smith was "so enraged" by being called a liar by a man named Bagby that he "followed him a few steps, and struck him two or three times."[55]

Smith often boasted of his ability at wrestling. One can only wonder why a man claiming to be a man of God found it necessary to establish his physical prowess. It appears that while he may have been strong physically, nevertheless he chose his opponents carefully. He has been described as six feet tall, weighing about 180 pounds,[56] stout in appearance with recessed searching blue eyes and round-shouldered. His complexion was smooth, lips thin, below a Roman type nose which he inherited from his mother Lucy Mack. His thick brown hair sloped back across his head covering a high forehead.[57]

A passenger who boarded a steamship owned by the Nauvoo Saints at Fulton City, Illinois, gave his observation of Smith. There were those on board who criticized the Prophet which was conveyed to him by his spies. Seizing the opportunity he proclaimed himself to be a "discerner of spirits" and proceeded to browbeat those who criticized him and refused to acknowledge him as a Prophet.[58]

Some writers have charged Smith with being mentally unstable. Others have suggested that he was an imprudent counterfeit. He may have been a conscious imposter who, in spite of his brazen disposition, never expected to be a successful leader. There seems to be some of all these elements revealed in his brief life. He was not satisfied to be named President and Prophet of the Church; he also had himself appointed Lieutenant-General of the Nauvoo Legion and additionally had himself crowned King. He constantly took to himself titles to bolster his ego. Just before his death he announced himself as candidate for president of the United States, sending out church officials all over the country to campaign for him.

The earliest psychological study of Joseph Smith was done by I. Woodbridge Riley at the turn of the century. Riley compared the opposing opinions of Smith: "To sectarians Joseph Smith appears an ignoramus, a fanatic, an imposter, and a libertine; to his followers—a prophet, a seer, a vicegerent of God, and a martyr." He concluded that Smith acquired his visions from epileptic seizures giving way to occult practices, faith healing and demonic exorcisms. It must be remembered that Riley wrote when psychology had reached its heyday.[59]

His eminent Mormon biographer Fawn Brodie raises what is perhaps the most intense and searching question concerning Smith. Was young Smith suppressing an unholy impulse as he worked out the first religious text of Mormonism? Later, as he grew in power, he privately endorsed the teachings of plural marriages while publicly denying that which would become the hallmark of early Mormonism. The inner struggle of his life is noted:

> *The Book of Mormon thus provides tantalizing clues to the conflicts raging within Joseph Smith as to the truth or spuriousness of his magic powers and his visionary claims. But it serves only to suggest the intensity of conflict, not to explain it. Why was this gifted young man compelled to transform his dreams into visions, to insist that his literary fantasies were authentic history engraved upon golden plates, to hold stoutly that the hieroglyphics on the Egyptian papyri he bought from Michael Chandler were*

actually words of the patriarch Abraham? Why did he feel compelled to resort to such obviously transparent devices as to write into both his Book of Mormon and his corrected version of the Bible prophecies of his own coming?[60]

Educationally, the fact that the prophet of Mormonism was limited is readily admitted, if not relished, by the Mormons. They accept it as a badge of authentication to his prophetic position. Orson Pratt, his able apologist, in a pamphlet described his ability to "read without much difficulty, and write a very imperfect hand" with little understanding of the basics of arithmetic.[61]

Although Smith had little formal education, he was not without ability. The landscape of history is dotted with individuals that lacked in academic excellence yet excelled in leadership. For example, Napoleon graduated low in his class at the military academy and Lincoln was virtually a self taught man. What Joseph lacked in education, he made up in assimilation, possessing a keen discernment of leadership in others. He later recognized that some of his leaders served as a threat to his own leadership. When this happened, he conveniently conveyed a revelation that sent them off on some mission or project. Martin Harris, insisting on proof of the plates, was sent to New York with a piece of paper bearing strange symbols to be authenticated. Oliver Cowdery and Hiram Page were sent to Canada, during the pressure to get the *Book of Mormon* printed, under revelation that they would copyright it there. Their trip ended in failure creating questions in the minds of the early leaders as to his prophetic ability.[62] Joseph's lack of prophetic skills was offset by his creative supplemental revelations. He admitted that some revelations came from God, others from man and a few from the devil.

In the beginning of the Mormon movement, Rigdon was given to excess in spiritual gifts. The prophet soon saw these gifts in conflict with his position as revelator. So Rigdon among other principal elders was sent west on preaching missions in search of

20

the New Jerusalem. This resulted in the establishment of Independence, Missouri as the "Land of Zion," the central point of all activity. All other works established were called stakes as an extension of Independence. True, Joseph had limited academic credentials, but he did excel in elocution. Even his critics granted him that. Pomeroy Tucker, who scathingly described Joseph in his early years an "indolent," "prevaricating" and "vagabondish" acknowledged that he evidenced rapid development of thinking on his feet and bequeathed to him a flair for uttering "the most palpable exaggeration or marvelous absurdity with the utmost apparent gravity."[63] Though unpolished in eloquence, he commanded the capacity to communicate, often weaving some humorous statement into his talk and punctuating it with graphic descriptions furnished by his lively imagination. Once when required to perform a miracle by a prospective convert, he mockingly inquired of his solicitor what he would like to see happen to him as an evidence of the prophet's power. Smith asked if he should call upon the Lord to paralyze or strike him blind. When the inquirer challenged his suggestion, Smith answered with contempt that he wasn't going to ask the Lord to strike someone else with a malady just to convince him of his powers.[64]

On the young American scene, mainline denominations contended for the truthfulness of their particular Christian doctrines. The Methodist, Presbyterian, and Baptist denominations flourished in Palmyra during the early 1800's. At this same time the Disciples of Christ were started by Alexander Campbell. Campbell rejected the idea of modern revelation, holding only to the Bible as the source of authority. He opposed the idea of creeds, which he adopted from the Baptists, after leaving the Presbyterians. Early in the Campbellite movement Walter Scott popularized the term "restoration," coined by Campbell, by which he meant the recovery of the New Testament pattern and practices and claimed the Disciples as the restored church.[65]

Sidney Rigdon, undoubtedly the most eloquent if not the

most eccentric of the early Mormon leaders, had joined the Baptists at the age of twenty-four in his hometown of Library, Pennsylvania. As a young boy he was injured while riding a horse which threw him off, dragging him for some distance. His brother, Dr. Loammi Rigdon, a physician, credited his often eccentric behavior as a boy to the blow sustained by the fall from the horse. While retaining his mental abilities he was known to be inclined to extreme visionary views on many subjects.[66] Two years after he joined the Baptist church he was ordained to the ministry and at the age of twenty-nine became pastor of the First Baptist Church of Pittsburgh. The year following his installation as pastor (1824) he was relieved of church duties and membership for teaching heretical views.[67]

Before joining Campbell, in that same year (1824) Rigdon, with the help of a young school teacher by the name of Walter Scott, established a reformed Baptist Church at Pittsburgh, Pennsylvania. In 1826, Rigdon accepted an invitation from the Mentor Baptist Church, near Cleveland, Ohio, to preach for them. They were so impressed with him that they extended a call to be their pastor. Alexander Campbell pastored a church affiliated with the same Mahoning Baptist Association. Shortly after accepting the call to Mentor Baptist Church, Rigdon led them to follow the teaching of Campbell to seek "restoration of the ancient order of things."[68]

Campbell, like Rigdon, had been a Regular Baptist but separated from them because of his views on baptism, believing the ordinance to be essential to the salvation of an individual. The Baptists held that baptism, while important to obedience, did not save but rather was emblematic or symbolic of salvation.

In 1830 Rigdon fell out with Campbell over several issues. The idea of communal living, a concept that all property was to be held in common, was introduced by Rigdon to his congregation in the Mahoning Baptist Association before joining Mormonism and later incorporated into Smith's church at Kirtland. Rigdon also took issue with Campbell over the teaching of "Spiritual Gifts," such as speaking in tongues, healing by the laying on of hands, discernment of wicked spirits, and the reception of visions. He maintained that in order to be restored to the early church dispensation, the church would by necessity have to observe these gifts of the Spirit. Campbell held that the gifts ceased after the Apostolic age.[69] The powerful Campbell, who commanded leadership over the Association, attacked Rigdon's ideas as heretical, driving him from it.

Parley Parker Pratt, also a Campbellite preacher, had heard about Smith's book while on his way to New York City. Detouring by the Smith home, he met Hyrum, Joseph's brother, who presented him a copy of the new publication. A few days after his appointment, Pratt returned and requested baptism by Hyrum. Later, he brought his brother Orson into the new church.[70] Pratt, along with Rigdon, became important influences upon Joseph Smith. Mormonism cannot be understood as a religion apart from these major personalities that became a part of the early life of the church and influenced Joseph Smith.

Carried over into Mormonism from Campbellism by Rigdon was the restoration idea that became the driving force to Smith's new church. Leonard J. Arrington and Davis Bitton, both Mormon scholars, acknowledge the influence of the restoration teaching of Campbell upon the early Saints.[71]

Following a dispensational view of revelation, Milton R. Hunter wrote,

> *It is evident from scriptures that the dispensation of the Gospel in the latter days is to be one of restoration and restitution... The Prophet Joseph Smith not only received the keys of the Priesthood from those in authority who held them last in each of the Gospel dispensations, but he also was given revelation upon revelation explaining the various principles and ordinances of the Gospel. Through this American Prophet, Jesus Christ again established His Church upon the earth and endowed it with all the power requisite for the*

salvation of the human family...Therefore, the Church of Jesus Christ of Latter-day Saints is the only organization in the world which is officially recognized by God as having the power, authority, ordinances and doctrine requisite to bring men back into the presence of the Eternal Father and the Only Begotten Son and to exalt them with a glorious eternal life. [72]

Rigdon has been called "Smith's theologian."[73] John Hyde, who left the Mormon Church at Utah because of the inconsistencies he observed in the life of Brigham Young, identified Rigdon as the true source of Mormon teaching. "The compiling genius of Mormonism was Sidney Rigdon. Smith had boisterous impetuosity, but no foresight. Polygamy was not the result of his policy, but of his passions. Sidney gave point, direction, and apparent consistency to the Mormon system of theology. He invented the forms and many of its arguments."[74] It is believed by many that Sidney, rather than Joseph, wrote the "Lectures on Faith," which prefaced the early *Doctrine and Covenants*. The doctrine of a three-storied heaven was declared by Smith on February 16, 1832. In this revelation concerning the state of the redeemed after the resurrection almost everyone is saved.[75] Rigdon is named by Smith as assisting him in the development of this revelation based partially on I Corinthians 15:40.[76] In this text from the Bible the Apostle Paul spoke of "celestial bodies" and "bodies terrestrial" (KJV). The pair coined an additional word "telestial" to describe what they called a third "kingdom." Specific discussion will be given to the exact meaning of this passage in Chapter Four on doctrine.

David Whitmer, who later withdrew from the church, attributes the idea of the Aaronic and Melchizedek Priesthood to Sidney Rigdon. He insisted that there was no mention of the priesthood from the discovery of the "golden plates" in 1827 until two years after the establishment of the Church in 1830.[77]

A comparative examination of the early church records and

histories with later editions of the same accounts reveal the inconsistencies. Nevertheless, Rigdon had been instrumental in mapping out much of the church's original organizational and theological direction. Under the leadership of Brigham Young, Rigdon has been either virtually written out of the records or portrayed in a dishonorable way.

Certainly, Sidney Rigdon played an important role in the Mormon saga during the years he was associated with them. When the Mormons moved to Illinois, he would develop a sharp difference with Smith. A hot debate ensued between Smith and Rigdon in June 1838 after what has been referred to as "Sidney's Salt Sermon" in Far West, Missouri. Rigdon had ranted against the dissenters of the church for over an hour taking his text from Matthew 5:13. His inflammatory rhetoric became the contributing factor that caused the citizens of Caldwell County to rise up and expel the Mormons from Missouri in 1833.[78]

On July 4, 1838 Sidney lit the fires of antagonism again in Gentile Caldwell County where he threw out a challenge to the Gentiles to cease their opposition that would be viewed as an ultimatum.[79]

Despite his previous rejection by Smith as First Counselor, Rigdon was chosen in 1843 as Smith's vice-presidential running mate. Joseph Smith was running for the office of President of the United States. Rigdon was away stumping for the election when Joseph Smith was killed along with Hyrum at the Carthage, Illinois Jail on June 27, 1844.[80]

Following Smith's death, Rigdon returned to Nauvoo to present his appeal to become the next president of the Church. After a failed attempt, he gathered some followers together whom he took back to Pennsylvania in a vain attempt to establish a new church. One by one he lost his membership to orthodox churches while some returned to follow Young west.[81] Finally, he retired to Friendship, New York, where he died in 1876.

Chapter Three
KINGDOM OF A CONFLICTING CHARACTER

Woven deeply into the fabric of Mormonism are their eschatological claims to world dominance through the coming millennial reign of Christ. They saw themselves as the chosen of God through which that reign was to be carried out. This was most favorable to them, perhaps due to their consistent material losses in the beginning of the movement and because they saw in the millennial teachings hope to rise above their Gentile enemies.

The concept that Smith's church was uniquely endowed by the hand of God and held exclusive rights as His divine instrument was sustained by every other strange sect of his day.[82] Oliver Cowdery, who was second only to the prophet in the early years of the church, was baptized by Smith and then in turn baptized the prophet, after claiming to have received the Aaronic priesthood in an appearance by John the Baptist. It must be noted, since ordination set the pattern for future Elders of the Church to follow, that according to the Church record John the Baptist baptized neither Joseph Smith nor Oliver Cowdery. Thus when Smith baptized Cowdery he was yet unbaptized himself. Since according to Mormonism the Holy Ghost comes upon a candidate at baptism, we now have a Prophet baptizing without the Holy Ghost.

In the developing accounts of this ordination the story

changes significantly. The 1842 history account records "We were baptized and ordained under the hand of the messenger" but was later altered to read "We were ordained under the hand of the messenger and baptized." Later the pair was confirmed in the Melchizedek Priesthood by the biblical Apostles Peter, James and John. The exact date Smith claimed that the three apostles appeared conferring the Melchizedek Priesthood is uncertain. B.H. Roberts dates the event between May 15, 1829, and April 1830, when the church was organized, but admits the date is not exact. Richard L. Bushman, respected Mormon historian, seems to suggest that the ordination took place after the organization of the church, thus leaving the newly formed church of Smith without the authority of apostleship through the Melchizedek Priesthood for a period of time. Joseph Smith III, president of the Reorganized Church of Jesus Christ of Latter-Day Saints, and son of the first Prophet, said "There is no historical evidence of such an event. Nor is there any evidence that Peter, James and John were present either when the instruction was given to ordain or when the ordination took place..."[83]

Immediately Smith and Cowdery began to recruit members for the new church. By April 1829 they had begun to announce the revelation of "a great and marvelous work" which would reveal the "everlasting salvation in the kingdom of God."[84] They were already identifying the unique work God would do through them as His chosen to their followers. Later, Sidney Rigdon would graft onto this concept of uniqueness the idea that they possessed the "restored gospel."

A final phase of this exclusive philosophy became their distinct place in the future millennial kingdom. Ultimately in the mind of Smith, the coming Kingdom of Christ and the city of Zion to be established at Independence, Missouri would become synonymous.[85] With Independence as the hub, the other strategic Mormon settlements became known as "stakes."

Cowdery fell into conflict with Smith when he understood that his plans exceeded a spiritual kingdom to include a physical dimension that would rival the nation's government. He was excommunicated from the church for rejecting the authority of Smith.[86]

In the Spring of 1844, shortly before his death, Smith established the Council of Fifty, a secret group of supporters inoculated with the idea of a revolutionary takeover of the nation.[87] Openly, the official church paper in England began to promote the philosophy that "all the political, and all the religious organizations that may have previously existed, will be swallowed up into one entire union—one universal empire—having no laws but God's law and saints to administer them".[88] This theme would later be continued in Utah where the United States government threatened to take over the state because of the practice of polygamy. Parley P. Pratt thundered, "The day will come when the United States government, and all others, will be uprooted, and the kingdom of this world will be united in one, and the kingdom of our God will govern the whole earth."[89]

What Smith taught empirically to the Council of Fifty was extended in Utah under Young, and is today held selectively by the more elite Mormons. Technically, Mormons presently hold what evangelical theologians would type as postmillennial views. Though they believe that Christ must return to reign at Independence, they maintain the way must be prepared for his coming by *their* good works.

That the Mormons serve as a formidable threat today to religious pluralism and that they are aggressively moving toward a goal of the ultimate takeover of the government of the United States is clearly demonstrated and documented by Heinerman (a Mormon) and Shupe. They succinctly state:

> *The Mormons, we maintain, represent such a group. They constitute a formidable economic force in the late twentieth century America. Important owners of public utilities and mass communications, they also exercise corporate strength as a powerful lobbying force in the nation's capital . . . Mormons are making*

important strides behind the scenes toward fulfilling the promise of post-millennialism.[90]

They not only have large holdings in the communications industry and corporate investments, but they also have key representatives in the political and intelligence community, the armed forces, and in many other government agencies. These representatives not only use their positions to advance the cause of Mormonism by favoring their own members for promotions, but they also protect the vested interests of the Church by overlooking and at times covering up failures by their fellow members.[91] Through their requirement that all faithful members tithe, they have over the years amassed a tremendous financial fortune for "Zion." The Mormons not only believe themselves to be the only true church but that they will ultimately triumph over all Gentile peoples of the world.[92]

The life of Joseph Smith was a patchwork of "divine revelations" and immorality. He claimed to be a man of God receiving revelations from heaven; therefore, his life as well as his testimony must be examined in light of historical facts. Beyond any claims for himself lie the indisputable records. Smith was an adulterer[93] and drinker,[94] deceiver[95] and fraudulent businessman,[96] a hypocrite,[97] a false prophet,[98] a law breaker,[99] an occultist,[100] a plagiarizer,[101] and prevaricator.[102] While it is not necessary to judge every modern day Mormon in light of Smith's behavior, it is important to understand the true character of their founder.

On February 27, 1833, Smith introduced by way of revelation the *Word of Wisdom* at Kirtland, Ohio. It was commended to the Saints as appropriating both "temporal and spiritual blessings." Adherents would receive "health to their navel and marrow in their bones" but a veiled threat concluded the revelation "that the destroying angel shall pass by them, as the children of Israel, and not slay them. Amen." The revelation forbade the use of wine, except in the sacraments, strong drink, tobacco, and hot drinks (such as coffee, tea or chocolate).[103] Brigham Young later revealed the circumstances behind the revelation. The Prophet and Elders of the church met in an upstairs room above the Smith home. When the meeting concluded, Emma found the floor splattered with tobacco juice. Her complaints initiated the revelation on *Word of Wisdom*.[104]

In August 1835 at Kirtland, Ohio, Elder Almon W. Babbitt was brought before the "Council of the Presidency" to answer charges that he had broken the *Word of Wisdom*. Specifically charged for drinking, he acknowledged that he had erred but cited the same behavior in the "Prophet and others." Followed by a mild rebuke, he was excused and admonished to keep the *Word of Wisdom*.[105]

Smith performed a marriage ceremony January 19, 1836, at the John Johnson home for Susan Lowell and Elder John F. Boynton where he blessed three glasses of wine and partook of it until filled.[106] Smith's general store in Nauvoo offered "sugar, molasses, glass, salt, tea, and coffee," all purchased in St. Louis.[107] Yet previously at Far West, Missouri, in 1837, Sidney Rigdon in a strong temperance sermon led the church to vote not to patronize any store where items were sold that violated the *Word of Wisdom*.[108] A pretentious statement appears in the church record of April 17, 1840. "This day the Twelve blessed and drank a bottle of wine at Penworthan...held a Council meeting and ordained Peter Melling, Patriarch."[109]

Again, unabashed, Smith wrote on May 3, 1843, "Called at the office and drank a glass of wine with Sister Jennetta Richards, made by her mother in England."[110] While Smith was Mayor of the City Council of Nauvoo, on December 11, 1843 they passed an ordinance permitting him to sell liquor.[111] Recorded in the *Saints' Herald*, church magazine for the Reorganized Church, Joseph Smith III, in what seems to be a reference related to the action of the Council, describes in his memoirs that a bar was built by his father in the new Nauvoo mansion while his mother Emma was away in St. Louis. She was indignant when she returned to discover the addition, stocked with all the accessories and managed by Orrin P. Rockwell. She ordered the bar removed under the threat that she was moving back across the street with the children to the old residence. Joseph quickly complied.[112] Not long afterward, across the street, Smith began to build a frame structure to house the bar and barbershop.[113] During his incarceration in the Carthage Jail, facing what he conceived as his final destiny, Smith toasted in wine his fellow Mormons John Taylor and Willard Richards.[114]

Philastus Hurlbut, a medical doctor who was a member of the original "Church of Christ," (the first name of Smith's church), became disenchanted with the religion accusing Smith of deception. He was dismissed from the church in 1833, and twelve years later, in an attempt to discredit him, he was accused in the *Times and Seasons* of using obscene language around young ladies. It wasn't unusual for apostates to be branded with charges of immorality. No doubt some deserved the charge but there is no evidence that Philastus Hurlbut was anything other than an honorable man.

Encouraged by Kirtland residents who had a disdain for Smith, Hurlbut returned to the Palmyra area interviewing and obtaining over eighty sworn affidavits by local residents who knew Joseph Smith and his family. In 1843 these statements were first printed in *Mormonism Unveiled* by E.D. Howe, a newspaper editor in Painesville, Ohio, who was an eyewitness observer to the birth and growth of Mormonism. Some twenty-six years later, two brothers named Kelly, members of the RLDS, attempted to disprove the testimonies that Smith was a man "entirely destitute of moral character, and addicted to vicious habits."[115] Their spurious attempt was weak and without weight, but a second attempt to discredit the testimonies was launched by Mormon scholar Hugh Nibley in more recent times. His arguments were typical of one trying to defend his prophet.

In 1970, Richard L. Anderson, professor of religion at Brigham Young University, defended Joseph Smith by accusing Hurlbut and Howe of using leading phrases such as "money diggers," "lazy," and "visionary" or by actually imposing this language upon the statements of those interviewed. Anderson's work, while superior to the former attempts to explain the affidavits, is yet lacking in sufficient validity to disqualify them. In answer to the defending article, "Joseph Smith's New York Reputation Reappraised," appearing in a Brigham Young University studies booklet by Richard L. Anderson,[116] a young Mormon freelance writer, named Roger I. Anderson, who specialized in nineteenth century religions, wrote a scholarly rebuttal to the attempts of the Kellys, Nibley, and Anderson in a book entitled *Joseph Smith's New York Reputation Reexamined.* Roger I. Anderson shows conclusively that these derogatory terms appear in other sworn statements, articles and writings that Hurlbut could not have influenced and that he likely used a set of standard questions for each person interviewed allowing for the recurrence of certain terms. The fact that these statements were sworn to by the individuals carries no little weight. E.D. Howe also verified these statements. While there are some minor mistakes in transmission of information, there is nothing to support any charges of fraud.[117]

Although the *Word of Wisdom* as a revelation had restricted the use of coffee and tea by the Mormons, for twelve years following a *Bill of Particulars*, listing items to be taken west with them, included both coffee and tea. Some of the thirty items listed in the church newspaper were cayenne pepper, sugar, flour, various spices, dried fruits, seeds and various other practical items including coffee, tea, coffeepots and teapots.[118]

Sociologically, Joseph Smith, Jr. was a specter of his environment. Historically, he was a product of his time. Psychologically, he was affected by the neurotic behavior of his own family. Educationally, he was an eclectic of powerful personal influences. Ethically, he was a "Pandora's box" of immoral habits and pretense to religion. Smith left a history of hypocrisy, fraud, false promises, occult practices, sensuality, and violence that are forever woven into the warp and woof of Mormon history.

PART TWO

EXPLORING THE PAST
OF MORMONS

"No man knows my history. I cannot tell it; I shall never undertake it. I don't blame anyone for not believing my history. If I had not experienced what I have, I could not have believed it myself."

Joseph Smith
From a funeral sermon at Nauvoo
April 7, 1844

Chapter Four
VISIONS OF AN ANGEL

Without question the first vision of Joseph Smith stands as the chart and compass to the genuineness of all his subsequent revelations. In the official account of his conversion experience Smith went into the woods of Palmyra, New York, near his home when he was fifteen years old. Disturbed by the controversy of contending denominations during a time of revival when "great multitudes united themselves to the different religious parties," he began reading the Bible and was struck by the force of James 1:4 *"If any of you lack wisdom let him ask of God."* Following a prayer for deliverance from an oppressive wicked spirit, "two Personages whose brightness and glory defy all description" appeared in the air standing above him. When he asked with which of the current denominations he was to unite, he was instructed to "join none of them, for they were all wrong, and the Personages who addressed me said that all their creeds were an abomination in his sight; that those professors were all corrupt..."[1]

There are several accounts of this first vision by Smith and others close to him that differ significantly, raising serious questions to his authenticity as a prophet. In the first known record appearing in Smith's 1832 diary, he records in his own handwriting, seeing the single person of Christ who announced that his sins had been forgiven. There is no record of angels and no conversation concerning which church to join.[2] Three years later on November 9, 1835, in an interview with a "Jewish minister," Smith relates that "no person" appeared and that he saw "many angels in his vision," but there is no question as to which church he should join. In a third diary record, five days later, there are no personages mentioned other than a visitation of angels.[3] Joseph Smith began dictating his history of the church to James Mulholland on June 11, 1839. Not until March 1, 1842, twenty-two years after the event, in the *Times and Seasons*, do we find the mention of two personages appearing simultaneously, which has become the official account of the first vision.[4]

In the various accounts, Smith claims to have been different ages when the vision appeared. He avows to have been sixteen years old in the first diary account,[5] fifteen in another,[6] and as young as fourteen in two other diary accounts.[7] In some of the first accounts, a "pillar of fire"[8] is seen but in the official version, not only is the reference to a "pillar of fire" missing but Smith adds a "thick darkness that gathered around" him.[9] There are also conflicting details as to instructions he received. In one of his accounts Smith is instructed by a personage that his sins are forgiven, but no question as to what denomination he should join is included. None of the earliest accounts contain a reference to a revival in the Palmyra churches accompanied by a condemnation of all religious groups (found in today's official version). The early accounts of the first vision in the archives of the Utah leaders record Smith seeing only angels.[10]

Yet Joseph Fielding Smith, sixth president of the LDS, compared the account of the first vision's importance to the resurrection of Christ when he wrote: "The greatest event that has ever occurred in this world since the resurrection of the Son of God ...was the coming of the Father and the Son to that boy, Joseph Smith."[11]

David O. McKay, ninth president of the LDS, regarded the vision as critical to all Mormon doctrine. "The appearing of the Father and the Son to Joseph Smith is the foundation of this church."[12]

John A. Widtsoe, Mormon Apostle, measured everything that followed by the validity of the first vision. "The First Vision of 1820 is of first importance in the history of Joseph Smith. Upon its reality rest the truth and value of his subsequent work."[13]

For more than 130 years the diaries of Joseph Smith, Jr. were kept secretly locked away in the archives of LDS headquarters in Utah. Only after Mormon scholars revealed their presence and released excerpts of the different accounts of the first vision, and were subsequently published, did the Church Historian's Office acknowledge their genuineness.[14]

It is significant that in 1859 when Joel Tiffany interviewed Martin Harris, one of Smith's first secretaries and the financial backer for the printing of the *Book of Mormon*, concerning the foundation of Mormonism, the first vision was never mentioned.[15] It appears that Harris had no knowledge of this experience that was to become the chief cornerstone of Mormonism or he would, no doubt, have related it.

In addition to the different accounts, there is the matter of inaccuracy of the date for the first vision. Smith consistently dates his conversion in the woods of Palmyra during 1820 while a great revival was taking place in the area. The late Wesley P. Walter, Presbyterian minister and respected researcher of Mormonism, proves conclusively that the revival referred to by Smith took place four years later in 1824. Records from the churches in the Palmyra area reveal no significant revival prior to 1824. Reverend George Lane, a Methodist minister and a Reverend Benjamin B. Stockton, referred to in an account of the first vision by Smith's brother William Smith, both pastored in Palmyra no earlier than 1824.[16]

In today's Authorized Version, Joseph Smith claimed to have seen God the Father and Jesus the Son during a time of prayer in the woods. Yet, in 1832 he gave revelation for the priesthood, which all males are expected to enter, that no man can see God without the priesthood.[17] It was not until May 15, 1829, that Smith and Oliver Cowdery avowed that John the Baptist appeared to ordain them into the Aaronic Priesthood.[18] No date is recorded in Mormon history for the confirming of the Melchizedek Priesthood but most scholars consider May or June

1829 as the time.[19] There is a direct conflict between the vision of 1820 and the revelation of 1832.

In 1821 a young lawyer in Adams, New York, by the name of Charles Grandison Finney, wrestled with conviction of sin. North of town, young Finney entered a woods to pray, eventually surrendering his heart to Christ. Endowed with new power he ran back into town declaring his newly found faith to offices, homes and in the street. Within twenty-four hours, no less than twenty-four people had professed faith in Christ due to his testimony.[20] Shortly after his conversion, Finney began to preach, first in a revival at Evans' Mill, then on to Antwerp, Western, Auburn and Rome. In 1830 a revival broke out in Rochester that continued for six months. Although Finney employed a similar invitation previously, it was in Rochester that he formally introduced the "anxious seat,"[21] where people were invited to come to the front and pray for their souls. The Methodists already employed a type of altar call in Rochester before Finney arrived. No little stir spread over the entire state and throughout the country concerning these revivals and the new method of inquiry.[22]

As early as 1824, news from Evans' Mill and Antwerp in Jefferson Country, New York about the apprentice lawyer turned evangelist and a certain man who exhibited unusual power in prayer, dubbed "Father Daniel Nash," swept the nation. Mighty conversions of those who opposed the revivals resulted as answers to prayer. It was one of the big news stories of the day, second only to the opening of the Erie Canal. In 1825 revival broke out in Oneida County. These revivals have been termed the "western revivals."

News of Charles Finney's "new measures" became a source of big debate between him and noted ministers of the area. A pamphlet criticizing the meetings, printed by a ministerial association, only served to flame the fires of interest in the Finney meetings. By 1826, some thirty-five miles from Palmyra, a mighty revival swept over the town of Auburn, as well as nearby communities. Joseph Smith would have had to be a veritable hermit to fail to hear and read about the revivals and the unusual conversion testimony of Finney. It is altogether possible that Joseph Smith attended one these early revivals in which he heard Finney's impressionable testimony first hand.

Reports of the 1830-1831 Rochester Revival were printed in the *Rochester Observer* and in some religious journals such as the *Western Recorder*, printed in nearby Utica. From the Rochester Revival (1830-1831), only twenty-five miles from Joseph Smith's hometown of Palmyra, an estimated 100,000 people united with churches. *The New York Evangelist* estimated that "almost every town within forty or fifty miles of Rochester is favored more or less with the presence of the Lord."[23]

Around the potbellied stove of grocery stores, whittlers philosophized concerning these "new measures" employed by Finney and details of Finney's conversion. Joseph Smith likely carried in his fertile mind the story of Finney's conversion, or may have reviewed a printed account, which he incorporated into his own conversion experience, and recorded for the first time in his diary sometime between July 20 and November 27 of 1832.

By comparing the conversion account recorded in Finney's *Memoirs* and taking Smith's first two diary accounts of the vision in the woods, the reader may note the similarities. Both Finney and Smith had been reading the Bible seeking truth. Both Finney and Smith became distressed over their sinful states. Both Finney and Smith were struck with the inadequacy of current denominations. Both Finney and Smith went into a "grove" to pray. Both Finney and Smith record thinking someone was approaching them and looked up to see if it were so. Finney wrote, ". . . again I thought I heard someone approach me, and I opened up my eyes to see . . ." Smith wrote, in one account "I heard a voice behind me like some person walking toward me. I. . .sprung up on my feet and looked around . . . " Both Finney and Smith, in the second account, describe an inability to pray. Both Finney and Smith experienced an unusually bright light. Both Finney and Smith saw the Lord Jesus. Both Finney and Smith were filled with the Holy Spirit. Both Finney and Smith described the twin sensations of "love" and "joy."[24]

Why did Joseph Smith wait some twelve years (1832) before recording his first vision, that is considered by Mormonism today to be so crucial to their other teachings? Was it as one writer has suggested, "a literary creation"[25] which bore no support by those who knew him best at the time it was supposed to have taken place? Was he at a critical place in his career as a prophet "facing division in his own ranks and strong opposition from the established churches" which drove him to fabricate the story to boost his image? It may have been invented as a necessary shift in theology from his initial concept of God as one, seen clearly in the *Book of Mormon*, to a plurality of gods.[26] For whatever reason, it seems likely that Smith was aware of the details of Finney's conversion experience as he wrote his own first vision. Smith was regularly given to expediency, calling up a vision to suit the occasion or declaring a new revelation to correct some error in a former one.[27]

Many Mormon scholars have lost faith in Smith as a Prophet and the *Book of Mormon* as they study the historical records. Some academicians wish merely to reform the Church by dealing forthrightly and objectively with the contradictory accounts and obvious problems of Mormonism. Yet they often resent non-Mormon scholars writing about their church. They look back to their ancestry driven from Missouri and Illinois, pulling carts across the foreboding mountains and plains to the Salt Lake basin and forging a home from the rugged frontier wilderness. For them, the church has ceased to be a matter of faith but rather their history and heritage.

The second vision of Joseph Smith must be understood, not only apart from the first vision but in light of the treasure digging activities of his family. In 1822 Willard Chase, neighbor of the Smiths, employed Joseph and Alvin to assist him in digging a well. In the process of digging they discovered a strange looking stone resembling a child's foot. Young Joseph studied the stone, placed it in his old hat and buried his head in the rim, claiming he could see things by means of it. The stone has been described as having "a whitish, glassy appearance, though opaque, resembling quartz."[28] After borrowing the stone from Chase for two years, Smith established quite a reputation for being able to discover hidden or lost items, a reputation no doubt fostered by his boastful family.[29]

During this time Josiah Stowell (Stoal), an honest but naive Dutchman, while visiting in the Palmyra area, heard rumors of Smith's ability to divine lost treasures by means of a mysterious stone. Smith convinced Stowell that he knew of "a bar of gold, as big as his leg, and about three or four feet long," residing in a cave near Stowell's home. In November of 1825, Joseph, his father and some others boarded at the Isaac Hale home while they searched for treasure on the nearby farm of Josiah Stowell.[30]

Escapades of this kind would later come back to haunt Smith and damage his credibility as a prophet. He sensed this later and tried to cover up these occult practices by denying that he had been a money-digger. His version of the event said that Stowell enlisted him to dig. "Hence arose the very prevalent story of my having been a money-digger."[31] In addition to directing the digging for gold by use of his seer stone, Smith was also observing Emma, twenty-one year old daughter of Isaac Hale, where he was boarding. Although Joseph claimed to be able to find lost items, no success stories have fallen out to sustain his pretense. From items present and items missing he would ultimately claim ability to divine things, future, mysterious and miraculous. When he returned empty-handed to Palmyra, he left a disappointed Josiah Stowell in South Bainbridge and a disillusioned Isaac Hale in Harmony. Over the next two years Joseph would return to visit Emma at length, mustering up the courage to ask Isaac for her hand in marriage. Isaac Hale was a devout Methodist of impeccable moral character who would reject his daughter's suitor knowing his penchant for occult use of the stone.

However, Smith was not to be refused. In a short time he returned when Isaac was away from home to entice Emma to elope with him. In January of 1827 they were married by Justice of the Peace Squire Tarbill (Tarbel) in South Bainbridge, New York.[32]

Fearing to face his strong willed father-in-law, Joseph took his new bride to the impoverished home of his parents. If Emma complained of the conditions, there is no recorded whimper. It became the first of many experiences that would forge in her the steel to stay with Joseph. In time, Emma was to write her father asking for some of her furniture, clothing and household items that had been left behind at her elopement. Hale received the request with favor and in due time the couple stood before the tearful eyes of a now mollified father. Peter Ingersoll, friend and confidant of Smith, accompanied the pair to the Hale home, assisting them in moving the items.

The couple was not to depart, however, until Hale extracted a commitment from young Joseph that he would cease and desist in his occult practices of stone-gazing, a pledge he confided in Ingersoll that he planned to keep. The sincerity of Joseph's commitment cannot now be known, but his expressed fear to Ingersoll was that his family would make the promise very difficult to keep.

His resolve, if sincere, was nevertheless short-lived. Once home, what he later related to his friend as a joke on his family, became his first steps back into occult practices. While passing through the woods, he discovered some unusually beautiful white sand in a hollow log. Immediately, he tied up several quarts in his frock coat. Upon entering the house, his family at the supper table began to quiz him on the contents. He told them it was a golden Bible retrieved from the earth, an idea Smith told Ingersoll he got from Canada.[33]

While Smith slept on September 23, 1823, he claimed to have received a visit from an angel with a message that would deny almost every major doctrine that Christians have held since the first century church. Accordingly, he awoke to see the angel standing beside his bed announcing his name as Moroni, the angel son of Mormon for whom the *Book of Mormon* is named. The angel told Smith of some golden plates which had been buried in a hill near his home. Martin Harris, secretary to Smith and financier of the printing of the *Book of Mormon*, related what

Smith had told him about the plates.

> *These plates were seven inches wide by eight*
> *inches in length, and were of the thickness of*
> *plates of tin; and when piled one above the other,*
> *they were altogether about four inches thick; and*
> *they were put together on the back by three silver*
> *rings, so that they would open like a book.*[34]

These "plates" were found in a stone box. They were together with two stones set in silver bows which were "fastened to a breastplate, constituting what is called the Urim and Thummim" to be used for translating the plates.[35] All the items were hidden in a hill he called Cumorah, not far from Smith's home.

The following day, Smith went to the hill in order to find the golden plates and the "seer spectacles," though he was not allowed to take them at this point. He was instructed by the angel to return to this spot each year for the next four years. On September 22, 1827, Smith claimed he was permitted by the angel to take the treasure from the hill Cumorah.

During the time that Smith claimed to have found the golden plates, he was arrested and found guilty of the charge of "glass looking" in the town of South Bainbridge, New York.[36] Smith, aware that someone might associate him with the indictment, sought to dismiss the incident by including in his history, "Hence arose the very prevalent story of my having been a money-digger."[37]

It must also be pointed out that in the early editions of his history, one of the very damaging contradictions is the name of the angel which came down to Smith in the second vision. According to the handwritten manuscript by Smith for *Times and Seasons*, where the history of the church was first printed, the angel that appeared to Joseph at his bedside was named Nephi.

He called me by name, and said unto me that he was a messenger sent from the presence of God to me, and that his name was Nephi.[38]

The name "Nephi" in the original handwritten manuscript has been struck and replaced with the name "Moroni." In the current record of this account, as it appears in *The Pearl of Great Price*, the name "Moroni" appears.

He called me by name, and said unto me that he was a messenger sent from the presence of God to me, and that his name was Moroni.[39]

On September 22, 1827, four years after Smith was allowed to see the plates in the hill near his home, he was permitted by the angel Moroni to take the golden plates, Urim and Thummim, as well as the breastplate home. A strict injunction was given the Prophet by the angel that he was "responsible for them" and that if he allowed them to be lost through neglect he "should be cut off."[40]

Smith reports that soon after the discovery of the plates persecution abounded from every direction. Lucy Mack Smith records an incident concerning the plates that had been hidden in a rotting birch log for protection. Retrieving the plates from the log, Smith wrapped them in a white linen frock and placed them under his arm as he passed through the woods to his home. The story goes that a man leaped from behind a log where he had been waiting to apprehend the plates from Smith. Young Joseph is said not only to have succeeded in knocking the man down, but overcame two others on the way.[41] This was quite a feat if former Mormon John Hyde, Jr. was correct in describing the plates as weighing nearly two hundred pounds, not including the large brass breastplate.[42]

Numerous other visions would later be claimed by Joseph Smith, but these two set the Mormon movement into motion. Today, over 165 years later, the specter of Mormonism looms on the horizon of human history as a formidable contender for the souls of men. It matters little to many that the authority for Mormonism arose from such a questionable beginning.

Chapter Five
KEY FIGURES JOIN THE PROPHET

S mith had taken a new wife who was accustomed to much more than he had to offer in the impoverished home of his family. In his own words he admits "my father's worldly circumstances were very limited, we were under the necessity of laboring with our hands . . . and by continuous labor were enabled to get a comfortable maintenance."[43]   Apparently "laboring with our hands" did not suit Smith's disposition to hard work. Before long he and Emma planned to return to her father's home in Harmony, Pennsylvania. In Smith's own version, the return was precipitated by widespread persecution to obtain the plates, a story repeated by Mormons today.

The fact is that Smith had a reputation for prevarication in the community. Affidavits taken from the people of Palmyra reveal that any story of golden plates delivered by an ancient angel was not taken seriously by his neighbors. So "being very poor, and ... there was no probability that we would be otherwise,"[44] along with their meager possessions and what was claimed to be golden plates, he prepared to return to the home of a distrustful father-in-law in Harmony.

The neighborly exception was Martin Harris, the eccentric and naive land owning farmer of the area from whom Smith obtained a loan of fifty dollars. This was likely no easy extraction from the tight-fisted farmer, but obviously Joseph was up to the challenge, promising rich rewards from the sales of a golden Bible. Later when Harris was planning to sell a piece of land to finance the printing of the *Book of Mormon*, his wife Lucy challenged his good judgment. "What if it *is* a lie?" he retorted, "If you will let me alone I will make money out of it!"[45] The speculative farmer envisioned a large return on his investment.

While visiting the family home in Palmyra, Harris became convinced Smith was a prophet. Harris was sitting on a rail fence picking his teeth with a pen when it fell into the shavings on the ground. When it seemed not to be found, he challenged Smith to discover it with his seer stone. Smith pulled the stone from his pocket, placed it in his old white hat, and put his face over the opening, pretending to see the pin. Producing the pin from the shavings, Smith handed it over to Harris who was immediately convinced.[46]

Harris became essentially the earliest convert to Mormonism, with the exception of the Smith family, after having been "first Orthodox Quaker, then a Universalist, next a Restorationer, then a Baptist, next a Presbyterian and then a Mormon."[47] He is said to have been an ardent student of the Bible who could quote lengthy passages from it. He nevertheless had a propensity for the sensational.

Soon after his arrival in Harmony, Joseph claims to have begun translating the plates by use of the Urim and Thummim with Emma as his first secretary. It became an easy transference from digging for buried treasure to digging up golden plates. It seems evident that in the beginning the statements concerning the plates were "varied and modified from time to time." From a solid gold Bible the plates became merely engraved. Then they became metallic plates embossed with gold letters.[48] Not until 1835, some eight years after the plates were taken from the earth, was an angel attached to the story.

It wasn't long before Martin Harris traveled to Harmony to secure his investment. A frugal, if not an avaricious man, he was not willing to risk further investment without some evidence of the authenticity of the plates. Smith informed Harris they were written in the "Reformed Egyptian" language, supplying him with a piece of paper containing some of the characters from the plates.

He in turn carried this inscription to some language authorities back east. Perhaps the best known was Charles Anthon of Columbia University. The professor was apparently rather ambiguous, not wanting to discourage the simple farmer, but rather advised him that the matter needed further investigation from legal authorities. Harris may have taken this as an authentication since he returned to report the characters were Egyptian hieroglyphics. In numerous articles and letters, Anthon denied verifying the characters as genuine. In a letter to E. D. Howe, editor of the *Painesville Telegraph* of Painesville, Ohio, he described Harris as a "simple hearted farmer" who approached his door with a piece of paper that contained what appeared to be various letters of Greek, Hebrew and Roman alphabets with crosses and flourishes, which was anything but Egyptian hieroglyphics. Further, he regarded the situation to be a "hoax" on the farmer.[49]

Harris, however, would not be deterred in his mission and, perhaps by sheer resolve not to look foolish, assured himself that the script was too mysterious to be understood by even the learned professor. After all, Smith had proven himself a prophet by retrieving his pen.

After completing 116 pages, Harris convinced Smith to permit him to show the translation to his wife back in New York. Reluctantly, Smith agreed. Harris apparently hoped to convince his disbelieving wife by submitting the translation for her examination. The original 116 pages disappeared but Mrs. Harris never revealed how she disposed of them. It has been suggested she probably threw them into the fire knowing her husband was being taken for a fool in the matter. Later Harris returned to announce that his wife had lost the pages. This threw Smith into a panic. Distraught, Smith paced the floor complaining that if he made a mistake in retranslating the lost pages, his enemies would imagine him a fraud. After a time, Smith recovered from his loss and subsequently fabricated a revelation in which God told him not to worry about the lost pages, that He would supply additional plates to translate essentially the same story.[50]

In April of 1828, Oliver Cowdery was boarding with the Smith family in Palmyra while teaching at a nearby school. Although Cowdery had apprenticed as a blacksmith in his youth, he had attained enough education to become an itinerant schoolteacher.

He had heard about the mysterious golden plates around the family fireplace and packed up his meager belongings to travel to Harmony. When he knocked at the door, Joseph must have immediately perceived his distant cousin Oliver as an answer to a great need. Within two days he became a convert to the prophet's religion and replaced Harris as scribe.

Cowdery was to play an important role in the formation of the *Book of Mormon*, yet it troubled him that Smith had not been formerly ordained. In May 1829, the pair retreated to the woods to pray and returned declaring that John the Baptist had appeared conferring the Aaronic Priesthood upon them. The heavenly messenger then commanded them to baptize each other in the Susquehanna River. First Smith baptized Cowdery and then Cowdery baptized Smith.[51] Soon, thereafter, Peter, James and John were said to have appeared to the two men, laying anointing hands upon them and conveying the Melchizedek Priesthood on them.[52]

Isaac Hale no doubt was distressed by the fact that his son-in-law was not working and began to prod him to support his new wife. It was not long before the group found it convenient, if not necessary, to move to the home of Peter Whitmer in Fayette, New York.

The completed manuscript was submitted for publication sometime in 1929 to E.B. Grandin, publisher of the *Wayne Sentinel* in Palmyra. At first, he declined the offer and attempted to persuade Harris not to mortgage his farm. When a Rochester, New York, printer by the name of Elihu F. Marshall agreed to print the book, Smith appealed to Grandin on the basis that it would be printed anyway and that it would be more conveniently printed at home. Grandin finally agreed to print five thousand copies for $3,000. John H. Gilbert, overseer of the printing, described the book as poor in grammar, spelling, capitalization, punctuation and paragraphing, and refused to continue the work unless he was allowed to correct these items. Reluctantly Smith agreed. By early 1830 the book was printed.[53]

The traditional Mormon story places the founding of the new church in the Peter Whitmer home on April 6, 1830, following the *Book of Mormon's* completion. This founding took place with six members. The first name of the church was "Church of Christ." Mormon historian H. Michael Marquardt contends that the Manchester log home of Joseph Smith, Sr. where Hiram's family was living, rather than Fayette, was the site where the church was organized. A baptismal service of some of the early leaders in the Crooked Brook stream, just outside Manchester, followed the organizational meeting. The Fayette meeting, Marquardt argues, was merely an extension (or branch) of the church previously organized in Manchester.[54] At this meeting, Smith appealed to the others present to accept his teachings along with Cowdery, to which they consented.[55] Cowdery then became the first Elder ordained in the new church, second only to Joseph.[56] On December 5, 1834, Cowdery was elected Assistant President, the only time in the history of the church that an assistant was elected.

After completion of the *Book of Mormon*, Harris pressed Smith to see the plates. David Whitmer, along with Oliver Cowdery and Martin Harris, formed a trio of witnesses who went into the woods where the plates were said to have been revealed. On a witness stand later in Utah, Harris admitted that he had never actually seen the plates other than through the eyes of faith.[57]

Harris was to become a continual thorn in Smith's side, at times maligning the character of the prophet, and transferring his allegiance to a would-be prophetess that arose among the ranks. Harris had a propensity for prophecy himself, often rivaling Smith. He described the devil as appearing to him with short hair like a mouse and resembling a jackass. Jesus, he claimed, manifested Himself in the form of a deer that talked with him as he walked through the woods.[58]

Sidney Rigdon brought charges against Harris for his rancorous conduct before A.C. Russell. His charges stated that Joseph Smith drank too much liquor while translating the *Book of Mormon*, that he wrestled too many men and that he (Harris) knew the content of the *Book of Mormon* before it was translated. But the imaginative Harris stated, when arraigned before the Council, that Joseph drank before he became translator of the book. Harris also admitted that he had talked too much. The Council forgave him with a slight rebuke.[59]

During the tumultuous times in Kirtland, while Smith was away on banking business in Cleveland, Martin Harris and David Whitmer entertained the prophecy of a young woman who gazed into a black stone and predicted that after a third of their number apostatized from Smith, one of them (Harris or Whitmer) would succeed him. It was too enticing for the ears of either, for they knew that Joseph was upon troubled times. A regular Thursday meeting was held to hear fresh revelation from this young woman who "would jump out of her chair and dance all over the floor, boasting of her power, until she was perfectly exhausted."[60]

Obviously her revelations appealed to Harris and Whitmer who circulated a petition gathering the names of many of the Saints against Joseph. Eventually Smith returned to dissipate the meetings. There was a reluctant repentance on the part of some of the chief leaders. As a result, Harris was disfellowshiped from the Church in 1837. In later years, when many of the Saints immigrated to Utah under the leadership of Brigham Young, it is reported in Mormon history that Harris rejoined the Church. At Clarkston, Utah, on July 10, 1875 at the age of ninety-three, with his family standing around his deathbed, it is said that Harris muttered something about the *Book of Mormon*.[61] It is very noticeable that B.H. Roberts, eminent historian of the Mormon Church, never mentions any reentry by Harris into the Church nor does he record any final confession to the truthfulness of the *Book of Mormon*. Neither are such records found in the regular *History of the Church* under the name of Joseph Smith nor Robert's *Comprehensive History of the Church* which would have been extremely important to Mormon history since Harris was one of the first three witnesses to the *Book of Mormon.*

Harris was not to be the only rival to the prophet. Late in August 1830, Joseph and Emma returned to Fayette from Harmony to discover that Hiram Page had taken up the gift of prophecy by aid of a seer stone. His revelations pertained to church government and the expansion of Zion. This prompted Smith to issue a revelation addressed to Oliver Cowdery, admonishing him to forbid Hiram Page from bringing further revelations and establish that only the Prophet was to receive revelations from God.[62] In a conference of the church on September 26, 1830, Smith figuratively threw the dice to determine his position as Prophet, calling for a vote of confidence by the people to sustain him. The gauntlet was cast down and even Hiram Page disavowed his former claim to the power of prophecy, along with the rest of the congregation.[63]

In an additional revelation, Parley P. Pratt, Oliver Cowdery, Peter Whitmer, and Ziba Peterson were sent from the conference on a mission to the Lamanites (American Indians).[64] On their way west they stopped to see a former associate of Pratt, who was pastor of the Mentor Baptist Church near Kirtland, Ohio. Sidney Rigdon was given a copy of the *Book of Mormon* with a request that the two missionaries be permitted to address his worship service that evening. It was a rather unusual thing for a Baptist church to permit men to bring a doctrine so foreign to their own. Rigdon, however, agreed to let them speak.

As noted earlier, Rigdon had fallen out with Alexander Campbell over the matter of communal living, the doctrine of millennialism and spiritual gifts which culminated in a confrontation before the Mahoning Baptist Association meeting that year. The popular preacher at Mentor was no match for the powerful presence of Campbell, who charged him with heresy before the association, driving him from the meeting, angry and defeated. Thus when the missionaries arrived at his doorstep, Rigdon no doubt saw this as an opportunity to save face and to promote his ideas in this new church. Without ever meeting this new Prophet, Rigdon and his wife Phebe were baptized along with some other Mormon converts in a river near Kirtland. His church in Mentor was appalled by their pastor's behavior and immediately dismissed him from his duties.[65] A communal group established by Rigdon prior to coming to Smith, was baptized into the new church under Cowdery.

In December 1830 Rigdon and a friend by the name of Edward Partridge traveled to New York to meet Joseph Smith. Partridge was not yet a convert to the new church but was baptized before they returned to Ohio. In 1831 he was appointed Bishop of the Mormon Zion—Independence, Missouri. Smith immediately recognized the abilities of Sidney Rigdon, a fiery speaker and imaginative leader. As Sidney described the possibilities of Kirtland, where already several converts had been baptized into the new church, Smith saw an opportunity to escape his unwanted reputation in western New York.[66] It was difficult to add new converts in a place where all the tales of his treasure hunting by use of the "peep stone" were so prevalent, his unsavory behavior as a youth haunted him, and the general notoriety of his family prevailed.

Chapter Six

THE CHURCH MOVES TO KIRTLAND

O ver the objections of many in the church, Joseph received a revelation calling the church to establish in Kirtland, Ohio.[67] By February 1831 Smith had led the faithful to the "land of promise, and...the place of gathering...".[68]

The conversion of Sidney Rigdon spread like wildfire over the Kirtland area, drawing the curious and the impressionable to investigate the claims of Mormonism. Among these was a bright young man by the name of John Corrill, who by his own admission, was greatly influenced by Rigdon's entrance into the new church. In reading the Bible, he writes that he began to notice references to certain seers in the Bible, concluding that Joseph Smith claimed to be a seer, God could have given another revelation through such a modern day prophet. Corrill joined the Mormons and remained with them for six years until they were driven out of Missouri. He became disenchanted with the futile leadership of a false prophet who "pretended to visions and revelations" but had no actual direction from God.[69] Corrill ultimately became an influential leader in the Missouri Legislature.

The worship services in Kirtland just prior to the arrival of Smith and Rigdon were marked by exaggerated visitations of angels and Indians. The church became a circus of excess and uncontrolled emotions. Mysterious light filled the air. Young men imagined themselves as ministers, leapt upon stumps to address fanciful congregations. Tongues were common phenomena, followed by falling, fits, and the appearance of fictional characters.[70]

Rapid growth swelled the membership of the new church to one thousand by September of 1831.[71] When Smith and Rigdon arrived, they were able to curb much of the exaggerated behavior in the services. The expansion of the church continued over the next few years, at the same time raising the ire of the community.

The pair began to "translate" the Bible before leaving New York and continued the work in Ohio. Smith contended there were missing books in the Old and New Testament respectively. When the manuscript was completed on February 2, 1833, Smith "sealed it up, no more to be opened till it arrived in Zion."[72] It was not until 1867 that the manuscript appeared in printed form. Emma Smith, after her husband's death, gave it to her son Joseph Smith, III, President of the Reorganized Church, and they subsequently published it. LDS scholars deny it as a true translation of the Bible but call it rather a revision.[73] Though they do not regard the *Inspired Version* of the RLDS as authoritative, it is cited extensively in their version of the King James.[74]

Smith claimed that he wanted to deliver a correct translation in a "plain and simple manner" and show that "there is but one God that pertains to us."[75] Thus, the first object of his revision is discovered. He wanted to make the King James Version agree with his "many gods" revelation which came after the printing of the *Book of Mormon*. Certainly the Word of God teaches there are many false gods without life and hope (Habakkuk 2:18-20), yet it also clearly teaches that there is but one true God (Deuteronomy 6:4).

In addition, Smith sought to portray himself as a prophet predicted in the Scriptures themselves. The book of Genesis closes with Joseph, Jacob's son, embalmed and placed in a coffin in Egypt (Genesis 50:26). Smith revised the passage to include a prophecy of himself coming as a seer to write the word of the Lord. In the book of Isaiah, Smith extended the twenty-ninth chapter to include a reference to himself translating a sealed book (*Book of Mormon*). In the "Book of Moses," included in *The Pearl of Great Price*, Smith has Noah commanding the people of the antediluvian time to repent and be baptized for the filling of the Holy Spirit.[76] Thus the doctrine of baptismal regeneration, promoted by Alexander Campbell as early as 1825, is forced upon the preaching of the Old Testament patriarch Noah.

Increased growth among the Kirtland saints brought with it extended problems. Within the new church Joseph experienced resistance and apostasy. Ezra Booth, a sometime Methodist exhorter, joined the Mormons, though not with complete conviction. Simonds Ryder also joined with many reservations. When Smith misspelled his name in an official communication conferring the office of Elder upon him, Ryder entertained grave doubts to the genuineness of a prophet who could not spell his name correctly.[77] There was a growing resentment to the methods of Smith by the surrounding communities. Forces of hostility merged into a mob on the night of March 25, 1832.

While the Smiths were staying in the home of a farmer by the name of John Johnson in Hiram, just outside of Kirtland, the mob burst into the bedroom where the couple had retired for the night. The exhausted pair had been caring for a set of twins taken in by Emma after their mother, wife of John Murdock, had died. On the day of their birth, Emma had lost a set of twins herself. Nine days later Emma brought the twins home. Now eleven months old, they had come down with the measles. Smith was asleep upon the trundle bed when some of the mob broke into the room. They dragged Smith from the bed while Emma screamed "murder." As the angry mob carried him away from the house, he saw Sidney Rigdon, a victim of their brutal beating, stretched out on the frozen ground. After stripping Smith, the mob tarred and feathered him. Bruised and badly shaken, Smith limped back to the Johnson home where Emma and friends peeled the tar from his body late into the long Saturday night. The next day with visible burn marks on his face, he emerged to preach before his congregation.[78]

Such vigilante behavior must always be condemned by any civilized society. It must, however, be remembered that these were the pioneering days where differences were often settled by the fist and gun rather than by the law. Certainly, one must wonder why such violent action was taken against the Smiths' new religion when the area had tolerated numerous other strange beliefs.

Simonds Ryder, named by Smith in his history as being a member of the mob, provides an explanation for the severe treatment. Certain papers left behind by Mormon missionaries in Hiram describing the takeover of Gentile properties by the "restored church" were discovered.[79] Coupled with the unrestrained boosting of the Saints and arrogant declarations of the Mormon preachers,[80] fuel was furnished to the already smoldering fires of resentment flourishing throughout the community.

Not long after the tar and feathering experience, Brigham Young, a robust and jovial young man, Smith's senior by four years, traveled to Kirtland to meet the Prophet. That meeting would leave an indelible impression upon Smith. Immediately he was struck with Brigham Young's clever views of policy, and generally instinctive knowledge of character. No other person Smith would receive into the church would be so loyal a defendant of the prophet.

Young had a very hard life as a youth. His mother died when he was fourteen years of age. Deprived of a mother, he knew nothing of the social graces, including a formal education. Although his father was a staunch disciplinarian and pious man, Young became tainted in his early life with such worldly habits as swearing, which in later years spilled over into his pulpit discourses.

At twenty-three Brigham married Miriam Angeline Works, his first wife, and took up the trades of painter, glazier and carpenter. In the summer he hired out as a farm laborer in order to provide for his family. In the spring of 1829 he moved his wife and two daughters to Mendon, New York, near his father.

Although Young believed in God and the hereafter, he exhibited little interest in formal religion before he was married. After marriage, Young joined the Methodist church but was never really active.[81] Miriam later contracted tuberculosis rendering her a semi-invalid.

Peddling a new religious book, Samuel Smith, brother to Joseph, passed through Mendon. At an inn there, Samuel Smith met Phinehas Young, a traveling Methodist exhorter, brother to Brigham. A copy of the *Book of Mormon* was placed in the hands of Phinehas[82] that led the family to discuss this new religious phenomena. When Mormon missionaries returned later, Brigham saw a demonstration of speaking in tongues accompanied by what was claimed to be an interpretation of the strange language. It was enough to impress the uneducated Brigham Young who later claimed that he had been seeking a sign as to the authenticity of this new religion by praying that the missionaries would come to his home and bless his sick wife. In due time they arrived at his doorstep, which Young took as an answer to his prayer. On April 15, 1832, at the age of thirty, Brigham was baptized by the Mormons in his own mill stream. Miriam was later baptized, due to her infirm condition, when the weather was warmer.

In September of 1832, Miriam Young died of tuberculosis. Following her death, Brigham, with his two daughters, moved in for a brief period with his good friend Heber C. Kimball and his wife.[83] The Kimballs had also joined the Mormons. Soon Young and Kimball traveled to Kirtland, Ohio, to meet the new prophet. Smith was chopping wood with some of his brothers when they arrived. At the Smith home they discussed matters pertaining to Mormonism. When Smith called on Young to dismiss the meeting with prayer, he burst out in tongues. Those around expected Smith to condemn the gift but Smith called it "pure Adamic language."[84]

On July 23, 1833, the cornerstone for the Kirtland Temple was lain. Almost three years later the temple was dedicated on March 27, 1836. It was built of stone quarried outside the city. The massive building was 60 x 80 feet outside measurement and

65 x 55 feet on the inside corridor. It was 110 feet tall with two stories, including the spire.[85] The stone was covered with cement stucco. Twelve windows adorned each side of the building with an attic used for classrooms. The imposing structure cost $40,000, not including the volunteer work, which was considerable, done by the Saints themselves.[86]

At the dedication of the Temple a full choir sang a capella. An organ was not installed until later. Sidney Rigdon read Psalms 24 and 96 and brought a discourse, two and a half hours in length, on Matthew 18:18-20, but it was Oliver Cowdery who stood beside Smith, in the twin pulpits, as the veils descended around them. When the veils lifted, Smith claimed to have seen the Savior and quoted freely from the first chapter of Revelation describing Him. Moses, Elisha, and Elijah were also said to have appeared to Smith and Cowdery. Smith concluded the formal service with a lengthy prayer, after which the choir sang. Church leaders made brief remarks but Brigham Young, not to be outdone, broke out in tongues at the close of the service.[87]

Kirtland was the site where the first Twelve Apostles were appointed, and the *Book of Commandments* was first distributed. After the destruction of the printing press in Jackson, Missouri, where the *Book of Commandments* was first published in 1833, additional revelations including the Articles of Faith were added to the book and the title was changed to *Doctrine and Covenants*.

Caught in the throes of land speculations and charged with discrediting the true Church by changing its name from the "Church of Christ" to the "Church of Latter-day Saints," Smith was faced with distrust and apostasy. Warren Parrish led a group in opposition to the leadership of Smith. It was so widespread that Brigham Young had to enlist the faithful to be present at Conference on September 3, 1837, to sustain the Prophet.[88]

Typical treatment of dissenters to Smith's leadership was to receive the acid tongue of the Prophet through his publications, accusing them of some immoral behavior. The *Elder's Journal* (Mormon newspaper) carried his searing charge calling Parrish an "animal" producing "groaning and gruntings". Leonard Richri was typed a "drunkard" and John F. Boynton as "a man notorious for nothing, but ignorance, ill breeding and imprudence." Luke Johnson was charged with being a "thief" who stole from his father.[89]

Business failures in Kirtland included a general store, though never a profitable one, owned by the church. The store maintained scarce supplies. Purchases were often charged by the Saints, many of whom never paid their accounts. Additionally, a printing shop, a tannery, and a saw mill all failed.[90]

There seemed to be no end to Smith's business adventures. His worst failure was the establishment of a bank, one that would ultimately send the Mormon leaders scurrying out of town under the protection of darkness. On November 2, 1836, Smith established "The Kirtland Safety Society Bank" that was anything but safe and far from being a bank in the normative sense. Oliver Cowdery, sent to Philadelphia to purchase printing plates for the new bank bills, returned with $200,000 in preprinted certificates. Orson Hyde traveled to the state legislature in Columbus, Ohio, to secure the proper papers for incorporation.[91] A hitch developed in the scheme when the legislature refused to grant Smith a charter for his new bank. The preprinted bills were thus rendered illegal. A clever, yet devious plan was adopted in the January 2, 1837 bank reorganization meeting of the Mormon leaders. The name on the bills of "Kirtland Safety Society Bank" were changed by stamping, in lowercase letters, "anti" as a prefix and "ing" as a suffix to the word "Bank," rendering it the Kirtland anti-Bank-ing Company. Smith claimed $4,000,000 as capital for the bank and a divine revelation for its establishment, admonishing in the name of the Holy Spirit that "the brethren abroad, to call on us, and take stock in the Safety Society."[92]

Charges were brought by Samuel D. Rounds against Smith and Rigdon, as President and Treasurer of the Bank respectively, their names appearing as such on the bills, that the bank was not legally incorporated. Following their arrest, bond was set and raised by friends, but before the court could reconvene, the bank went under. Both fled under cover of darkness for Far West,

Missouri, another Mormon settlement, leaving behind many Saints and non-Mormon investors holding the worthless notes.[93]

Although Smith in his history blamed the times generally for the bank failure, he specifically blamed Warren Parrish, who had been a clerk of the bank, as well as a faithful member of the church. Parrish fell out with Smith over changing the name of the church, became an apostate and led a group out. It became convenient for Smith then to blame him for the collapse of the bank.[94]

When Smith demanded a search warrant to investigate the contents of the trunk of Warren Parrish, Squire Frederick G. Williams refused to grant it, probably because he recognized it as a subterfuge by Smith to cover his own tracks. Smith in turn discharged Williams from the office of magistrate.[95]

The church membership in Kirtland was reported at one thousand, but Smith was looking beyond Kirtland as a final resting place for the Mormons. A year before in New York, he had sent Parley P. Pratt, Oliver Cowdery and two others on a mission west to the Indians. Reaching the western border of Missouri, in the winter of 1830, they remained through 1831 settling in Independence (Jackson County), Missouri. There they presented the Mormon teachings to the Indians of the surrounding area.

Chapter Seven
MIGRATION TO MISSOURI

W hen the church conference was held in June 1831, according to Mormon records, two thousand followers gathered in Kirtland, where Smith received a revelation designating Missouri as the next conference site with the instruction that he and Rigdon travel to the area to survey the work there. Meanwhile, a group of sixty Colesville, New York Saints, after a short tenure near Kirtland, moved just outside Independence. When the Prophet arrived, they laid the foundation of the first log house and a revelation was recorded declaring Independence as the specific place of the city of Zion. The next day Smith dedicated the future temple site just west of the courthouse.[96]

        With the large influx of Mormons into Independence, the older citizens began to feel threatened. More than a third of Jackson County became populated by extremely poor, voting Mormons. The original settlers saw the immigrants rapidly becoming a majority who would rule the county. Tensions mounted as the church grew. The zeal of many of the Saints was intemperate and so was their language. Those already living in the area soon discovered that the Mormons planned to take over the entire area in obedience to a revelation of their prophet. That the Mormons intended to purchase the land for the future city of Zion may well have been misunderstood by their Gentile neighbors. As the Mormons grew in Jackson County, so did their opposition. Conflicts among themselves and confrontation with the original settlers, who were taught that their creeds were wrong and their doctrine an abomination unto the Lord, did not set well with these orthodox Christian believers.[97]

Tensions increased between the settlers and the Mormons who claimed direct revelation from God and possession of the New Testament gifts. Opposition also arose from the merchants of the area because the Mormons patronized their own store, refusing to buy from them. The Mormon newspaper, *The Evening and Morning Star*, edited by W.W. Phelps, made it clear from its beginning that Independence was Zion where the Saints would be gathered. B.H. Roberts, church historian, admitted it was too plain a word of the Saints' intention and that overzealous members had declared that the Lord would give them the state of Missouri. In July 1833 *The Evening and Morning Star* further agitated the older citizens of Jackson County by stating,"...no matter what foolish report the wicked may circulate to gratify their evil disposition; the Lord will continue to gather the righteous and destroy the wicked, till the sound goes forth, IT IS FINISHED." In addition, the paper printed what was perceived as a reprimand to the people of Missouri concerning a law prohibiting "free people of color" from entering the state.[98]

Rumors spread among the slave holding residents that the Mormons wished to extend an invitation to the "free people of color," being the Negro or mulattos that had been set free or purchased their freedom. This created such a stir that the Mormon newspaper printed the Missouri law regarding free people of color and advised church members not to offend Gentiles in this matter.[99]

Countercharges were traded, tempers flared and Mormon homes were fired upon, rocked and generally assaulted. Citizens gathered at the courthouse in Independence and drafted an ultimatum demanding the Mormons leave Jackson County. In the town meeting at the courthouse, about two hundred citizens formulated a manifesto ordering the Mormons to leave Jackson County. When the Mormon leaders requested time to consider the manifesto, the mob was in no sympathy to wait. They proceeded to raze the Mormon printing office and tar and feather Edward Partridge and a man named Allen.

When the Mormons were finally driven from Missouri, Partridge later became Bishop of Nauvoo, Illinois, where he died of fever.[100] The two daughters of Partridge, Emily and Eliza, were taken by Smith into his home and later became two of his many polygamous wives.[101] Smith once described Partridge "a pattern of piety, and one of the Lord's great men..."[102] An appeal to Governor Daniel Dunklin by the Mormons brought only advice to apply to the local courts for assistance, courts controlled by Gentile citizens.[103]

Continued mob violence broke out against the Mormons, who with no due recourse, moved to nearby Clay County where they were received with general hospitality, a hospitality that would be short-lived. The citizens there understood that the settlement would be temporary, but after two years of buying land, the Mormon situation appeared permanent. Essentially the same charges were brought against the Mormons of Clay County. A solution was presented to them offering to divide Ray County into two additional parts, naming them Caldwell and Daviess counties. The Mormons were offered Caldwell County as their own. Existing settlers in Ray County would be offered an opportunity to sell their land to the Mormons, which some did. The proposal was agreed upon and the Mormons moved to Caldwell County where they established the town of Far West as a main settlement,[104] under the leadership of Edward Partridge.

Back in Kirtland, apostates volleyed for leadership over the remaining saints, but none had the charisma of Smith. Five hundred and fifteen souls, many of which had lost their finances in the failed Bank, packed up their wagons and headed out of town for Far West, Missouri,[105] returning Kirtland to the sleepy little community it was prior to the Saints first arrival. There, on the hillside behind the wagon train, rose the majestic temple they had labored so hard to build.

Joseph Smith departed Kirtland penniless. Had it not been for the ingenuity of Brigham Young, whom he met up with on the way to Far West, he would have entered the new Mormon settlement broke. Young shared the Prophet's plight with a brother in the church who had recently sold a piece of land and was obliged to give a gift of three hundred dollars, which Young handed over to Smith, sufficient to deliver him with his family to Far West.[106]

When Smith pulled into town, his spirits were revived when welcomed with a brass band, a cheering crowd and a favorable following. Whatever Smith lost in his humiliating failure back at Kirtland, he quickly regained as he entered Far West. Though the conditions there were far more primitive, he wasted no time in looking over his new kingdom. There were few homes in the new settlement which were nothing more than log cabins with dirt floors, windows without glass and the simplest living conditions. For a time Smith had to satisfy his family in a tent until a cabin could be constructed. He took note in his diary that in camping out, rattlesnakes, though not numerous, were native to the area.[107]

Soon after Smith arrived in Far West, he traveled eighteen miles north, staying close to the river, crossing Wright's Ferry into Daviess County. When a member of the party discovered a pile of curious rocks, Smith broke out in revelatory enthusiasm, immediately declaring the place to be Adam-ondi-Ahman "the place where Adam shall come to visit his people, or the Ancient of Days shall sit, as spoken of by Daniel the Prophet." This was in fact, declared Smith by the authority of the Lord, an ancient altar of Adam where the patriarchs associated with him, offered up sacrifices and angels "instructed them in heavenly truths."[108] He also taught that it was the original spot of the Garden of Eden where Adam blessed his children[109] and was buried.[110]

If Smith was receiving revelations, he was at the same time receiving criticism from some of his original leaders in the movement. Oliver Cowdery was charged on April 11, 1838, with eight counts, including encouraging lawsuits against the brethren, accusing the Prophet of committing adultery, absenting himself from meetings and refusing to be governed by "ecclesiastical authority or revelations..."[111] Cowdery refused to appear before the Council to face the charges, withdrawing his name from the church.

By April 13th, David Whitmer was also charged by the Council with "not observing the *Word of Wisdom*," neglecting to attend meetings," and corresponding with dissenters in Kirtland criticizing "the character of Joseph Smith." He also refused to appear before the Council and withdrew his name from the church roll. Both Cowdery and Whitmer are listed today as two of the three witnesses in the *Book of Mormon* as having seen the plates from which the translation was made.[112] Martin Harris, previously dismissed from the Church, was the third witness.

The waters were further troubled by the 4th of July celebration sermon by Sidney Rigdon against the dissenters of the church, typed as "Sidney's Salt Sermon." The sermon, taken from Matthew 5:13, charged the dissenters as being "good for nothing, but to be cast out, and trodden under the foot of men." The message, committed to print, was distributed and fell into the hands of some of the non-Mormon settlers, who interpreted the message as directed to them, firing their already charged emotions against the Mormons.

Ebenezer Robinson, a printer, joined the Mormons at Kirtland and ultimately, along with Don Carlos Smith, established the Mormon newspaper *Times and Seasons*. Robinson left the Mormons when the doctrine of polygamy was introduced at Nauvoo. In 1889 he edited *The Return* in Iowa after joining David Whitmer's Church of Christ. In *The Return*, Robinson remembers that "Rigdon was not alone responsible for the sentiment expressed in his oration, as that was a carefully prepared document previously written, and well understood by the First Presidency...This oration, and the stand taken by the church in endorsing it, and its publication, undoubtedly exerted a powerful influence in arousing the people of the whole upper Missouri county".[113]

The strain between the two parties grew from bad to worse. A fight broke out between them at a political election, where a Mormon by the name of Samuel Brown was attacked. In response, Smith, along with several of his men, visited Justice of the Peace Adam Black of Daviess County, obtaining a statement over his signature, declaring his intention to uphold the law. After they left, Judge Black swore an affidavit against Smith and Lyman Wright, stating that he felt his life threatened by the visitors had he not signed the document.[114] As a result, state troops were called in.

Following the excommunication of some of the leading members of the church, a secret organization was established called the Danites, a name taken from the tribe of Dan in the Bible. The Danites were a brotherhood of key Mormons committed to defend their Prophet, right or wrong, at all costs, by use of threats or even physical force.

According to David Whitmer, the creative genius behind the Danites was Sidney Rigdon.[115] Their assignment was to put down non-Mormon resistance and punish apostate Mormons. John Ahmanson, a Danish Baptist who converted to Mormonism in 1850, became disillusioned with the church and in 1876 wrote an exposé detailing some of the hidden secrets of Mormonism, including the Danite movement. Ahmanson wrote that Smith planned to take over Missouri, then the entire United States, and ultimately the world.[116] Later in Nauvoo the Danites served as bodyguards to Smith. Twelve men were named by the Prophet to this post, not the least were three who would identify themselves as violent defenders of the faith: John D. Lee, Orrin Porter Rockwell, and William Hickman.[117] A victim of grand delusions, Smith would be guilty of heinous crimes in the name of religion, under the protection of this fraternity of fearless men. Finally, in Utah, this band of "destroying angels" would continue to be used by Brigham Young to bring disloyal Mormons and Gentiles into line.[118]

Charges and countercharges were exchanged between the Mormons and the original settlers of Missouri. Tensions peaked when Thomas B. Marsh, President of the Quorum of the Twelve Apostles and Orson Hyde, also a member of the Twelve fled Far

West to Richmond, Missouri, to swear out affidavits disclosing the plans of the Danites. They also revealed Smith's angry threat to become the "second Mohammed" if hostilities continued."[119]

The Mormons were now poised in the settlement of "Di-Ahman" and Far West to defend themselves. In south Caldwell County, under the leadership of a Captain Samuel Bogart, forty soldiers of the state militia searched the Mormon home of a man by the name of Pinkham, arresting three men. News of the arrest filtered into Far West where Caldwell County Judge Elias Higbee (Mormon) called for a militia to be raised to rescue the three Mormon prisoners. [120] Approximately seventy-five men advanced on Bogart's encampment at Crooked River killing one man and wounding six others. Bogart's militia fled to the surrounding woods but not before mortally wounding Mormon Captain David W. Patten.[121]

Report of the attack upon Bogart's company at Crooked River spread like wildfire through the counties of Caldwell, Daviess and Ray. Mormons now sensed a foreboding of what was to come. The original settlers feared the worse at the hand of the Mormons. Word reached Governor Lilburn W. Boggs that the Mormons had burned Gallatin and Mill Pond and were preparing to burn Richmond. Boggs, familiar with the troubles in the area, including the previous threat by Sidney Rigdon in his Fourth of July address at Far West where he stated "it shall be between us and them a war of extermination, for we will follow them till the last drop of their blood is spilled, or else they will have to exterminate us," dispatched what would be the most infamous letter of the civil war between the Mormons and the Missouri settlers. Designated as "the order of extermination" it was addressed to General John B. Clark, Headquarters of the Militia, City of Jefferson and dated October 27, 1838. The letter instructed the General to treat the Mormons as enemies and that they "must be exterminated or driven from the State, if necessary for the public good."[122]

The conflict peaked on October 30th when the Missouri militia of two hundred and forty men marched on Haun's (also spelled Hawn's) Mill, ten miles east of Far West at Shoal Creek. The Mormons had been advised to collect at Far West for protection but the settlement at Shoal Creek was convinced that their buildings would all be destroyed once vacated, so they decided to remain to defend their properties.[123] Colonel William O. Jennings of Livingston County led the Missouri militia in an attack upon the Haun's Mill settlement, sending the women and children scurrying into the nearby woods, as thirty armed men and a boy ran to the blacksmith shop to defend themselves. The militia poured round after round into the poor barricade killing seventeen men outright and wounding twelve others. When the firing ceased, a trembling boy was retrieved from under a bellows where he hid for safety. Mercilessly, a militiaman named Rogers murdered the boy. An old man by the name of Thomas McBride, trembling, surrendered his rifle, saying, "Spare my life; I am a Revolutionary soldier". The soldier took the weapon, still loaded and discharged it into the veteran's breast. Another soldier mangled his body with a corn knife leaving his white hair stained by blood.[124] Thus a dark and shameful chapter is entered in Missouri history because of the callused leadership of Colonel W.O. Jennings, who acted virtually on his own in the attack.[125]

Apprehension filled the residents of Far West as numerous forces gathered about the city. A Mormon militia of eight hundred men formed a line south of the city to meet the advance of the enemy. The state militia offered no quarter, demanding the surrender of Joseph Smith Jr., Sidney Rigdon, Lyman Wright, Parley P. Pratt and G.W. Robinson. They demanded they be taken into custody; that the Saints surrender their arms, make financial restitution for damages and agree to leave the county under protection of the Missouri militia. The five hostages were transferred to the Liberty Jail. W.W. Phelps, Colonel Hinkle, John Corrill, John Whitmer and Danite leader Dr. Sampson Avard all testified against the Prophet and Rigdon. These five were subsequently excommunicated from the Church at Quincy, Illinois, on March 17, 1839. Both Phelps and Marsh subsequently were accepted back into the church.

Under the charge of "treason, murder, arson, larceny, theft and stealing" the five asked for a change of venue which was granted for Boone County. In the transmission of Smith and the others, the sheriff with his guards were bribed with a jug of whiskey. A final guard escorted them out of camp, to escape to Illinois, after the others drank themselves to sleep. Attempts to extradite Smith by Missouri officials failed numerous times.[126]

Chapter Eight
ILLINOIS MIGRATION

Beginning in October of 1838, the wagons, horses, sheep and cattle from twelve to fifteen thousand Saints, made their way in a winter exodus to Quincy, Illinois. A few of the Saints settled in nearby Iowa. By late March almost every Mormon had left Missouri. On April 20th the last Mormon departed.[127] They had been given three weeks to collect their crops for the trip. The trip itself could take as long as three weeks to reach Quincy. Some made it in eleven days, and the quickest was in nine days, all in the bitter cold of winter. [128]

Illinois was a rugged country where the Saints gathered temporarily around Quincy. It was a state in deep debt and filled with lawless conditions. The Mormons were viewed by the politicians as an opportunity to gain votes.[129] Simply to increase the population, Quincy was both quick to welcome the migrating crowds to Illinois and to condemn their treatment at the hands of the people of Missouri. People were a premium to these frontier states. Sidney Rigdon received letters of commendation from President Martin Van Buren, Governor Wilson Shannon of Ohio and Governor Thomas Carlin of Illinois. Yet the politicians and people would soon see the folly of their invitation.

There was considerable concern among the Saints about living together in a collective commune, due to their previous experiences in Missouri, but Smith soon prevailed in convincing them that they could find a peaceful and safe residence. The settlement of Commerce, Illinois was selected as a permanent residence of the Saints. Commerce consisted of two blockhouses, two framed dwellings, and one general store. Land was purchased and the town's name was changed to Nauvoo, a Hebrew word claimed Smith, meaning "a beautiful place." A beautiful place, it was lying on the east bank of the Mississippi River, high on a hill looking out toward Iowa. Nauvoo grew rapidly with many Saints gathering there from all parts of the country, some emigrating from Great Britain to stand with their Prophet against oppression of their enemies.[130]

Immediately facing Smith was the need for land in the new settlement. Seemingly able to convince his most dubious creditors, two men initially accepted his grandiose proposals. Smith also traded properties he could never reclaim back in Missouri with Dr. Isaac Galland, who provided "a considerable portion of the city plot" on "very reasonable terms and on long credit,"[131] later became a Mormon in Nauvoo. An additional 500 acres were purchased from H.R. Hotchkiss who took a note for $53,500, half of which was to be paid in ten years and the rest in twenty.[132]

The town, symmetrically laid out in plots of 180 x 200 feet facing the river, grew rapidly. By January 1, 1841, Smith estimated the population to be 3,000. A request for incorporation of the city of Nauvoo and the establishment of a seminary was placed before the Illinois Legislature.[133] In December of 1841 the city was granted a charter.

From different parts of Europe converts flocked to Nauvoo, swelling its population to an estimated 14,000 by 1842, according to Mormon sources,[134] which may have been closer to 10,000, making it yet the state's largest city. Soon after the Mormons settled in Nauvoo, Joseph Smith, Sr. died at sixty-nine. Don Carlos, brother to the Prophet, died shortly following the death of his father.

On April 1841 the cornerstone for the Nauvoo Temple was laid. With the gathering of the Saints to this new location also came new revelations defining the doctrine of Smith's church. Along with the laying of the cornerstone the doctrine of baptism for the dead was instituted, also referred to as salvation for the dead, which offered opportunity for departed family members to be brought into Mormonism by proxy baptism.[135] In many ways this heterodox teaching would appeal to prospective proselytes offering hope for their loved ones after death. Essentially, it became the equivalent to the Catholic doctrine of prayers for the dead in purgatory and limbo. Comparatively, baptism for the dead is theological universalism, a provision for every soul. Unfortunately, little could be farther from the truth of Christian Scriptures.

Traditional Christian teaching taught from the beginning of the church that couples united in marriage were joined "until death do us part," but Smith introduced a new philosophy termed synonymously "celestial marriage," or "eternal marriage," which purported to join couples not only upon the earth in time but also for all eternity.[136] A convenient extension of this teaching became the plurality of wives, better known as polygamy. This single teaching, which would create havoc in the hearts of many Mormon women and become an affront to non-Mormons, was given in a revelation and was read to Joseph's wife Emma by his brother Hyrum. Warned by Joseph, his brother returned to say that Emma had given him the worst "tongue lashing" such as he had never experienced and that she was "very bitter and full of resentment and anger." As Joseph placed the revelation in his pocket and prepared to leave, he reminded Hyrum that he had warned him that such would be her response.[137] The revelation wouldn't be read into the commandments until July 12, 1843, but it is stated in the official account that the Prophet had conceived the idea as early as 1831.[138]

Publicly, Smith preached one man for one woman for one lifetime but privately he taught his most intimate leaders the plurality of wives principle. William Clayton, Smith's private secretary in Nauvoo, recorded six journals of detailed information during 1840 to 1853, one of the most important eras in Mormon history. George D. Smith, in a valuable introduction to the publication of those journals writes, "Although he eventually married more than forty women, Joseph Smith never publicly acknowledged that he practiced polygamy . . . Even while the prophet issued denials, Clayton recorded his secret marriages."[139]

In July of 1838 Smith responded to the question, "Do Mormons believe in having more wives than one?" He answered, "No, not at the same time." Even marrying soon after the death of a spouse was rejected by Smith.[140] In October 1842 he wrote:

> *Inasmuch as this church of Christ has been reproached with the crime of fornication, and polygamy: we declare that we believe, that one man should have one wife; and one woman, but one husband, except in the case of death, when either is at liberty to marry again. We have given the above rule of marriage as the only one practiced in this church, to show Dr. J.C. Bennett's 'secret wife system' is a matter of his own manufacture; and further to disabuse the public ear...[141].*

At first he shrouded the teaching by claiming that they were only "spiritual" wives, as indeed a few may have been. In the beginning the majority of Saints believed any consummation of these marriages would take place in the after life of eternity. The *Book of Mormon* strictly forbids polygamy, calling it an abomination before the Lord, [142] yet the Mormons practiced it for over fifty years and some fundamentalist Mormons still practice polygamy today.

The Reorganized Church does not hold polygamy as a teaching and has blamed other leaders of the church for the idea. Officially, the RLDS in their publications, has blamed Dr. J.C. Bennett as the originator of the plural wife system. Others have cited Brigham Young as the instigator.[143] Bennett has been described as a man "excessively vain and pompous," of "questionable reputation"[144] and the "greatest scamp in the Western county... debauched, unprincipled and of profligate character."[145] Previously an Ohio physician, he had moved to Illinois to become Quartermaster-General of the State, where he joined the Mormons in August 1840. In one of his extremely flawed judgments, the prophet appointed Bennett as Mayor of Nauvoo in February 1841 and later gave him the title of Major-General of the Nauvoo Legion.[146] When his character was assailed in several Illinois newspapers, Sidney Rigdon defended him as dutiful and dedicated. Bennett would ultimately be excommunicated from the church May 17, 1842 but would return after the death of Smith to support the inauguration of Rigdon as the next president, a battle which would be lost to Brigham Young and his Twelve Apostles.[147]

Just what actually happened between Smith and Bennett that drove a wedge between them is not clear. Both were strong willed leaders, each contending for power. It is likely Smith recognized too late that he had opened a Pandora's box in heaping too much leadership on Bennett and all too quickly. He now regretted his hasty action. Trust invested in some men only serves to heighten their avarice, a truth Smith must have realized. From the minute that Bennett was read out of the church, he became a constant thorn in Smith's side, filing the Illinois papers with vituperative letters, traveling on a lecture circuit and finally producing an exposé of the prophet and Mormonism. Smith continued to experience the growing reactions of Bennett and hastened to retaliate. Smith labeled Bennett as "an imposter and base adulterer" teaching "promiscuous intercourse between the sexes."[148] Further, he recorded that a communication from a reliable source had informed him, soon after Bennett had joined the church, that he was showing too much attention to the young ladies of Nauvoo, while maintaining a wife and children back in McConnelville, Ohio.

This reference has been interpreted by the RLDS to mean that Bennett instituted polygamy. Even though Smith says he received this letter immediately following Bennett's acceptance into the church, he later appointed him Mayor of the city and Major-General of the Legion.

The revelation in the *Doctrine and Covenants* requires the Saints to obey the doctrine of plural marriage at the peril of their salvation. Temple Mormons, through the endowments cannot reach the highest order in glory unless they obey this commandment. This commandment "pertaining to principle and doctrine of their having many wives and concubines" stipulated "For behold, I reveal unto you a new and everlasting covenant; and if ye abide not that covenant, then ye are dammed; for no one can reject this covenant and be permitted to enter into my glory."[149]

Sidney Rigdon objected to the teaching of plural wives so strongly that it caused a rift between him and Smith. It was also his rejection of polygamy that may have figured as a factor in his rejection by Young and the Twelve Apostles to become the head of the church after Smith's death.[150]

William E. McLellin, an original member of the Quorum of the Twelve Apostles, was closely associated with Joseph Smith.[151] While with the Mormons, he kept detailed accounts of events surrounding their beginning days. Early on it troubled him that Smith, while claiming to be a prophet receiving revelations directly from God, often altered these revelations before they entered the *Doctrine and Covenants* for printing.[152] He lost faith in Smith when he discovered that he had committed adultery with Fannie Alger, who was taken in by Emma and ultimately driven from the house when Emma learned of Joseph's relationship with her. Alger is listed as Smith's first plural wife.[153] McLellin, once a devoted follower of the prophet, was excommunicated in 1838 and became a bitter enemy of the church, but not before leading a group of forty-two dissenters to Kirtland where he published a paper called *Ensign of Liberty*.[154]

Smith, on October 25, 1831 had issued a revelation regarding McLellin, commissioning him to "go forth and preach, ... heal the sick," but charged him to "commit no adultery, a temptation with which thou has been troubled."[155] It was Smith's subtle way of assaulting his character through a veiled revelation. Yet, there is not a single thread of evidence that McLellin, though misguided, was anything other than an honorable man.

During the 1988 Mark Hofmann investigation in Salt Lake City, Utah, it was revealed that part of the McLellin collection of journals, letters and documents, which he was supposed to have been trying to sell to individuals in the church, had been secretly hidden away in the vault of the First Presidency since 1908.[156] These documents threaten to reveal embarrassing details surrounding the life of Joseph Smith. Hofmann was the Mormon forger who sold thousands of dollars worth of fake documents to the LDS church and killed several individuals with brown paper sack bombs.

Joseph Smith, fraught with arrogant ambition and driving dreams, projected his aspirations for the Presidency of the United States. Appeals were made to John C. Calhoun, Fort Hill, South Carolina and Henry Clay, Ashland, Kentucky who refused a pledge of redress for the Mormon against the State of Missouri.[157] He now conceived himself as a temporal prince and spiritual leader to his people. Openly denouncing the government of the United States as completely corrupt, he offered himself as presidential candidate for the nation. Surrounded by his Danite band, who pledged to support him to the death, he had himself anointed King of Nauvoo.

Peter Cartwright, fervent Methodist circuit rider, met Joseph Smith on a trip to Springfield, Missouri. A friendly conversation turned into a heated exchange between them. "I will show you, sir," thundered Smith, "that I will raise up a government in these United States which will overturn the present government, and I will raise up a new religion that will overturn every religion in this country!"[158]

Smith established a proposed platform to cut Congress by half, pay the members $2 a day plus board, pardon all convicts, free all slaves, establish a national bank and bring in equal pricing as a means to make cities solvent.[159]

Smith accused Sidney Rigdon, since their departure from Missouri, of being disloyal to the prophet. Charges were brought against Rigdon by Smith on the second day of a special conference on October 6, 1843, called to discuss Rigdon's present standing with the church and progress on the building of the temple. Rigdon was charged with corresponding with apostate John C. Bennett, former Mayor of Nauvoo, and ex-Governor Thomas Carlin; mismanagement of the Nauvoo Post Office; betrayal of information to the Missouri officials as to the whereabouts of Smith, and his general failure in the position of First Counselor to the prophet. Rigdon, in a pitiful plea, threw himself on the mercy of Smith and the Council giving some explanation for a few of the charges, and denying that he had ever written apostate Bennett, other than a business correspondence of which Smith was aware.

On October 8th, after a brief period of adjournment due to inclement weather, the Council heard Rigdon further defend his actions in Missouri. Finally, Smith, perhaps after some diminution of his paranoid suspicion and having obtained additional information concerning the matter, rose and explained the correspondence of Rigdon with ex-Governor Carlin to the satisfaction of the Council. Then, in a rare gesture of clemency, Smith expressed willingness to retain Rigdon in his present office, providing he would magnify it with integrity, but concluded with a lapse back into protectionism, conceding that he hardly felt it possible due to Rigdon's past actions.[160] Was it the expression of a magnanimous spirit by the prophet or was it that he remembered that Rigdon was privy to information that could be used against him if he so chose?

Shortly after the conference, Rigdon was sent back to his home state of Pennsylvania to campaign for the upcoming election. As proof of Smith's unabashed temperament, he also sent two or three thousand missionaries throughout the eastern United States campaigning for him.[161] James Arlington Bennett of New York was first chosen to be his vice-presidential running mate but was disqualified by the fact that he was not American born. Next, Solomon Copeland of Paris, Tennessee, was asked to be Smith's running mate, but declined. Perhaps still taunted by possible repercussions from the hand of Rigdon or in a move to unify his forces, Rigdon was finally chosen to become his vice-presidential running mate.[162]

The Mormons continually sought evidence to support the *Book of Mormon*, such as plates with inscriptions hidden in the earth. In 1843 six hatchet-shaped plates with curious characters were reported found near Kinderhook, Illinois. Having a hole near the top of the smaller end of each plate, they were held together by a ring. It was reported that Robert Wiley, a merchant of the area, found the plates while digging among the ashes and human remains of a mound of earth. When Smith was shown the plates, he immediately declared them to be a history of the descendants of Ham, son of Noah.[163] Facsimiles of both the fronts and backs of the plates are pictured in the *History of the Church*. Years later in a sworn affidavit, Wilson Fulgate, before Justice of the Peace Jay Brown of Mound Station, Illinois, declared that the plates were a hoax, made up by Robert Wiley and Bridge Whitton, a blacksmith who cut the plates out of some pieces of copper. Wiley and Whitton made the hieroglyphics by creating impressions on beeswax and filling them with acid, after placing them on the plates. Nitric acid, old iron and lead were used to create an effect before binding them with a piece of hoop iron.

The trio further conceived of burying the plates and then digging them up in the presence of two Mormon elders, one of which proclaimed that the Lord had led them to the digging. Ultimately the plates were placed in a St. Louis, Missouri museum where they later disappeared.[164] In 1920 one of the plates turned up in the hands of Mormon history professor Stanley B. Kimball, who after extensive testing determined that the plates were fake.[165] It is interesting to note that neither B.H. Roberts, in his *Comprehensive History of the Church,* nor present Mormon historians, refer to the Kinderhook plates as evidence for the *Book of Mormon*, although Smith declared them to be a record of the descendants of Ham.

Chapter Nine
FATAL DECISION AT NAUVOO

Not far from Nauvoo, the *Warsaw Signal*, under the perspicacious pen of Thomas Gregg, hammered away at the advancing threat of Mormonism with a prophet that taught the degrading concept of polygamy. William Smith, brother to the prophet had precipitated the fight in his first issue of *The Wasp* by calling Thomas Sharp, co-editor with Gregg, "a contemptible demagogue" and a "complete Jackass of an editor." Sharp retorted saying "The Wasp" would be better named the "Polecat." "It is needless to inform our readers that we don't fight with such animals - nature giving them a distinct advantage."[166] Back and forth between the papers the verbal missiles were launched at each other, no doubt to the amusement of their readers.

Within the church, among others, William Law, an intelligent and wealthy man, had come to Nauvoo from Canada with his brother Wilson. Law, a devout follower of Smith and a man of notable character, advanced to the position of Second Counselor where he began to recognize the unsavory business practices of the prophet. But what troubled him the most was the teaching of Smith concerning "plural wives." He watched with horror as the spectacle of "spiritual wife" teaching turned into physical wife polygamy. It was more than he could abide when Smith approached his own wife Jane to become his "spiritual wife."[167]

William Law begged Smith to abandon the idea of

polygamy but Smith persisted. When private imploring to cease the teaching failed, Law turned to public exposure in order to reform the church and its prophet that he viewed as fallen. The Law brothers, Dr. R.D. Foster, Francis M. Higbee, Chauncy L. Higbee, and Charles A. Foster, who became its publishers, established the *Nauvoo Expositor* that was to know only one issue. While Law wrote with restraint, he nevertheless issued a clarion call for repentance and righteousness.[168]

The paper barely left the hand of Smith when he ordered Hyrum to summon the City Council into session. The *Expositor* was summarily condemned as a public nuisance and the City Marshall was dispatched, backed up by the Nauvoo Legion, who broke into the paper, and carried the type trays into the street where they were burned. The press was completely destroyed.[169]

Destruction of the paper set off a tidal wave of reaction in the community and surrounding area, deploring the attack upon free speech and the violated rights of private property. Recognizing that he had unleashed a formidable reaction, Smith called in from the field all apostles and representatives who were out stumping for his election as president of the United States. He mobilized the Legion and sent to Governor Thomas Ford an imploring letter to come to Nauvoo.[170] Governor Ford, influenced by the Laws, Foster and Higbee, returned a summons for Smith's arrest to face trial in Carthage, fifteen miles away. Smith responded to the summons by planning an escape with Hyrum. This brought charges of abandonment and cowardice from Joseph's wife Emma and others.[171]

As the conflicts increased in the Mormon haven of Nauvoo with his Gentile neighbors, Smith began to formulate a plan for settling elsewhere. A new Zion would have to be developed far beyond the reach of their anti-Mormon adversaries and the intrusion of the national government. Sentiment continued to mount against Smith because of the destruction of the *Nauvoo Expositor* and the flourishing reports of polygamy. On June 22, 1844 Joseph, his brother Hyrum, Willard Richards, and Orrin P. Rockwell entered a skiff about midnight and rowed until they reached the Iowa side the next morning.[172]   Amidst his planned escape came an imploring letter from Emma and reported charges of cowardice causing him in resignation to return to Nauvoo.[173]

As Smith passed down the streets of Nauvoo, he perceived the mixed reaction in the faces of the Saints. Many were relieved to see him, feeling a bit safer for his return. Others viewed his presence with foreboding fears of reprisals from the government due to the destruction of the *Expositor*. Some glared from their doorways at a prophet who had fled in the night leaving them to face the eventful future alone. He could sense their deep disappointment. Even the children playing in the street felt the menacing mood of disaster.

On the desk of Smith lay an unopened letter from Governor Thomas Ford in response to a request petitioning protection against the angry threats of his Nauvoo neighbors in Carthage and Warsaw. In his letter to the governor, he had defended his actions of destroying the paper as necessary to the protection of the city. Ford's letter promised protection but demanded his immediate surrender, warning that nothing less than the Illinois militia would guarantee it.[174]

The Nauvoo Legion anxiously assembled before the reviewing stand as the Prophet mounted the steps dressed in his general's garb with gilded buttons, epaulets on his shoulders and a sword at his side. In his brassy speech he warned them that they were as much a target of the enemies' contempt as he was, declaring his willingness to stand against them till death. A roar of response filled the air in a shout of support from the Legion.[175] The women quietly prepared for a hasty move to another unknown destination. Back at the mayor's quarters, a core of clerks copied reports of threatened violence against the city of Nauvoo to send to the Governor's office.

Governor Ford visited Carthage to investigate the reports against the leaders of Nauvoo where he met an infuriated assembly ready to advance on Nauvoo. He charged the group to act only within the law of an orderly force. A committee from Nauvoo set before him their defense of the destruction of the *Expositor*, which helped cement his understanding of the matter. Conditions of a declaration held out protection for the Prophet and his associates, providing their surrender.[176]

Joseph and Hyrum balefully entered Carthage around midnight, met by the jeers and threats of the townspeople still left in the streets. The next day they appeared before Justice Robert F. Smith on charges of riot and treason, by virtue of declaring martial law and calling forth the Nauvoo Legion. Along with Smith and Hyrum appeared thirteen members of the Nauvoo City Council. They were all released on the charge of riot after posting bond of $500 each, pending their appearance at the next Circuit Court. As the hour was late, the charge of "treason" was not mentioned.[177]

The Smith brothers remained at the Hamilton House while the other members of the City Council returned to Nauvoo. Joseph and Hyrum were rearrested by Constable Bettisworth that same evening and taken to jail. Governor Ford accompanied the defendant's lawyers to the justice because the Smiths received no hearing before they were first jailed. The justice explained that he had placed them in jail to protect them from the rebel rousers in the city. Governor Ford requested that the prisoners be kept in the large area on the second floor which had no bars and they could receive friends, one of which later passed them a six-shooting revolver.[178] This was originally denied in the church newspaper[179] and is never mentioned today by Mormon guides at the Carthage Jail. With the Smiths were Willard Richards and John Taylor, two others having been sent on errands.

The Mormons make much of the fact that Governor Ford failed as promised to take Joseph and Hyrum with him when he went to Nauvoo to investigate the report of a counterfeiting press. Ford had hoped to display enough force to discourage the Saints from retaliation for the arrest of their prophet. The Governor received word from some of his officers that it would be "highly inexpedient and dangerous" to take the Smiths with him in light of the many hostilities among the Hancock militia and reports that they were spoiling for a confrontation with the Mormons. Ford perceived the death of many innocent women and children in such an event and decided not to take the Smiths with him. He considered them safer in jail, having secured the "word and honor, officers and men, to do their duty according to the law" from Justice Robert F. Smith, head of the Carthage Greys, who guarded the jail.[180] Ford felt assured that no vile action would be taken by the troops knowing it would expose his troops to the open vengeance of the Mormons in Nauvoo.

With a company of only seven hundred soldiers, two companies left behind to guard the jail and a larger number having been dismissed and sent home, the Governor marched into Nauvoo. Had there been an upheaval in Nauvoo the Mormons outnumbered the Governor's soldiers three to one? In Nauvoo, he addressed the issue concerning the destruction of the *Expositor's* printing equipment, placed the city under martial law, and, noting the heavy armament of their Legion, warned that any outburst in defense of their leaders would only result in the needless bloodshed of innocent women and children.[181] Veiled threats passed between the two parties but no demonstration of force took place on either side. The troops passed through Nauvoo back to Carthage. About three miles out of town George D. Grant and David Bettisworth brought news of the attack on the Carthage Jail.

While Captain Robert F. Smith and his Carthage Greys camped on the town square, a young townsman by the name of William Hamilton placed atop the courthouse cupola, watched for any sign of a mob. Down at the jail, John Taylor sang "A Poor Wayfaring Man of Grief" to his friends. The prisoners shared some wine they had ordered, not as a sacrament as has been suggested, but says John Taylor, to "lift their depressed spirits."[182]

Late in the afternoon of June 27, 1844, young Hamilton spotted a group of men advancing on the jail, dragging their concealed guns behind them. He ran to take the news to Captain Smith but the mob had already reached the jail before he found him.[183] Most of the men in the mob were from the Warsaw regiment but the evidence reveals that the Carthage Greys were joint conspirators in the attack. Only a sergeant and eight men stood guard over the jail, part of which were reported in compliance with the action about to be taken. Advancing on the stairs, a shower of bullets passed up to the second floor followed by rapid footsteps. John Taylor, Joseph Smith and Willard Richards placed themselves against the door leading to the steps and sprang away when bullets passed through the door between them. Hyrum, positioned directly facing the cracked door, was hit by a bullet on the side of his nose. Another ball, hitting him from the window, passed through his side, shattering his pocket watch. "I am a dead man," were his final words as he fell motionless to the floor. Joseph snatched up the revolver from his dead brother's side and fired down the steps. Taylor and Richards, with their walking sticks, assisted the prophet by knocking muskets down as they were poked through the opening in the door.

Taylor ran to the window preparing to leap out when a bullet from the doorway hit his leg, sending him sprawling back upon the floor. He drew himself under a nearby bed as another bullet struck his pocket watch, stopping the movements at 5:16. Joseph leaped into the window, as bullets continued to ricochet around the room. Four balls struck the prophet, two from the doorway entering his back, one in the breast and another in the right collar bone. He cried, "O Lord, my God" as he fell out of the window and died.[184] At that moment, those on the stairs retreated to the outside. Fabricated stories of the prophet resting up against a well as additional bullets riddled his body[185] and of a man who threatened to cut off his head are mere fiction.

Inside the jail, Taylor was dragged by a disquieted Richards from the larger room to a nearby cell, and covered with a mattress, fearing of the mob's return. Outside the mob disbanded, returning hastily to their quarters. Near midnight the wounds of Taylor were tended by the town doctor. Willard Richards quickly sent word back to Nauvoo that both the Prophet and Hyrum were dead, Taylor was wounded and that he was well. He called upon the Saints not to retaliate but keep the peace. The citizens of Carthage fearfully and hastily evacuated the town by ferry, leaving only a few families behind.[186]

The bodies of Joseph and Hyrum Smith were taken back to the Nauvoo Mansion by wagon, prepared for burial and placed in pine coffins. After the family had viewed the remains, the townspeople passed by the coffins in a tearful procession. At the close of the day, the bodies were removed from the coffins and buried by night in the basement of the unfinished Nauvoo House. In the coffins were placed bags of sand, nailed shut, carried to a mock funeral and buried, fearing the prophet's enemies might dig up his body. In the fall, the Smiths were exhumed and buried side by side near the Nauvoo Mansion overlooking the Mississippi, at the request of Emma.[187]

Chapter Ten
FACTIONS OF THE FAITHFUL

T here have been 216 splinter groups formed from the original Mormon organization established by Joseph Smith in 1830.[188] Many of the groups lasted only a short time, ceasing with the death of their founder. Others continued into the second and third generations while a few merged with other factions of the church. There are still in existence several of the sects formed around a follower of Smith who claimed to receive additional revelations. In some instances, they saw Smith as a fallen prophet or at least felt the church, which had become apostate under the leadership of Brigham Young, was in need of reform. All of these groups, with no known exceptions, accepted Joseph Smith as a prophet and the *Book of Mormon* as sacred.[189] Five figures stood in the forefront as contenders for the position of president of the church, all of which failed to achieve recognition of the larger group controlled by Brigham Young, but not without taking a fraction of the group with them.

No person so influenced and contributed to the formation of the Mormon doctrine as did Sidney Rigdon. Standing by Smith's side, he forged the framework of much of the teachings in the Mormon church. Having fallen out with Alexander Campbell over communal living and the place of gifts of the Spirit in the modern church, but not without being greatly influenced by the teachings of Campbell, he took up with the Mormons. No one was closer to Smith for fourteen years, directing the course of Mormonism. Rigdon was the only surviving member of the First

Presidency after Smith's death.

On August 3, 1844, Sidney Rigdon arrived back in Nauvoo from Pittsburgh. There he met with Apostles Parley Pratt, John Taylor, George A. Smith and Willard Richards. In a rather rambling and incoherent fashion, he declared in a sermon that he had received a vision from the Lord in Pittsburgh that a "guardian" should be appointed to head the church and that the Lord had further revealed that he was the divinely appointed "guardian". A recommendation from Willard Richards proposed that such a decision be held until the other apostles returned.[190]

Brigham Young, in a special called meeting August 8th, after Rigdon had presented his plea in a morning meeting, placed before the Saints a choice between the leadership of the Twelve Apostles and that of Sidney Rigdon. In a very clever tactical move on the part of Young, President of the Quorum of the Twelve, perhaps knowing at that moment he could not win the office for himself and that the Saints at this juncture would feel more comfortable with twelve men over one man leading them, suggested the choice between the Twelve and Rigdon. Both Emma Smith, the prophet's wife and his mother Lucy Mack Smith supported Rigdon in his attempt to gain leadership of the Church. The people under the strong influence of Young chose the Twelve to lead them.

Rigdon, who pretended to accept the will of the Twelve, met with groups of his supporters, leading them to Pittsburgh where he established a new church. At first they took the name of Church of Jesus Christ of Latter-day Saints but at a conference meeting on April 1845 changed it to Church of Christ. After the conference, Rigdon began to print his church paper *Messenger and Advocate of the Church of Christ* which survived almost two years.[191]

On September 8, 1844, Rigdon was voted out of the church at Nauvoo under the leadership of the Twelve. In an attempt to build up his church, Rigdon visited former settlements of the Saints to little avail. Over the next two years the church dwindled, with many joining orthodox churches in the area. By

1847 only a handful remained. In 1869 Rigdon tried to reorganize a formal following in Attica, Iowa, but failed there, too. When John Rigdon, son of Sidney, visited Salt Lake City, Utah, in 1863, Young sent word by him to Sidney that there was a place for him there. The invitation was never acknowledged due to Rigdon's strong feelings against polygamy. Rebuffed by his old antagonist, Young had Rigdon reduced to a minor player in the history of the church. On July 14, 1876, at eighty-three years of age, Sidney Rigdon died in Friendship, New York.[192]

Some historians consider Jesse James Strang, later to be changed to James Jesse Strang, to be the initial bidder for the church leadership. Born in Scipio, New York, on March 21, 1813, his childhood was filled with sickness. He was slight of frame all of his life and never reached above five foot three and one half inches tall, not a height of commanding presence. While young his teachers thought him an idiot, a judgment likely derived from his frail physical condition.[193] His head was unusually large for his body, hair brownish red, and his face finely chiseled with pronounced cheek bones.[194]

Though Strang enjoyed little formal education due to illness in childhood, he did become a prolific reader. As he grew up, he continued to study on his own and in 1836 he was admitted to the New York Bar of Chautauqua County. Strang, raised in a Baptist home, married the daughter of a pioneer Baptist preacher, the sister of his best friend Benjamin Pierce.[195]

In 1843, Strang journeyed with his family to Burlington, Wisconsin where he became acquainted with the Mormons through a brother-in-law, Aaron Smith. Together they traveled to Nauvoo in 1844 where they met Joseph Smith and Sidney Rigdon, becoming converts to Mormonism. He was baptized by Joseph Smith, sealed to the Melchizedek Priesthood and ordained an elder in the church.[196] Strang had only been a member of the church four months when Smith was killed at the Carthage Jail.[197]

On June 27, 1844, the day of Smith's death, Strang claimed that an angel appeared to him anointing his head with oil, ordaining him to rulership over the Saints of Earth. In support of this vision he received a letter on July 9th from Joseph Smith, having been written, he claimed, from the Nauvoo Jail, appointing him to be his successor. The letter dictated over Smith's signature on June 18, 1844, nine days before his death, appointed Strang to establish a new stake in Zion in Voree, Wisconsin, and, in effect, named Strang his successor.[198]

On September 1, 1843, Strang claimed that an angel disclosed to him the whereabouts of eighteen plates, inscribed with characters, buried in the roots of an old oak tree. The plates of Laban, as they were called, retrieved in the presence of witnesses, were translated by use of the "Urim and Thummim," *The Book of the Law of the Lord*, which obligingly brought a new revelation of polygamy and concluded with a reference that conveniently noted him as the prophet to succeed Joseph Smith.[199]

Strang's translation, *The Book of the Law of the Lord*, was originally printed in an eighty-page booklet in 1851,[200] but interpretative commentary brought the number of pages to around three hundred, revealing the teaching of a theocracy, "based upon principles of unmitigated absolutism".[201] Strang, who later led his church to Beaver Island, Michigan, had himself crowned King, now possessing a divine document that authorized his rule.

For several years a distinguishing factor between the Strangites and the Brighamites was the doctrine of polygamy. Strang had strongly denounced this teaching but in 1849 began to practice it by taking Elvira A. Field, a young schoolmarm, as a second wife. To conceal their secret, Elvira cut her hair and wore clothes resembling a man. Accompanying Strang on preaching missions, she was presented as his nephew Charles J. Douglass. Ultimately the secret was exposed and he reluctantly admitted the truth.[202]

After Young was elected president in 1847, Strang led the largest group of dissenters to Voree, Wisconsin. Included in the group were such notables as William Smith, brother to the Prophet, John C. Bennett, and John E. Page, a member of the Council of the Twelve Apostles. In Voree, Strang organized a church and established the *Voree Herald*, a church paper furnishing guidance to his followers. Ultimately he brought his group by revelation to Beaver Island, Michigan, where the *Voree Herald* became the *Northern Islander*. After organizing the islands into the county of Manitou, he represented it in the Michigan state legislature for a number of years.[203]

Like Smith, Strang led his followers by revelation. Plates dug from the earth were translated, and he had himself named as the official head of Beaver Island. Most of his followers disbanded after he was killed in 1856 by a mob, as a result of a falling out with Dr. Hezekiah D. McCulloch, a one time leader in the Strangite church.[204] Today the Strangite church numbers around 200.

William Smith, the only living brother to the prophet, then the presiding Patriarch of the Church, returned to Nauvoo in 1845. On October 6th in a meeting of the Twelve Apostles, his name was presented for the position of Apostle. Orson Pratt objected saying that he was unfit for the position. The vote was unanimous against the recommendation. A second recommendation asked that he be sustained as presiding Patriarch of the church. Again, he lost unanimously. William became bitter, printing a tract against the Twelve, for which he was promptly excommunicated. He then fell in with J.J. Strang for a short time but was later dismissed from Strang's church.[205] William had a stormy history in relation to the church, particularly with Joseph. Their relationship had been strained throughout the prophet's tenure,[206] even coming to blows on at least one occasion.[207]

In 1850 William founded a group that assembled at Covington, Kentucky, and began publishing the *Aaronic Herald* on February 1, 1849.[208] He declared himself "President Pro Tem" asserting that Joseph's son held the right to be president of the church, but because he was too young, William insisted that he should act as president until such time as young Joseph was able to take office. The movement was, however, short-lived. Identifying loosely with the Reorganized Church of Latter-Day Saints, he died in Oserdorck, Iowa in 1893.[209]

Among others who broke away and formed still additional

groups were Lyman Wright, Granville Hedrick and David Whitmer. Wright led a group to Wisconsin and Hedrick established in Independence, Missouri as The Church of Christ (Temple Lot). Three years following the death of Smith, David Whitmer, whose name appears in "The Testimony of Three Witnesses" in each copy of the *Book of Mormon*, became President of "The Church of Christ" founded by William E. McLellin, one of the original Twelve Apostles, but was excommunicated in 1838 at Far West by Joseph Smith. Following a break with McLellin, accusing him of error, Whitmer refused to move to Kirtland from Missouri and was dismissed from the church. McLellin then published *The Ensign of Liberty* at Kirtland, Ohio in 1847, which was to know only seven issues.[210] Whitmer died in 1888 shortly after a failed attempt to reorganize his followers.

On April 6, 1860, sixteen years after the death of Joseph Smith, many remaining behind after the migration to Utah officially formed the Reorganized Church of Jesus Christ of Latter-Day Saints (RLDS). Joseph Smith III was ordained as their president at Amboy, Illinois, with headquarters first established at Plano, Illinois, and later moved to Independence, Missouri.[211]

The Church of Joseph Smith, now divided into several factions, witnessed many of their members taking an introspective look within. Isaac and Sarah Scott, who later followed J.J. Strang into Wisconsin, wrote of their disillusionment to their family back in New England:

> ...*The Church is now divided, and part go for Sidney Rigdon and William Law, the only Presidents left the Church. The other part hold to the Twelve, who arrogate to themselves the authority to lead the Church. Rigdon and Law are honorable, virtuous men; therefore you see they would not do to teach polygamy, adultery, fornication, perjury etc. which is and has been*

abundantly taught in the Church. I have heard it taught I presume, an hundred times; I will be mistaken if Nauvoo before long don't be laid as waste as ever Jerusalem was; the wickedness of this people exceeds anything on record.[212]

Chapter Eleven
WESTWARD BOUND

At Carthage, Sheriff Minor Deming attempted to arrest those involved in the murders of Joseph and Hyrum Smith. Only five of the nine accused were located. Separate trials were set for each of the murders. Remembering their past history in Missouri, the Mormons were disdainful that the state would prosecute the defendants in the trial. John Taylor, writing in the *Nauvoo Neighbor*, expressed with biting force, "Until the blood of Joseph and Hyrum Smith have been atoned for...no Latter-day Saint should give himself up to the law."[213]

Rumors flourished that should the courts bring back an unsatisfactory verdict, then Carthage could expect retaliation from the Mormons. The fact that no eye witnesses to the crime could be produced by the prosecutor Josiah Lamborn made it virtually impossible to establish guilt beyond a reasonable doubt. According to common-law rule in Illinois during this time, any person participating in the attack on the jail was criminally accountable. The jury, made up of twelve non-Mormons, heard witnesses both for and against the defendants, listened to intense speeches by both lawyers for six long days and on May 30, 1845, at two o'clock returned a not guilty verdict, acquitting the defendants. A factor that no doubt frustrated the prosecuting attorney was the failure of Mormon leaders to assist him in securing more witnesses because the Mormons wanted to avoid further jeopardizing the public peace.[214]

During the trial, the Saints worked feverishly back in

Nauvoo to complete the Temple, in order to observe their endowments, their leaders staying under cover to avoid arrests because of floating warrants against them. On May 24th, Brigham Young engineered the capstone on the southeast corner of the temple into place, before a hushed crowd below. After Young pronounced the temple complete, the congregation shouted, "Hosanna, Hosanna, Hosanna, to God and the Lamb".[215] Two factors now made it evident to the Mormons that it would be impossible to remain in Nauvoo, the continual harassment from meandering bands of mobocrats attacking them in outlying areas and perennial indictments plaguing the leadership. In the Morley settlement alone, twenty-nine houses were torched, crops were destroyed and the inhabitants driven out. Unaided by their Gentile neighbors, even by those who bore them sympathy for their trials, the Mormons organized a posse of several hundred men to protect their property.[216]

A letter from Governor Ford suggested that if they were to know worship in a peaceful setting, they might consider removing to California.[217] In an unprecedented move, the state legislature repealed the Nauvoo city charter on January 21, 1845.[218] Rumors that federal troops in St. Louis planned to seize Mormon properties persisted, though now believed to be circulated only to induce the Saints' relocation sooner than they had planned.[219]

When plans to remove from Nauvoo were formally announced, preparations began immediately. The streets were filled with the business of trading tangible items incumbent to travel for more practical items such as wagons and animals. Blacksmiths beat their heavy hammers late into the night, forging the red-hot metal into form. Speculators hurried to Nauvoo to take advantage of bargain sales by the evacuating Mormons.[220] Brigham Young attempted to sell the entire city, offering it for one million dollars, half of its value, a plan that never materialized.[221]

On February 4, 1846, Charles Shumway, a staunch member of the Council of Fifty, made his way across the Mississippi to mark out a campground at Sugar Creek, Iowa, some seven miles from Nauvoo.[222]   Seven days later, approximately four hundred families left Nauvoo, headed for the camp.[223] On February 15th, Brigham Young, along with Lorenzo Snow, Apostles Willard Richards and George A. Smith, turned their backs to the disturbing events of Nauvoo in pursuit of a new frontier of freedom. They arrived in Sugar Creek where a large group of Saints awaited them.[224]

As the "Camp of Israel" pitched its tents at Sugar Creek, the ship Brooklyn pulled out of New York harbor on February 4, 1846, with 238 men, women and children, making its way to Yerba Buena in San Francisco, as the Mormon Battalion marched by land to California. A little more than half of the Brooklyn party ever made their way to Utah, many of them apostatizing and a few joining other Mormon colonies.[225] Other companies followed throughout the next two months until near the end of April when the greater part of the Mormons had evacuated Nauvoo.

Though Joseph Smith had suggested a possible future move to California or Oregon, he never viewed such a move as imminent since he was campaigning for president of the United States right up until the time of his death. Even Brigham Young was uncertain of their ultimate destiny as Lorenzo Snow, who became one of the Twelve Apostles of Young in Utah, wrote: "On the first of March, the ground covered with snow, we broke encampment about noon, and soon nearly four hundred wagons were moving to we know not where."[226]

After a brief time at Sugar Creek, allowing the Saints to gather, they soon moved to Council Bluff, Iowa, some four hundred miles northwest of Nauvoo.   Along the way they attempted to establish encampments, planting seeds for future immigrants that would follow, but they were a poverty-stricken people who had little possessions to do with. Many of them had sold their properties for a pittance or traded for any tangible item to equip them for travel. Martha S.H. Haven wrote her mother in Massachusetts: "We have sold our house for a trifle to a Baptist minister. All we got was a cow and two pairs of steers, worth about sixty dollars in trade."[227]

By July the main force arrived in Council Bluff. All along the way the Mormons sought work from the farmers or in some building trade. Facing the elements of snow and rain, they did what they could to provide for themselves. Young raised a Mormon battalion of some five hundred men and boys to assist the Federal Government, under President James K. Polk, due to a declaration of war with Mexico. Their pay, after expenses, was to assist the Saints in Utah. In a hardship march, after outfitting in Fort Leavenworth, Kansas, they marched to California, arriving a year later.[228] Some of them continued on to Salt Lake and others remained in California, separating from the Mormon church.

On April 8, 1847, Young organized a pioneering company of "one hundred forty-three men, seventy-two wagons, and one hundred and seventy-five head of horses, mules, and oxen, with rations for six months, agricultural implements and seed grain, manfully set out in search of a home beyond the Rocky Mountains."[229] Passing up the left bank of the Platte river, crossing at Fort Laramie, proceeding over the mountains of the South Pass, on July 21, 1847, they reached the Great Salt Lake. On the 24th the presidency along with the main body arrived, selected a portion of ground, consecrated it in prayer, and proceeded to plant crops. Young had contacted mountain fever and was severely ill, delaying his arrival. Author Conan Doyle, years later having traveled to Salt Lake, described it "as a barrier against the advance of civilization."[230]

Not long after the Mormons arrived, an area was marked out and surveyed for what was to become Salt Lake City. By 1848 a grist mill and two saw mills were erected. After a particularly devastating winter the Mormons began to formally organize a government, plant crops and erect houses. The maturing crops were ready for spring harvest when invading hordes of crickets advanced on them, leaving clean fields behind. Attempts to drown, burn and trample the crickets failed. Nothing seemed to work in getting rid of the pests until flocks of sea gulls from the area of Great Salt Lake swept in, gorging themselves on the crickets. For several weeks the gulls pecked away at the crickets until large portions of the crops were saved. The Mormons, regarding the coming of the sea gulls as a miracle, have reproduced the story in music, drama, sculpture and art. Actually, the cricket plagues continued into the 1870's.[231]

If Nauvoo became the "city of Joseph" then Salt Lake City must rightfully be called the "city of Brigham". By the winter of 1848 the Salt Lake area was swollen to almost five thousand in population. With the 1849 gold rush in California, some Mormons began advancing further west seeking fortune. Brigham Young saw the danger of so many Mormons leaving Utah and checked the westward movement by tempered speeches. Like most pioneer cities, Salt Lake experienced progress and failure together. The Tabernacle, their first building of worship, was completed April 6, 1852, four years after the Mormons arrived in the Salt Lake Valley. One year later, on April 6, 1853, the cornerstone was laid for the Temple but was not completed until forty years later in April of 1893.[232] Immigrants poured into Salt Lake City from England, Germany and Scandinavia over the next few years.

By 1855-1856, Brigham Young and his advisers, discussing cheaper ways of transporting the poor European immigrants to Zion, devised a plan to bring them across the plains by hand carts, built of hickory and ash, weighing approximately sixty pounds. The long distance of the trip, overbearing weather, and poor construction of many of the carts created disaster for many of the Saints along the trail. Sand often got into the bearing of the hubs, wearing them out. What was lauded by Church leaders as a divine plan revealed from heaven, became for the immigrants a devastating procedure. Women, children and the elderly faltered under the sheer burden of the trip. Flour for bread gave out, stock stampeded and were lost, promised provisions from Utah failed to materialize, and fatigued by toil, many were lost in death. Finally, three days out of Salt Lake, the emigrants were met by wagons of food and supplies.[233]

What was hidden, secret, and publicly denied in Nauvoo became open, revealed, and declared in Salt Lake. Five years after the Mormons arrived in the new territory of Utah, polygamy was announced as a revelation.[234]   The Mormons, now in their own land and virtually free of Gentile interference for the time being, established their independence. Brigham Young declared, "I live above the law, and so do this people".[235] The doctrine of plural marriages took on a ludicrous defense by Orson Pratt, an original leader in the church, claiming that "The fleshly body of Jesus required a Mother as well as a Father...hence the Virgin Mary must have been, for the time being, the lawful wife of God the Father... it may be that He [God] only gave her to be the wife of Joseph while in this mortal state, and that he intended after the resurrection to again take her as one of his wives, to raise up immortal spirits in eternity".[236]

His defense is further flawed by contending that Jesus was a polygamist, having several wives, Martha, Mary and Mary Magdalene taken as His bride at the wedding of Cana of Galilee, place of the first miracle. "If all the acts of Jesus were written," he wrote, "we no doubt should learn that these beloved women were his wives."[237] In Salt Lake City, as President of the Twelve Apostles, Pratt stood in the Tabernacle and declared:

> *...Jesus was the bridegroom at the marriage of Cana of Galilee... Now this was actually a marriage; and if Jesus was not the bridegroom on that occasion, please tell me who was... We say it was Jesus, who was married, to be brought into the relation whereby he could see his seed, before he was crucified... I shall say here, that before the Savior died, he looked upon his own natural children, as we look upon ours...[238]*

Orson Pratt maintained that the principle of polygamy was first taught by Joseph Smith in 1831, but that he did not practice it until 1841, ten years later.[239]   Yet Oliver Cowdery accused Smith of adultery as early as April 11, 1838.[240] One of several women writers chronicled the horrors of "cruel degradation" and "humiliation" in a lengthy book about the struggles of Mormon women with the teaching of polygamy in early Utah. Fanny Stenhouse wrote the following as a former Mormon in 1875:

> *Mine, in one sense, is the story of a wasted life. From the day when I linked my destiny with that of a Mormon Missionary Elder, to the time when, after long weary years of trial and endurance, I adjured the faith of the modern Saints, I suffered a constant martyrdom. Poverty, self-denial, and suffering, I gloried in, when I believed myself the humble instrument in the hands of the Almighty for proclaiming the 'Fulness of the Gospel' to those who were walking in the darkness of unbelief.*[241]

Numerous books by Mormon women, voluminous articles in magazines and newspapers, a constant haranguing by non-Mormons, and frequent court battles kept a sharp focus on polygamy in the Utah territory.[242] President Rutherford B. Hayes in 1880 appointed Eli Murray, a Kentuckian and former cavalry commander in the Federal Army during the War Between the States, as governor of Utah. Murray served in this capacity until 1885, reporting all the evils of polygamy to Congress and using his influence to see the practice brought to an end.[243] After several failed attempts by others to ban polygamy, Senator George F. Edmunds from Vermont, introduced an amendment to the Anti-Bigamy Act of 1862. Aimed at disqualifying George Q. Cannon as the Utah territorial candidate to Congress, it was signed into law in 1882.[244] It has been estimated that there were 3,500 polygamous families in the Utah territory during this time, 3,500 men and 11,500 women. The Edmunds law was strengthened by the Edmunds-Tucker Act in 1887.[245]

The phenomenon of polygamy has been traditionally explained in two ways. Mormon writers explain it as the natural consequence of an over population of women, which certainly was not the case in Utah. Non-Mormon writers explain polygamy as the result of the sensual desires of Smith and Young.[246] A real problem arises when the plural wife principle is held as a direct result of revelation, often referred to as "the principle," in light of the 1890 Manifesto rejecting polygamy which was issued due to pressure by the national government. And, although the church leaders had no doubt discussed at length, the forthcoming declaration, it was not an issue they surrendered quickly or without reluctance. President Wilford Woodruff was convinced that the political and social pressure was too much to withstand, as did Young before him, lest the church crumble under the iron fist of Washington.

Another reason for the Manifesto, however implausible, might contend that within Mormonism there was enough pressure to force Woodruff to bring an end to polygamy. There is, however, no evidence the resisting monogamists among the Mormons wielded any type of power sufficient to influence the Church Leaders, nor was it their disposition to succumb to any type of resistance. Long after the Manifesto many church leaders practiced polygamy secretly.

The Manifesto by President Wilford Woodruff in 1890, which was said to have rejected polygamy, must be studied carefully. The *Doctrine and Covenants* contains only excerpts of three addresses by the President. Note that it is not addressed to the Saints but "To Whom It May Concern" nor is it declared a word of the Lord and is not classified an actual revelation but a "Declaration" from the President.

In spite of a Manifesto, announced by President Wilford Woodruff September 25, 1890, an act motivated to defuse pressure of the national government and a desire to gain statehood, polygamy still flourishes. Estimates project from 30 to 50,000 Mormons still practice polygamy in several western states, including Utah and Canada. These polygamists claim that Joseph Smith appeared to President John Taylor in 1886 forbidding the abandonment of polygamy. A copy of the revelation, recorded by Taylor, they claim, remains in the Utah church vault, which is denied by the LDS Historical Department.[247]

When the system of celestial marriage is weighed in the light of Scripture, it is found to be in error. The Sadducees, referring to the Jewish custom of a man taking the widow of his deceased brother as his wife, and seeking to trick Jesus, asked Him whose wife a certain woman would be in the resurrection. Jesus declared them ignorant of the Scriptures saying that in the resurrection, "they that arise from the dead, they neither marry, nor are given in marriage; but are as the angels which are in heaven."[248]

Though vigorously denied, and often ignored in the writings of many Mormons, the Danites were organized by Dr. Sampson Avard with the knowledge and approval of Joseph Smith and Sidney Rigdon.[249] Originally known as "The Daughters of Zion,"[250] their commission was to support one another, right or wrong, and to uphold the dictates of the president.[251] This secret group of men, more appropriately named "Destroying or Avenging Angels" as they were later called in Utah, under the direction of Brigham Young, dealt severely with apostates by administering the practice of "blood atonement." The principle, based erroneously on Hebrews 9:22, taught that a person involved in certain sins could be saved by shedding his blood. Joseph Smith first cited the principle in Far West in a heated discussion with John Corrill concerning discrediting his revelations, saying that Simon Peter hanged Judas for betraying Christ.[252] The principle later taught by Young in Nauvoo was practiced in Utah.[253] Such things as stealing, apostasy, revealing temple ceremonies and adultery were considered worthy of blood atonement. The Danites were also an active force in putting down resistance by non-Mormon sources by intimidation, destruction of property and bodily harm, including murder. None were more violent in this respect than Orrin Porter Rockwell, "the most infamous of all the Mormon assassins,"[254] William "Bill" Hickman[255] and John D. Lee,[256] all former bodyguards of Smith who followed Young to Utah.

In Deseret, title given to the new county to which the

Mormons had come, they developed an exclusive spirit. Brigham Young forbid trade with non-Mormons, minted their own coins, established Mormon schools, and created a special alphabet of 38 characters. A school primer along with the *Book of Mormon* was printed in it. And although in 1855 the Utah legislature subsidized the new alphabet at $2,500, it failed to gain wide acceptance.

Chapter Twelve
MOUNTAIN MEADOWS MASSACRE

One of the darkest stains on Mormon history is the Mountain Meadows Massacre that took place on the plains of southern Utah in September of 1857. The Fancher party of over 120 men, women and children were brutally murdered, their bodies left on the hot sands of the Meadows for the wolves and vultures to pick their naked bodies clean. Years later their bleached and scattered bones still remained as a testimony to one of the cruelest massacres in American history.[257]

The Fancher party, most of which were from Southern Arkansas, with one man from Illinois by way of Indiana and another from Tennessee, had encamped on the plains when a band of Indians, directed by a group of painted-face white men, posing as Indians, rushed down from the nearby hill, catching the emigrants by surprise. They quickly responded to the attack which lasted five days. On the second day three men were dispatched to nearby Cedar City for help by the Mormons there. One man, William Aden, a native from Tennessee, had previous associations with the Mormons and believed them to be trustworthy. Little did he know that behind the painted-faces were Mormon white men sent on a mission, not of mercy but of murder. Two of the men were savagely killed by Indians as they camped, say the Mormons, but many suspect it was the Mormons themselves that did the deed. A third man, John D. Baker, escaped temporally, only to be killed later by some Indians, led by Ira Hatch, a Mormon. Baker was carrying a list naming each member of the train and their possessions, including the animals. The list was destroyed when he was killed.[258]

With a treacherously calculated plan, divested of their Indian disguise, John D. Lee, and William Bateman rode into the Fancher camp under a white flag of truce. For reasons yet unknown, the emigrants surrendered their arms and abandoned their wagons to walk thirty-five miles under the protection of men about which they knew absolutely nothing. John D. Lee suggests that it was because they had very little ammunition left.[259] No doubt wearied by the persistent attack and possible lack of supplies, since the Mormons consistently refused to sell to them, they abandoned their wagons with the exception of two which carried their wounded men, women and children out ahead of them. The party was apparently made to believe that by surrendering their arms and leaving their wagons temporally behind, they could pacify the Indians and would be protected by the Mormons who promised to return their wares once in an area of safety.

About three hundred and twenty miles south of Salt Lake City, on the Southern Trail to California, they marched into the Meadows beyond Cedar City. The unarmed men marched single file alongside an armed Mormon until the signal by Major John N. Higbee, "Do your duty!" Each Mormon quickly drew down on the man beside him and brutally shot them while the Indians, at the sound of gunfire, bounded out of the bush where they were hiding, killing the wounded men, women and most of the children.[260]

The wagons, possessions and even the bloody clothes were stripped off the dead and carried to the tithing office in Cedar City and later sold at public auction. Some of the guns and cattle were distributed among the Indians who had assisted the Mormons. John D. Lee took a fine carriage to his own home from the raid.[261] Sixteen of the children from two to seven years of age, one of which died of wounds sustained in the attack, were taken to the nearby Hamblin ranch.[262] Two additional children were taken by other Mormon families. Later, a little boy was rescued from one of these homes when the children were returned east. But a little girl, Nancy Cameron, who was never discovered until years later, grew up in the home of a family that undoubtedly participated in killing her natural parents. When grown, she married a Mormon. After the children were taken to the Hamblin ranch, the assailants, ate breakfast, and returned to the scene to discover that the Indians had scalped the dead and crushed their skulls.[263]

An unsuccessful attempt was made by Federal Judge Jamison Cradlebaugh of Utah to prosecute some of those who took part in the murderous event. Frustrated by failure to prosecute those responsible for the heinous crime, Judge Cradlebaugh charged the Mormon church and civil officials with obstructing justice. For thirteen years the Mormon church suppressed the facts and blocked any investigation into the crime.[264] Finally, after public pressure and threat of government intervention, which Brigham Young feared the most, the blame was laid on a single individual who probably epitomized blind loyalty the most, John D. Lee. In the succeeding years Lee would be charged with the crime, convicted and returned to the spot where the crime took place to be executed by a firing squad. They that live by the sword must die by the sword. In a lengthy statement before his death John D. Lee declared, "I have been sacrificed in a cowardly, dastardly manner . . ."[265]

Sermons and speeches pouring out of Utah from Church leaders in the days preceding the Massacre were filled with hot anti-government rhetoric. Combined with the simmering hatred for the people of Missouri and Illinois, you have the making of a massacre.[266] Ill treatment in these two states was fostered and perpetuated by a Mormon idealism of taking over the nation in the name of their religion - a belief they frequently brandished before their Gentile neighbors.[267]

Some Mormon accounts blame the event partially on some purported remarks by a few of the emigrants[268] but they more likely were led to believe that the wagon train represented the larger government that they left behind. Brigham Young, along with others, vented their spleen from the Mormon pulpits. Major J.H. Carleton, in a report before the 57th Congress, who was sent to investigate the massacre, quoted several Indian chiefs and some Mormons who participated in the raid, saying that they had seen a letter from Brigham Young authorizing the mass murders.[269]

The Mountain Meadows Massacre has been called "one of the most calculated, pitiless and shameful mass murders ever perpetrated in the violent history of America's violent frontier." [270] William Wise, who chronicled the story, was convinced that Brigham Young was the man behind the event. He argues that nothing happened in Utah that did not at least come under the personal examination of Brigham Young.

Brigham Young has been described by his followers as the "American Moses"[271] of the Mormons and by his foes as "the most bloodthirsty"[272] leader of all time. He has been typed "visionary"[273] by one and "uncouth and illiterate"[274] by another. By his advocates he has been regarded as an "angel of light" but his adversaries regarded him as a "goblin damned".[275]

Speculation abounded during Young's life as to how many wives he had. The object of much humor, he was careful never to reveal the number. He had sixteen known wives by which he produced no less than fifty-seven children. Nine additional women, who were considered his wives, bore no children to him. Two women, having been formerly the plural wives of Joseph Smith, were sealed to Young in the winter of 1845-1846, but died shortly after their sealing.[276]

At the age of seventy-six, on August 29, 1877, Young died of complications, resulting from what was described as cholera morbus. More recently, it has been suggested that his condition was "a ruptured appendix." Two of his sons, Brigham, Jr. and John W. desired to succeed him as leader of the church but the die had been cast. Their own father, after the death of Joseph Smith, had led the church not to follow family succession and was elected President of the Twelve Apostles.[277]

> *As the first governor of Utah, Young established the state emblem, a beehive on a stand under the words "Holiness Unto The Lord," having been a Temple symbol long before it was introduced to the State. The symbol, carried into Mormonism from the Masonic Order,[278] characterizes the order and government which Mormons believe will exist through the administration of the Priesthood. Essentially it represents the power of Mormonism to ultimately control the nation, if not the world.[279]*

Joseph Smith certainly taught the demise of the national Constitution and a triumphant rescue by Elders of the Mormon church. President Ezra Taft Benson, addressing the 1987 Semiannual General Conference, said, "We are fast approaching that moment prophesied by Joseph Smith when he said: 'Even this nation will be on the very verge of crumbling . . . and when the Constitution is upon the brink of ruin, this people [Mormons]. . . shall bear the Constitution away from the very verge of destruction'."[280]

Eugene England chronicles a veiled remark at the dedication of the Oakland Temple, Washington, D.C. by former President Spencer W. Kimball who gave "a literally stunning vision of the Latter-day work sweeping to its conclusion."[281] This is described in the same issue of *Dialogue*, "we Latter-day Saints not only declare that the Constitution of the United States was divinely inspired but also think of ourselves as standing ready to make a prophesied defense, perhaps even a rescue, of it when it is in particular danger, at some time when it is to 'hang by a thread'."[282] Although the average Mormon may be unaware of this teaching, many Mormons have not surrendered the idea of world domination, taught in the Temple endowments and embraced by their leadership.

PART THREE

EXAMINING THE PHILOSOPHY OF MORMONS

"Of all the unorthodox theological systems that were introduced in the New York hinterland between 1800 and 1850, the only one that has become and important American religion is The Church of Jesus Christ of Latter-day Saints."

Jan Shipps
Journal of Mormon History
1974, page 3

Chapter Thirteen
CHURCH GOVERNMENT AND THE BOOK

That Joseph Smith from the beginning of his church had delusions of taking over the world through Mormonism is evident from church history.[1] Certainly not everyone in the church caught the vision but many did, proclaiming it before their non-Mormon neighbors. It was this type of irresponsible rhetoric that caused much of the stringent reaction from the non-Mormon communities. At Nauvoo, Illinois, the church paper arrogantly announced:

> *Nauvoo, then is the nucleus of a glorious dominion of universal liberty, peace, and plenty; it is an organization of that government of which there shall be no end—of that Kingdom of Messiah which shall roll forth, from conquering and to conquer, until it shall be said, that 'the kingdoms of this world are become the kingdoms of our Lord, and of his Christ.' 'AND THE SAINTS OF THE MOST HIGH SHALL POSSESS THE GREATNESS OF THE KINGDOM UNDER THE WHOLE HEAVEN.'*[2]

Woven into the coming of Christ by Smith was the controlling rule by the Latter-day Saints, a rule that would begin with their gathering to Zion, Independence, Missouri.

The government of the Mormon Church is a hierarchy in nature with authority flowing from the top to the bottom. As the church grew, it took on the polity of leadership over membership, always retaining the Prophet/President at the top. From 1831 to 1839 it was governed by the influence of congregational rule, a spill over from evangelical churches, which allowed for large scale apostasy and conflict.[3] Smith also began to face from some of his most intimate confidants a challenge to his uniqueness as a Prophet by their claim to the same gift of prophecy and special revelations. Martin Harris seems to be the first to make such a declaration for himself. Undaunted, he claimed to have conversed with Jesus who appeared as a deer walking more than two miles with him through the woods and to have seen the Devil, who appeared as a donkey having short mouse-like hair. He further prophesied that in four years the United States government and all religious denominations would be "gathered unto the Mormonites."[4] Oliver Cowdery, one of the three witnesses to the *Book of Mormon* and second elder ordained in the new church, not only claimed the same revelatory power as Smith but presumptuously assumed the right to recommend changes in the Prophet's revelations. This called up a revelation by Smith to Cowdery warning him to beware of pride[5] and later instructing him to be obedient unto Joseph.[6] Smith alone claiming the gift of translation which positioned him as the unique Prophet of the church. After Smith's death, J.J. Strang left Nauvoo to establish his own church and also claimed the gift of translation.

From the single office of Elders grew an elaborate structure of President, Counselors, Twelve Apostles, the Council of Seventy, Bishops, Stake Presidents and Ward Bishops. The Mormons claim that they have a "moral" government in distinction to "effective" government" which operates by human compulsion. This moral, Mormon government is said to have been built upon the will of God and consent of the people,[7] but the consent is conditioned by obedience to the President of the church, which must be sustained by the membership each year.

In order to understand Mormon church government, it must be viewed as the kinetic kingdom of God on earth,[8] administered by the Presidency and the Twelve Apostles. The church regards itself then as a theocracy. As the Saints moved to the Utah territory, they sought a refuge from the government of men, particularly those that would discredit the doctrine of polygamy and total self rule. It was the desire of Brigham Young and other church leaders to escape the intrusion of national government into the affairs of the theocratic government of Zion. In the beginning, respect for the laws of the land was written into the commandments of the church[9] but as they experienced oppression from state Gentile governments, a bitter hatred developed for Missouri and Illinois.[10] Then private revelations took on a new response to Gentile laws.

The government of Mormonism is evolutionary in development, beginning with Smith and his Council of Fifty and maturing into an organization that involves every "worthy male." There are two priesthoods which enlist every active Mormon male according to his age. The Aaronic priesthood is for males from ages 12 to 18 and the Melchizedek Priesthood for men 18 years of age and up. Under the Aaronic priesthood are levels of service beginning with the office of deacon, usually held by boys 12 years of age. They next proceed to teacher and after two or three years enter the priesthood. At age 18 or 19 they enter the Melchizedek Priesthood as an elder which also has three levels. A young Mormon is definitely introduced into the rank of elder before going on a mission assignment. After returning from the mission commitment he is usually elevated to the office of "Seventies." From the office of high priest a very limited few are elected to the office of patriarch, apostle and finally the presidency.

While the local ward leaders are unsalaried, they do receive a small expense stipend. The church officers and staff at church headquarters in Utah, now a large bureaucratic establishment, are all salaried[11] including the office of Patriarch of the church, who pronounces special blessings daily upon worthy individuals. This office is held in the Reorganized Church only by direct descendants of Joseph Smith but the Patriarch of the Utah Church traces his lineage through Hyrum Smith.[12] Mormon women and their daughters are expected to be involved in auxiliary organizations.

The philosophy of Mormonism is not only seen in their governmental structure but also in their "sacred writings." There are four works that set Mormonism apart from other religions. They are the *Book of Mormon, Doctrine and Covenants, The Pearl of Great Price* and Joseph Smith's *Revised Translation* of the Bible. Sometimes the first three books are included under one cover along with the King James Version of the Bible. The *Book of Mormon*, the first book produced by Joseph Smith, was printed in Palmyra, New York, in 1830. The crucial question debated by students of Mormonism is the authorship of this first work by Smith. Debate forms around three major theories. The first is that Smith indeed received the plates from the Hill Cumorah outside Palmyra and translated them into the *Book of Mormon*, the view held by loyal Mormons. A second view holds that Smith plagiarized an unpublished manuscript written by a Congregational evangelist/author by the name of Solomon Spaulding. A third view maintains that Smith created the book out of his vivid imagination by utilizing the major themes of *View of the Hebrews* by Ethan Smith, published seven years prior to the *Book of Mormon*.

The second theory, being the oldest and most circulated, contends that Smith plagiarized Solomon Spaulding's unpublished "Manuscript Found" to produce the *Book of Mormon*. Spaulding, a Congregationalist minister, was born at Ashford, Connecticut, in 1761 and died at Amity, Pennsylvania in 1816. He graduated from Dartmouth College where he studied for the ministry. Due to ill health he served less than ten years as an evangelist before becoming a sometime novelist. The theory contends that he wrote two novels similar in content which were fictionalized histories exploring the beginnings of the American continent. The first novel was put aside but a second novel "Manuscript Found" was submitted to Robert Patterson, a printer in Pittsburgh,

Pennsylvania, around 1813. The plot thickens with the association of Sidney Rigdon with J.H. Harrison, who worked in the Patterson Printery. Through Harrison, it is claimed that Rigdon secured the novel which had been resting on the shelves of the printery for sometime, passed it onto Joseph Smith, who used it in producing the *Book of Mormon*. This theory was first suggested by Philastus Hurlbut, a former Mormon, who was alerted to the connection between Spaulding's "Manuscript Found" and the *Book of Mormon* while on a preaching mission with Orson Hyde.[13] Hurlbut collected numerous affidavits concerning the nefarious character of Smith from neighbors who knew him personally and from the family of Solomon Spaulding, establishing a connection between the two writings. Smith promptly initiated excommunication procedures at Kirtland after accusing him of "unchristian conduct with women."[14] There is no real evidence that Hurlbut was anything but an honorable man. The affidavits he had collected were later sold to E.D. Howe, editor of the *Painesville Telegraph*, Ohio, for five hundred dollars, who subsequently printed them in *Mormonism Unveiled*.[15]

Charles A. Shook, former member of the Reorganized Church of Latter-Day Saints, collected additional affidavits in support of this view. He also sought to establish a connection between Joseph Smith and Sidney Rigdon prior to the latter joining Smith's church in 1830. Shook notes that both the "Manuscript Story" and the *Book of Mormon* were found under a stone. Both describe a great storm at sea where emigrants were transported from the Old World to the New by boat. Both record iron being on the American continent which was unknown before the coming of Columbus. Both employ references to the Great Spirit in connection with the Indians, which current authorities ascribe to the coming of the white man to America. Both mention the relation of the sun to the earth and the office of High Priests. The most conclusive is a reference to a seer stone in "Manuscript Story" which Joseph Smith later claimed to employ to discover hidden treasure and interpret the plates.[16]

Vernal Holly, a former Mormon of Roy, Utah, has made

a detailed comparison between the "Manuscript Story," now owned by Oberlin College, and the *Book of Mormon*. Holly notes that both books have similarities in cultural references, theological views, descriptions of wars and the exchange of letters. The literary style of both books are very similar, both employing the use of first person in the first part of the book and concluding in the third person. The use of chiastic sentences, invented names and explicit word combinations, redundancies, parallelisms, contradictory thoughts and terms are all noted by Holly.[17]

It is believed by defendants of this view that Spaulding wrote a first novel which he entitled "Manuscript Story." Setting the first work aside, he wrote a second work entitled "Manuscript Found"[18] which was the manuscript taken by Rigdon from Patterson's printery. Assisted by Joseph Smith, the manuscript was reworked by Rigdon into what became the *Book of Mormon*.[19] The "Manuscript Story," the first novel discarded by Spaulding but very similar to "Manuscript Found," was secured by Hurlbut with permission from Mrs. Spaulding, from a trunk on the Clark farm where it was stored. This has remained the most widely circulated view and, not withstanding its strong evidences, is not without challengers. The first manuscript remains in the possession of Oberlin College, Oberlin, Ohio.

The third view, first offered by Fawn Brodie, eminent biographer of Joseph Smith, is that Smith was indeed able to produce the *Book of Mormon* out of his fertile and imaginative mind. Smith's mother describes Joseph's ability to hold them spellbound around the evening fire with tales of the ancient inhabitants of America woven from his vivid mind.[20] Brodie favors the use of Ethan Smith's *View of the Hebrews*, published seven years prior to the *Book of Mormon*, as a basis for supplying the core idea for Smith's book. Oliver Cowdery had moved to New York in 1825 from Poultney, Vermont, where *View of the Hebrews* was first printed in 1823.[21] It is very possible that he carried a copy of *View of the Hebrews* with him and shared it with Joseph Smith. Both books make use of the idea that the Indian mounds were the result of great battles where they buried their dead, and that they buried a book in one of these mounds. Smith quoted this legend, presented by *View of the Hebrews*, in the Mormon newspaper *Times and Seasons*.[22] Further parallels include:

> *Both books opened with frequent references to the destruction of Jerusalem; both told of inspired prophets among ancient Americans; both quoted copiously and almost exclusively from Isaiah; and both delineated the ancient Americans as a highly civilized people. Both held that it was the mission of the American nation in the last days to gather these remnants of the house of Israel and bring them to Christianity, thereby hastening the day of the glorious millennium. View of the Hebrews made much of the legend that the 'stick of Joseph' and the 'stick of Ephraim'—symbolizing the Jews and the lost tribes—would one day be united; and Joseph Smith's first advertising circulars blazoned the Book of Mormon as 'the stick of Joseph taken from the hand of Ephraim.'*[23]

When prominent former LDS historian B.H. Roberts did "A Parallel" comparison of Ethan Smith's book, *View of the Hebrews* and the *Book of Mormon*, he found numerous similarities. After his death, members of Robert's family donated three major unpublished manuscripts and numerous letters to the Marriott Library of the University of Utah. Some Mormon scholars reject the idea that Smith copied ideas from *View of the Hebrews*, insisting that there were too many differences between it and the *Book of Mormon* and that critics have strained to find parallels between them. Yet, Roberts found what he considered to be many disturbing comparisons between the two books. His manuscripts and letters in the Marriott Library reveal that Roberts had many questions concerning the writings of Joseph Smith, whom he once held so highly. This, along with other facts, caused him to lose faith in the *Book of Mormon* as a divine book.[24] It is noteworthy that on the tombstone of B.H. Roberts is a cross, a symbol rejected by the Mormon Church.

It is difficult to decide which view holds the most weight, each offering seemingly conclusive evidence. The answer may well be that Smith, with or without the help of Rigdon or Cowdery, was able to write the *Book of Mormon* drawing on ideas from both "Manuscript Found" and *View of the Hebrews*. Certainly Smith was a great borrower from everything around him and the fact that the *Book of Mormon* lacks continuity caused Mark Twain to describe it as "chloroform in print."[25]

Objections to Smith's use of the Spaulding manuscript involve the 116 pages lost at the hands of the wife of Martin Harris. The argument goes that if he had copied the manuscript, he could have easily recopied it without the panic he experienced when told of the loss by Martin. There are two possible answers to this objection. First, it is possible that Smith destroyed the first 116 pages of the Spaulding manuscript as he "translated them," as security against anyone discovering his deceit. There is a second response to the objection that seems very plausible. Smith became distraught because he had so embellished the Spaulding manuscript with the major themes of Ethan Smith's novel that he knew he could not reproduce it in its original form, fearing that the wife of Harris would produce the first 116 pages and reveal him as a fraud. Of course, if Smith really had received the translation from God, then he certainly could have reproduced it in the exact original form. Joseph Smith gives a defining description of a scribe, which he claimed to be, as one that "bringeth forth out of his own treasure things that are new and old . . . For the work of this example see the *Book of Mormon*, coming forth out of the treasure of the heart; also the covenants given to the Latter-day Saints . . . "[26] This description of a scribe suggests the source of his book was his own mind rather than from God.

As early as 1799 Charles Crawford of Philadelphia, in an essay, maintained that the Indians in America had descended from the ten lost tribes of Israel. By 1816 Elias Boudinot, in *A Star in the West*, declared as his theme the mystery of the lost tribes. Caleb Atwater in 1820 speculated that Indians migrated to America during the time of Noah. In nearby Albany, New York, in 1825 Josiah Priest wrote *The Wonders of Nature and Providence Displayed* sustaining the idea that the American Indians were descendants of the Jewish race who came to America.[27] Smith cites Priest's work in *Times and Seasons*. This view was held by such noted ministers as William Penn, Roger Williams, Cotton Mather, and Jonathan Edwards.[28] In the first edition of the *Book of Mormon*, Smith describes himself as the "Author" on both the title page and the preface but in later printings, he is designated as "Translator".[29]

Joseph Smith claimed that "the *Book of Mormon* is the most correct of any book on earth, and the keystone of our religion, and a man would get nearer to God by abiding by its precepts, than any other book".[30] Oliver B. Huntington recorded an explanation by Joseph Fielding Smith, sixth President of the Latter-day Saints, as to how the Book of Mormon was recorded:

> *Joseph Smith did not render the writings on the gold plates into the English language in his own style of language as many people believe, but every word and every letter was given to him by the gift and power of God . . . The Lord caused each word [to be] spelled as it is in the Book to appear on the stones in short sentences or words, and when Joseph had uttered the sentence or the word before him and the scribe had written it properly, that sentence would disappear and another appear. And if there was a word wrongly written or even a letter incorrect, the writing on the stones would remain there. Then Joseph would require the scribe to spell the reading of the last spoken and thus find the mistake and when corrected the sentence or word would disappear as usual.[31]*

Even a cursory comparison of the first and later editions reveal thousands of changes in grammar and punctuation, but most importantly the addition and subtraction of words, changing the original text. In 1964 Jerald and Sandra Tanner reviewed the 1830 edition, noting 3,913 changes in the *Book of Mormon*.[32] Some additional 200 changes were made in the 1981 printing.[33] Originally church officials rancorously denied any serious changes, blaming limited mistakes on the printer and approved in a later edition by Joseph Smith,[34] but before losing faith in the book, B.H. Roberts, prominent LDS historian, ultimately admitted the errors, claiming that the book is infallible only in its message which was expressed in Smith's own words.[35]

Not only was Smith's English improved and the chapters and numbers rearranged in later editions of the *Book of Mormon* but significant changes were made in names, theological doctrines, and words that altered the meaning of the sentences. On page 200 of the first edition it reads that " . . . king *Benjamin* had a gift from God, whereby he could interpret such engravings . . . " which was changed in the 1981 edition on page 188 to " . . . king *Mosiah* had a gift from God, whereby he could interpret such engravings . . . " (Mosiah 21:28). On page 32 of the first edition, Christ "the Lamb of God is the Eternal Father and the Savior of the world . . . " but in the 1981 edition it reads "the Lamb of God is the Son of the Father, and the Saviour of the world..." (I Nephi 13:40). On page 214 of the first edition it reads "My soul was wrecked with eternal torment; but I am snatched, . . . " but in the 1981 edition it reads "My soul was racked with eternal torment; but I am snatched, . . . " (Mosiah 27:29).

Another problem that plagues Mormon scholars is the use of 1611 King James language in a book that was supposed to be translated from plates dating back from AD 384 to AD 421 when Mormon wrote them down. More than 2,000 verses lifted from the King James Version of the Bible, including the italicized words added to clarify words for the reader, were transported onto the *Book of Mormon* manuscript.

A third problem faced by Mormon scholars is the lack of

archaeological evidence to support the many claims of the *Book of Mormon* expansive buildings that covered the New World and the numerous people that populated it. The book describes in detail two civilizations on the American continent with items that existed prior to the coming of Columbus such as domesticated animals like horses, goats, cows and even elephants. Dr. Raymond T. Matheny, former professor of anthropology at Brigham Young University, insists that these anachronisms of domesticated livestock referred to in the Mormon bible dating as late as 600 B.C. demand a definite cultural level that did not exist in pre-Columbian America. He writes:

> *You just don't have a cow or a goat or a horse as an esoteric pet or something. There is a system of raising these things . . . domesticated animals and so forth in the New World.*[36]

Theologically, the *Book of Mormon* does not match the times it was supposed to have been recorded on the plates. Revival scenes describing people being overcome by the power of God and falling down (Jacob 7:124; Mosiah 4:1) have language and events taken directly from the times Smith was writing his book.[37] Infant baptism argued against in the *Book of Mormon* (Moroni 8:5) was not practiced until around 220 AD and only occasionally then. It was not in vogue until the 7th or 8th century, far too late to be reflected in the history of the Nephites. The *Book of Mormon* rather reflected the theological debate of Smith's time.[38]

Medically, references to the "circulation of the blood," discovered by Harvey in 1619, and "pores" could not have been known until after the invention of the microscope[39] by Dutch spectacle-maker Zacharias Janssen around 1590.

The *Book of Mormon* deals primarily with how the American Indian got to America. The premise of the book is that there were two major migrations of people who came to the Americas. The first migration took place approximately 2250

B.C. The immigrants are described in the Book of Ether as Jaredites who left their region around the time of the Tower of Babel (Genesis 11:1-9). They traveled, according to Ether 2:16-17, on eight barges. After founding a civilization, the inhabitants began to war with one another. Two million men fell in battle along with the women and children (Ether 15:2) until only two warriors were left. Their names were Coriantumr and Shiz. Ether 15:31 describes the remarkable event:

> *And it came to pass that after he [Coriantumr] had smitten off the head of Shiz, that Shiz raised upon his hands and fell; and after that he had struggled for breath, he died.*

In addition to Coriantumr, there remained a Jaredite prophet named Ether who recorded on twenty-four plates the history of his people before he died. It should be noted that there are four different sets of plates covering the period of history from 600 B.C. to A.D. 421, listed in the *Book of Mormon*, the plates of Nephi, the plates of Mormon, the plates of Ether and the brass plates of Laban. The final set of plates is claimed to have come to America from Jerusalem and appears in the form of extracts of a Nephite record.

After the extinction of the Jaredites, a second migration took place with a Jewish prophet named Lehi. Because of the wickedness of the Jews he, his wife and four sons moved from Jerusalem to an area near the Red Sea. At the command of God, they built a large ship which was guided by a compass-like object (1 Nephi 16:10). Nephi became the favored son of Lehi because he obeyed the Lord. The family of Laman, called Lamanites, along with his brother Lemuel, rebelled against the Lord and were cursed with a dark skin (2 Nephi 5:21). According to the Mormons, it is from the Lamanites that the American Indian descended and it was to them that Christ appeared on the American continent where He established twelve apostles, taught baptismal regeneration by immersion (3 Nephi 11:23-24), and expounded the Sermon on the Mount (3 Nephi 12-14).

In AD 385 the Lamanites and the Nephites met each other on the battlefield near the Hill Cumorah in New York state. All were killed with the exception of Moroni, son of Mormon, a Nephite Warrior, who had recorded the history of his people on golden plates. Moroni recorded two additional books - *Ether* and *Moroni*, burying the entire history in the hill Cumorah. According to the *Book of Mormon*, Moroni returned as an angel to Joseph Smith in 1823 revealing to him the whereabouts of the plates. In 1827 Smith was allowed to take the plates and translate them.

A third migration, given little attention by Mormon scholars, took place shortly after the Nephite migration in 600 BC It was led by Mulek, son of Zedekiah, a king of Judah (Mosiah 25:2; Helaman 6:10; 8:21)[40]

Originally, Joseph Smith taught that Lehi and his family landed in Chile, South America, and migrated to upstate New York where the great battle was fought.[41] Although this has been the traditional view of the church for over a hundred years, some modern Mormon scholars are challenging this view for what is called a "Limited Geographical View," placing the landing in Central America.[42] In this view, the Hill Cumorah is also placed in Central America, removing the problem of lack of archaeological evidence in America to support the claims of a great battle in New York State. It also removes any need for the armies to travel 6,000 miles north to do battle, which is described in the Mormon chronicle. The fact is, there is no archaeological evidence in Central or in North America to support the *Book of Mormon*. And if the great battle was fought somewhere other than in the State of New York, why would the angel Moroni transport the plates there and bury them?

Chapter Fourteen
ADDITIONAL REVELATIONS

The second sacred book to Mormonism was printed during the Kirtland years, covering the revelations of Joseph Smith from July 1828 to September 1831. Entitled the *Book of Commandments*, it contained sixty-five revelations and was printed in 1833. Doctrinally it is the first key to the Mormon system of beliefs.[43] In 1835 the *Book of Commandments* was expanded to cover an additional seventy-one revelations, deleting some parts, rewriting others in the original printing, and renamed *Doctrine and Covenants*.

The *Book of Commandments* was in the process of being printed at Independence, Missouri, where the church paper, *Evening and Morning Star*, was published. Townspeople were angered by the prognostications of their Mormon neighbors who freely stated their intent to take over the state but a more immediate concern was an editorial that hinted ex-slaves, received into the church in other states, would be welcomed among the Mormons in Independence. Some 500 men marched on the first floor printery over which W.W. Phelps and his family lived. The press, type trays and furniture were carried into the street where they were destroyed, along with all printed pages of the Book of Commandments they could find. Not content with the destruction of the press, the mob proceeded to tar and feather Charles Allen and Edward Partridge.[44]

Found in the *Doctrine and Covenants* are teachings exclusive to the book. Such teachings as the plurality of gods

(Section 121:28-32), God as an exalted man (132:20,37), the preexistence of spirit children before coming to earth (131:7-8), baptism for the dead (124:, 127:, 128:), eternal marriage (132:19-20), and polygamy or plural wives (132:1,39;61-62) are not found in the *Book of Mormon*. In fact, the *Book of Mormon* contradicts the *Doctrine and Covenants* on all these subjects.

Eighteen of the revelations relate to individuals such as Smith's father (Section 4), Oliver Cowdery (8,9,28), brother Hyrum (11), Joseph Knight, Sr. (12), David Whitmer (14), John Whitmer (15), Peter Whitmer (16), Thomas B. Marsh (32,112), Parley P. Pratt (32), Ezra Thayre (33), Orson Pratt (34), Edward Partridge (36), James Covill (39), Algernon Sidney Gilbert (53), W.W. Phelps (55), and John Murdock (99), but the later revelations refer to the church at large. One revelation pertains to Oliver Granger, declaring that his sacred remembrance will be held "from generation to generation forever and ever saith the Lord" (117:12). Granger was appointed at Kirtland to serve as Smith's representative after the Mormons moved to Nauvoo. When Mormons are asked today who Oliver Granger is, they usually look at each other and shake their heads, yet their Prophet gave a revelation he claimed was from the Lord declaring Granger's continual remembrance "from generation to generation, forever and ever . . . "

With the exception of the 136th revelation by Brigham Young at Winter Quarters, Nebraska, regarding the "organization for the westward journey," and the 138th revelation by Joseph Fielding Smith, son of Hyrum, at Salt Lake City, Utah, concerning "the Savior's visit to the spirits of the dead while his body was in the tomb," all the revelations are from the hand of Joseph Smith. Following the revelations, two "Declarations" appear. The first Declaration, issued October 6, 1890, by Wilford Woodruff, pertaining to polygamy, advised the Saints "to refrain from contracting any marriage forbidden by the law of the land." The second Declaration by Spencer W. Kimball, September 30, 1978, rescinded the prohibition against ordaining blacks to the priesthood.

It is disturbing for many Latter-day Saints to discover, that while their church teaches an unchanging doctrine, that, in fact—besides the rescinding of the two doctrines just cited—there are numerous changes that have been made between the original *Book of Commandments* and their present *Doctrine and Covenants*. Mormon scholar Karl F. Best distinguishes between simple changes made for the purpose of making the revelations more readable such as punctuation, grammar, spelling, changes in person, and clarifications from substantive changes. While suggesting that few of the changes are substantive, he does admit that "Joseph was then adding material that he had already decided was uninspired to a revelation he claimed to be from God." Claiming that the revelations came from God initially, he further admits "they were changed to fit the situation by a man who was influenced not only by the Spirit but also by circumstance, his associates and his understanding."[45]

A section on marriage which forbids polygamy and the "Lectures on Faith" in the 1833 edition have been deleted from editions after 1921. The "Lectures on Faith," delivered by Smith to the elders of the Kirtland Church, were dropped from the *Doctrine and Covenants* because they taught a different view of God which conflicted with the later teachings of Smith. In the "Lectures on Faith" Joseph Smith taught that God " . . . is omnipotent, omnipresent, and omniscient; without beginning of days or end of life;...".[46] Yet the Mormons teach today that God was once a man who progressed to godhood. Milton R. Hunter, Mormon writer, explains:

> *The Gospel of Jesus Christ teaches that God the Eternal Father is an exalted being . . . Mormon prophets have continually taught the sublime truth that God the Eternal Father was once a mortal man . . .* [47]

Hunter goes on to state that: "As early as February 16, 1832, the Lord revealed to Prophet Joseph Smith the sublime truth that 'men may become gods.'"[48]

One of several examples of the serious changes between the first and later editions is revealed by comparing Chapter Four from the *Book of Commandments* with its parallel as it appears in Chapter Five of the *Doctrine and Covenants* today. Between the two editions, fifty changes have been made. The most serious change was the altering of verse 2 in the original edition which states that Joseph Smith " . . . has a gift to translate the book [*Book of Mormon*], and I have commanded him that he shall pretend to no other gift, for I will grant him no other gift." Smith, in the original revelation, claimed the gift exclusively for translating the *Book of Mormon* and that there was no gift to receive additional revelations from God. It became obvious to Smith that if he was to produce the *Book of Commandments*, this revelation had to be changed.[49] In the 1982 version, this revelation reads:

> *And you have a gift to translate the plates; and this is the first gift that I bestowed on you; and I have commanded that you should pretend to no other gift until my purpose is fulfilled in this, for I will grant you no other gift until it is finished (Section 5:4, page 8.)*

Another example of changes in the revelations is revealed when Chapter 28 of the *Book of Commandments* is compared with the same revelation appearing in the 1982 *Doctrine and Covenants*, Section 27. The content has doubled in the later printing and significant changes have been made. When the *Times and Seasons*, May 1840, which carried a revelation of Smith from the Liberty Jail, is compared to the present rendering in *Doctrines and Covenants*, Section 124:1-4, it will be noted that most of the actual revelation has been deleted.[50] These changes and alterations in revelations that were claimed to have been given by God are disturbing to the thinking Mormon.

Some revelations were predictions concerning future

events. At the heart of Smith's teaching was the millennial reign of Christ upon the earth, particularly as it related to the Mormon Church. In Section 57 of the *Doctrine and Covenants*, Smith designated Independence, Missouri, as the place of "gathering of the Saints" when Christ returns to earth. Independence became the City of Zion and the place where the temple would be built. The Bible teaches that Jerusalem, not Independence, is the City of Zion. On August 1, 1831, Smith and a group of men held a service in which he laid a cornerstone for the temple to be built in Independence (Section 58:6-7). Later Smith prophesied by " . . . the word of the Lord concerning his church, established in the last days for the restoration of his people" that the temple would be built " . . . in the western boundaries of the State of Missouri, . . . in this generation" (Section 84:1-4).

Joseph Smith specifically designated Independence as the place where the temple would be built, even laying a cornerstone on a particular spot and prophesied that it would happen "in this generation." The fact is, no temple has been built on the temple lot where Joseph Smith said it would. Only recently the RLDS built a temple on a nearby lot. Smith, no doubt realizing the conflict, on January 1, 1841, in Nauvoo, Illinois, produced a lengthy revelation which included a section that absolved the Saints from building the temple when prevented by wicked hands (Section 124:49-54). The fact remains that over 160 years have passed in which everyone in Smith's generation has died and no temple has been built.[51] David Whitmer, early associate of Joseph Smith, also reported a prophecy that failed. Smith, looking into his hat at the seer stone, announced that some of the brethren should go to Toronto, Canada, where they would sell the copyright to the *Book of Mormon*. This, of course, never happened. The copyright was granted in America.[52]

Not one of the major doctrines of Mormonism today is found in the *Book of Mormon*, their first sacred book. In fact, the *Book of Mormon* contradicts the *Doctrine and Covenants* on every major teaching of the church. The *Book of Mormon* teaches that "the decrees of God are unalterable" (Alma 41:8) but the

Doctrine and Covenants teaches the opposite: "Wherefore I, the Lord, command and revoke as it seemeth me good;...and give a new commandment . . . " (Section 56: 4-5).

The *Book of Mormon*, Alma 11:27-29, teaches that there is one God:

> *And Amulek said: Yes, there is a true and living God.*
> *Now Zeezroom said: Is there more than one God?*
> *And he answered, No.*

Yet, the *Doctrine and Covenants*, Section 132:20 & 37, teaches that there are many gods:

> *Then shall they be gods, because they have no end; therefore shall they be from everlasting to everlasting . . .*
> *...they have entered into their exaltation, according to the promises, and sit upon thrones, and are not angels but are gods.*

The *Book of Mormon*, Alma 18:26-29, teaches that God is a Spirit:

> *And Ammon said: Believest thou that there is a Great Spirit?*
> *And he said, Yea.*
> *And Ammon said: This is God. And Ammon said unto him again: Believest thou that this Great Spirit, who is God, created all things which are in heaven and in the earth?*
> *And he said, Yea . . .*

Yet, the *Doctrine and Covenants*, Section 130:22, teaches that God has a body of flesh:

> *The Father has a body of flesh and bones as tangible as man's; the Son also; but the Holy Ghost has not a body of flesh and bones, but is a personage of Spirit . . .*

The *Book of Mormon*, Jacob 2:24, condemns polygamy or plural wives:

Behold, David and Solomon truly had many wives and concubines, which thing was abominable before me, said the Lord.

Yet, the *Doctrine and Covenants*, Section 132:1, condones plural wives as given by God:

Verily, thus saith the Lord . . . I, the Lord, justified my servants . . . Abraham, Isaac, and Jacob . . . as touching the principle and doctrine of having many wives and concubines . . .

There are many other contradictions to be found by comparing the *Book of Mormon* and the *Doctrine and Covenants*. Numerous contradictions between the *Book of Mormon* and teachings of the later Presidents of the LDS church may also be discovered by comparing them.

The third sacred book of Mormonism is *The Pearl of Great Price* composed of five sections; two sections are taken from the "translation" by Joseph Smith of the Bible in Genesis 1:6 and Matthew 23:39-24:51; a section entitled "The Book of Abraham" a section containing the first five chapters of Joseph Smith's history; and a final section containing the Articles of Faith.

During the Kirtland years, Joseph Smith claimed a revelation that Rigdon was to be his scribe in an assignment from the Lord to retranslate the Scriptures.[53] Smith claimed that the Scriptures had become flawed through the years of translation and needed to be restored. The work composed of additions, alterations, and expansions of the Bible was completed in 1833 at Kirtland but was not published until 1867 by the Reorganized Church, twenty-three years after the prophet's death. The "translation" contains a prediction of the *Book of Mormon* in Isaiah 29:11-12.[54] In Genesis 50:33 Smith predicts his own coming, specifically naming himself and declaring "they that seek to destroy him shall be confounded;..."[55] This prophecy failed since his enemies did indeed kill him. At least one writer believed the revised translation to be the product of Sidney Rigdon,[56] not Smith. The "Book of Moses," taken from Smith's revision of Genesis, found in *The Pearl of Great Price*, contains some heretical teachings, including the idea that Adam's sin was necessary to the procreation of the human race (*Book of Moses* 5:10-11), the existence of souls in heaven before birth (*Book of Abraham* 3:22-23), and that Satan offered to die to redeem mankind (Book of Moses 4:1.)

A portion of the "translation" in *The Pearl of Great Price* concerns the second coming of Christ found in Matthew 24. This "translation" was meant to keep alive the millennial position of the Mormon church which portrayed them as the focus of Christ's coming.

A section containing Chapters 1 - 5 of the early history of Joseph Smith first appeared in serial form in the Church newspaper *Times and Seasons*. His ancestry, the times in which he grew up, an account of the first vision, marriage to Emma Hale and the account of his translation of the *Book of Mormon*, are also contained in *The Pearl of Great Price*.

Thirteen in number, the "Articles of Faith" are general statements of faith meant to enlist sympathy for Mormon teachings. These articles were submitted to John Wentworth, editor of the *Chicago Democrat*, by Joseph Smith in response to the editor's request for a statement of Mormon doctrine.[57]

The most controversial section of the *Doctrine and Covenants*, if not the most embarrassing to Mormon scholars, is "The Book of Abraham." On July 3, 1835, Michael H. Chandler rolled into Kirtland with four Egyptian mummies and a few pieces of papyri inscribed with hieroglyphics.[58] Smith immediately claimed to translate some of the papyri, identifying it as the writings of Abraham. This act revived the confidence of his people in him, but it would prove to be an index to the true character of the man they revered as their Prophet. At first Smith told Josiah Quincy, who was in Nauvoo to interview him, that his

140

mother purchased the mummies at a cost of $6,000[59] but in his journal he stated that they were purchased by "some of the saints" in Kirtland for $2,400[60]

At the time of purchase, no one in America had the expertise to translate Egyptian hieroglyphics. Thirteen years before Smith claimed to have translated parts of the papyri, a Frenchman by the name of Jean Francis Champollion, who deciphered the writing on the Rosetta Stone, wrote a pamphlet containing the results of his work. This stone was discovered by an officer of Napoleon in 1799 and is now property of the British Museum. Not until years later did the translation of the script on the stone serve as a basis for deciphering Egyptian writings.[61]

Smith claimed to have translated the hieroglyphics on the papyri, thus reestablishing his tarnished past when he claimed to have translated the *Book of Mormon*. Examining the papyri, he determined that the writings were by Abraham, patriarch of Israel, while he was in Egypt. Another fragment was declared to be from the hand of Joseph, son of Jacob. The "Book of Abraham" presently appears in every copy of the *Doctrine and Covenants*, within the section designated *The Pearl of Great Price*.

After the death of Smith, the mummies were sold to the St. Louis Museum and placed on display.[62] From St. Louis they were taken to Chicago where they were thought to have been destroyed in the 1871 Chicago fire. In 1967 the original papyri that Smith was supposed to have translated were discovered in the Metropolitan Museum of Art in New York City. When the LDS church later acquired the papyri, Mormon scholars authenticated them as the fragments Smith had translated.[63]

Thomas Stuart Ferguson, a Mormon lawyer who spent much of his life trying to discover archaeological evidence to defend the geography in the *Book of Mormon*, authored several books supporting this premise. He was President of the New World Archaeological Foundation which sent explorations into Central America and Mexico in search of evidence to support the *Book of Mormon*. In *One Fold and One Shepherd*, Ferguson expressed enthusiasm and hope that eventually inscriptions would be found, evidence of some unique person or place recorded in the first sacred book of his church.[64] Year after year passed with no significant find relating to early Mormon history. His faith began to wane in the book he had spent his life trying to defend.[65]

The 1967 discovery of "eleven tattered pieces" of Egyptian papyri by a professor of Arabic studies at the University of Utah promised to be the answer to all his searching.[66] Ferguson obtained photographs of the papyri which he forwarded excitedly to Egyptologists for translation. His hopes were dashed when they turned out to be nothing more than the *Book of Breathings*, an Egyptian funeral text placed with the body of a man named Hor or Horus. This was the papyri from which Joseph Smith had claimed to have translated the entire "Book of Abraham." Ferguson's personal letters, now in a collection at the University of Utah, reveal that before his death he lost all faith in the writings of Joseph Smith, although he still advocated Mormon values.[67]

Chapter Fifteen
STRANGE NEW DOCTRINES

U nderstanding the Mormon doctrine of God is the key to unlocking their belief system. According to their teachings, God has a human body and was once a man who attained godhood by "obedience to the great law of progression."[68] Lorenzo Snow, fifth president of the Mormon Church, coined a phrase that expresses their belief that "As man is, God once was; As God now is, man may be."[69]

This doctrine is plainly contradicted by their own sacred books. In *The Pearl of Great Price* we read: "Behold I am the Lord God Almighty, and Endless is my name, for I am without beginning of days and end of years" (Moses 1:3). The *Book of Mormon* states, "For do we not read that God is the same yesterday, today and forever, and in him there is no variableness neither shadow of changing?" (Mormon 9:9). The Bible teaches that God is not a man (Numbers 23:19; Hosea 11:9) and that He is Spirit not flesh (John 4:24). Although God appeared in an anthropomorphic appearance as a man to Moses (Exodus 33:20) and revealed Himself as a man in Christ, He is Spirit. There are several figures used in the Scriptures to describe God's relationship with man such as Psalm 91:4 which says, "He shall cover thee with his feathers, and under his wings shalt thou trust" but God is not a bird nor does he have the body of a fowl. The terms "feathers" and "wings" are merely metaphorical figures used to describe His comfort and compassion.

Bruce R. McConkie, Mormon writer, defends the Mormon

doctrine of God by claiming that John 4:24, "God is Spirit" is a mistranslation according to Joseph Smith's "Inspired Version," but every other major translation translates it correctly "God is Spirit."

Mormons believe not only is there a Father god with a human body but that he is accompanied by a Mother god, who live together on a planet next to a great planet named Kolob (*Book of Abraham* 3:2-9). The concept of a Mother god seems to have begun with Joseph Smith in 1839.[70] Milton R. Hunter states, "The stupendous truth for the existence of a Heavenly Mother, as well as a Heavenly Father, became established facts in Mormon theology."[71] It mattered little to former Mormon President Joseph Fielding Smith that neither the *Bible*, the *Book of Mormon* nor the *Doctrine and Covenants* mentions a mother in heaven.[72]

The term "Father" is a metaphorical term suggesting relationship and love. Nowhere in the Bible is there a hint of a "heavenly Mother." "The God of the Bible is a sexless God," wrote Carl F.H. Henry. "When Scripture speaks of God as "he" the pronoun is primarily personal (generic) rather than masculine (specific); it emphasizes God's personality."[73]

Implicit in the Mormon teaching of a heavenly Father and Mother is the concept of "spirit children" produced by them. Bruce R. McConkie explains, "All men in pre-existence were the spirit children of God our Father, an exalted, glorified, and perfect Man . . . In a future eternity, spirit children will be born exalted, . . . ".[74] Yet, Jesus said, "For in the resurrection they neither marry, nor are given in marriage, but are as the angels of God in heaven" (Matthew 22:30.)

According to the Mormons their god is one of many gods. In their teaching, the godhead is composed of three separate gods. The *Book of Mormon* (Alma 11:26-32, 38-39; 2 Nephi 31:21) reflects the biblical view of God as one (John 10:30-33, 14:7-10; Hebrews 1:8). But when Smith wrote *The Pearl of Great Price*, his concept changed from God as one to a plurality of gods. In the "Book of Moses" (1:6), he teaches the oneness of God but, in the "Book of Abraham," (4:3-31) Smith teaches the concept of many gods. In the *Doctrine and Covenants* (Section 20:19,28), God is seen as one, but in the same book (132:20,37) Smith later taught the plurality of gods.

Joseph Smith officially declared the plurality of gods in the King Follett funeral sermon.[75] Yet in the front of every *Book of Mormon*, the concluding sentence of "The Testimony of the Three Witnesses" reads, "And the honor be to the Father, and to the Son, and to the Holy Ghost, which is one God. Amen." The Bible clearly teaches the oneness of God the Father, God the Son, and God the Holy Spirit (Deuteronomy 4:35, 6:4; 1 Corinthians 8:4).

Mormons sometime cite John 10:34 to support their teaching that man can become gods. Certainly, there are false gods to which the Scriptures testify but only one true God. Citing Psalm 82:6 Jesus quoted, "I said, 'Ye are gods, and all of you are the sons of the Most High God.'" This reference is what is called "a fortiori" argument to affirm His uniqueness as the Son of God. The reference is the scene of an earthly court where there are human judges or rulers. The word "Elohim" may be translated "god" or "judges" as in Exodus 21:6 and Exodus 22:8-9.[76] In Psalm 82:6 the word refers to unjust judges. This Scripture cannot be used by Mormons to support their view because this is an earthly scene. Jesus does not confirm the Jewish concept of a judge as god. He merely uses it as a defense against them.

Mormons teach that God is both Michael, spoken of in the Bible as an archangel and Adam, the first man (*Doctrine and Covenants* 27:11, 107:54, 116:1, 128:21, 138:38). Brigham Young taught that Adam was God, implying he came down to have sexual relations with Mary, producing Jesus, popularly called the "Adam-God" theory.

When the Virgin Mary conceived the child Jesus, the Father had begotten Him in His own likeness. He was not begotten by the Holy Ghost. And who is the Father? He is the first of the human family . . .".77

This same sermon was printed a year and a half later in the Mormon newspaper, the *Millennial Star*.[78] Hosea Stout, Captain of Smith's Nauvoo police force and a contemporary of Brigham Young in Utah, in his diary describes an evening meeting in which "President B. Young taught that Adam was the father of Jesus and the only God to us. That he came to this world in a resurrected body . . . ".[79]

On February 19, 1981, Mormon Apostle Bruce R. McConkie, one of the most definitive writers of Mormonism, admitted in a letter to Eugene England that "Yes, President Young did teach that Adam was the father of our spirits, and all the related things that the cultists ascribe to him. This, however, is not true. He [Young] expressed views that are not in harmony with the gospel."[80] Spencer W. Kimball, former President of the Church, warned, "We denounce that [Adam-God] theory and hope that anyone will be cautioned against this and other kinds of false doctrine."[81]

The doctrine of Christ taught by Mormon church leaders cannot be reconciled to the biblical view of Christ. Mormons deny that Jesus is coequal, cocreator and coeternal with the Father and Spirit. Yet, in John 1:1 Jesus is called "the Word" who "was God" and in John 1:3 says "all things are made by Him." Jesus said, "Before Abraham was, I Am" (John 8:58).

The *Book of Mormon* in Alma 7:10 reflects the biblical view of Christ's birth, (with the exception that Christ was born in Bethlehem, not Jerusalem), as uniquely conceived by Mary as a virgin:

"And behold, he shall be born of Mary, at Jerusalem [sic] which is the land of our forefathers, she being a virgin, a precious and chosen vessel, who shall be overshadowed and conceived by the power of the Holy Ghost, and shall bring forth a son, yea, even the Son of God."

Jesus is believed by Mormons to be the firstborn of the spirits produced by heavenly parents: "All men, Christ included, were born as his children in pre-existence."[82] He is also said to be the spirit-brother of Lucifer.

The appointment of Jesus to be the Savior of the world was contested by one of the other sons of God. He was called

Lucifer, son of the morning. Haughty, ambitious, and covetous of power and glory, this spirit-brother of Jesus desperately tried to become the Savior of mankind.[83]

The Christian view holds that Jesus is God (John 10:30), uniquely conceived of the Holy Spirit by a virgin girl named Mary and born in Bethlehem (Matthew 1:18; Luke 1:35; John 1:1-2,14). 1 Nephi 11:18, in the first edition of the *Book of Mormon*, calls Mary the "Mother of God," but in the present edition she is called "Mother of the Son of God . . . " Mormons teach that Jesus can only save for the sin of Adam but the Bible clearly teaches that He saves for all sin (1 John 1:7, 1:9.)

According to Mormon doctrine there is a distinction between the Holy Ghost and the Holy Spirit. John A. Widtsoe wrote:

> *The Holy Ghost, sometimes called the comforter, is the third member of the Godhead, and is a personage distinct from the Holy Spirit. As a personage, the Holy Ghost cannot any more than the Father and the Son be everywhere present in person.[84]*

The Holy Ghost is viewed as a personage, without a human body like God and Jesus (*Doctrine and Covenants* 103:22), who is the influence of God or "the power and the gift of that Personage".[85] He has the power "to fill the immensity of space," and to "quicken your understandings" (*Doctrine and Covenants* 88:6-13.)

According to Mormon theology the Holy Ghost is bestowed only by the Melchizedek Priesthood upon the obedient who "follow faith, repentance and baptism, and come through the laying on of hands."[86]

There is no distinction in the Bible between the Holy Ghost and the Holy Spirit. The same Greek words are used to refer to both and the Holy Spirit enters every believer at the moment of salvation (1 Corinthians 12:31; Ephesians 1:13.)

Gordon H. Fraser, tacitly evaluates the problem of Mormon teaching concerning the Trinity:

The reason Mormon thought cannot comprehend the oneness of the Trinity and at the same time personality of the Holy Spirit is because of their failure to recognize that all divine propositions cannot be confined within the limits of human expression.[87]

In order to comprehend the Mormon doctrine of salvation it is necessary to understand their teaching on sin. Mormons teach that the fall of man was essentially good because, if Adam had not sinned, he would have been confined to live forever in the Garden of Eden but death provided him a resurrection (2 Nephi 2:22-25). They also believe that God first taught baptismal regeneration to Adam after he was driven out of the Garden of Eden (Moses 6:51-54, 57-58.)[88]

"Salvation is twofold" according to Joseph Fielding Smith, former President of the Mormon Church, "General—that which comes to all men irrespective of a belief (in this life) in Christ—and, Individual—that which man merits through his own acts through life and by obedience to the laws and ordinances of the gospel."[89]

Mormonism teaches salvation by works. The death and resurrection of Jesus, according to them, only guarantees man's resurrection[90] but exaltation to godhood comes through works in the Mormon temples. In this system of belief essentially everyone will be resurrected except those vile types, along with Satan and the fallen angels. Even to these are offered hope of temporary judgment. James E. Talmage wrote,

"True, the scriptures speak of everlasting burnings, eternal damnation, and the vengeance of eternal fire, as characteristics of the judgment provided for the wicked; yet in no instance is

there justification for the inference that the individual sinner will have to suffer the wrath of offended justice for ever and ever."[91]

Thus, for Mormons, hell or eternal punishment is temporary with the exception of "apostates" who have denied the truth of Mormonism and forfeited their right to celestial glory.[92] The *Bible* teaches only those who have a personal experience with Jesus shall be saved (John 3:18,36). Although Mormons claim to believe in Christ, it is their obedience through works that brings salvation and exaltation. Loyalty to the local ward and faithful temple works will prepare one for ultimate exaltation (godhood) in the resurrection. Tithing, keeping the *Word of Wisdom*, obeying the commandments, faithful attendance, and service in the local ward are necessary to receive a Temple Recommend, admitting Mormons to perform endowments in the temple.

In the local wards, candidates are baptized by immersion, believed to be essential to salvation, bringing remission of sin, admitting the individual to membership, starting the person on the path to salvation and the means of personal sanctification.[93] Yet, in the "Articles of Faith," before baptism they are to express faith in Jesus Christ.[94] "But under certain circumstances there are some serious sins for which the cleansing of Christ does not operate . . ."[95]. However, the *Bible* clearly teaches that "the blood of Jesus Christ His Son cleanseth us from *all* sin" and "from *all* unrighteousness" (1 John 1:7, 9.) Faith in Jesus must be coupled with faith in Joseph Smith according to Mormon belief. Joseph Fielding Smith wrote under the heading "NO SALVATION WITHOUT ACCEPTING JOSEPH SMITH" that: "No man can reject that testimony without incurring the most dreadful consequences, for he cannot enter the kingdom of God."[96] Repentance, in Mormon belief, is connected to baptism by water.[97] Following baptism is the laying on of hands by two elders to bestow the Holy Ghost upon the candidate.[98]

Sacrament meetings are held each Sunday which usually cover a three hour period of time. During this time the sacrament of bread and water is taken after a song, a prayer, and a talk or lecture on doctrine or some motivational story. Originally wine was used in the sacrament services. In December 1836, Sidney Rigdon urged the Council to discontinue using wine in church services for either healing of sick or observance of the sacrament. The vote was unanimous with the exception that wine may be used to wash the body or occasionally might be used in the sacrament. Water was first substituted for wine by Joseph Smith in April 1837.[99] Wine was used in these services throughout Utah until the end of the 19th century.[100] It might be said whereas Jesus turned the water into wine, Joseph Smith turned the wine into water. Not only do Mormons not use wine or grape juice to represent the blood of Christ, it is noteworthy that a cross never appears on the steeple of any Mormon building.

After the sacrament meeting the congregation breaks up into classes of appropriate age levels to study the four major works of Mormonism-the *Book of Mormon, Doctrine and Covenants, The Pearl of Great Price*, and finally the *Bible*. The Priesthood for men and boys follows while the women organize around the Relief Society. Marriages for time are performed in the local ward but marriages for eternity are accomplished only in the temple.

Admission to the temple endowments is obtained by faithful attendance, obedience to Mormon teachings and loyal tithing in the local ward, which are open to everyone but only worthy Mormons are admitted to the Temple by a current Temple Recommend which is signed by the ward bishop and stake president.[101] Less than 20 percent of Mormons receive a Temple Recommend. Gentiles and regular Mormons are admitted to a temple only before it is dedicated and even then not into every part.

LDS temples are scattered throughout the United States and in some foreign countries. Usually they are located in large cities such as San Diego, Dallas, and Washington, D.C. Utah has several temples but the main temple is in Salt Lake City. In the temple, secret endowment ceremonies, also called ordinances, are performed, such as baptism for the dead, marriage for eternity, ordination for the priesthood and other sealing ordinances. These ceremonies or ordinances may be performed for the living or for the dead who are represented by a worthy and acceptable proxy.[102] James E. Talmage claims that "In this respect they [Mormon Temples] resemble Israel of olden times."[103] The fact is that there is no actual comparison between Mormon temples and the Temple of ancient Israel. Secret ritual was never a part of Jewish worship, nor were any Jews excluded from participation in the services. There was even a court for Godfearing Gentiles to view what took place. And certainly it would be unthinkable to an orthodox Jew that there could be many gods instead of One, including a Mother god.

Chapter Sixteen
KINGDOM OF THE CLANDESTINE

Brigham Young described the functions of the temple ceremonies in words taken directly from Masonic ritual: Your endowment is, to receive all those ordinances in the House of the Lord, which are necessary for you, after you have departed this life, to enable you to walk back to the presence of the Father, passing angels who stand as sentinels, being enabled to give them the key words, the signs and tokens, pertaining to the Holy Priesthood, and gain you eternal exaltation in spite of earth and hell.[104]

But when the *Book of Mormon* was written, it reflected the strong anti-Mason sentiment of the times (Ether 8:18-26; Helaman 6:18-30.) William Morgan, a former Mason during the time of Joseph Smith, had written a book entitled *Illustrations of Masonry*, exposing their secret rituals. Morgan suffered a series of mysterious persecutions while the book was in preparation. He was held by local officials for a debt claim while his house was searched for the manuscript. Attempts to burn down the print shop failed but soon afterward Morgan was kidnaped and never seen again. The Masonic Lodge was implicated, creating an anti-Masonic sentiment which spread across the county closing down thousands of Masonic lodges.[105]

The Masonic order was not originally introduced into Mormonism in Nauvoo as one writer has suggested.[106] Hyrum Smith entered the Mount Moriah Lodge No. 112 in Palmyra, New York, at the time Joseph claimed to be discovering the golden plates. Dr. Reed C. Durham, former president of the Mormon Historical Society, suggests that Smith and Morgan, contemporaries in time and by geography, knew each other. Durham cited Dr. Rob Morris, Masonic biographer of William Morgan who had written that Morgan "had been a halfway convert of Joe Smith, the Mormon, and learned from him to see visions and dreams."[107]

By 1832 new members of the Mormon church include W.W. Phelps, Brigham Young, Heber C. Kimball and Newel K. Whitney, all who had been Masons prior to entering Joseph's church. Smith likely wrote the anti-Masonic passages into the *Book of Mormon* because the plot for his own life story was taken from Jewish Cabalistic lore about Enoch which had been carried down into Masonic legend. No doubt Smith feared that those initiated into the ritual of Masonry would identify the similarities between his book and the Masonic legend of Enoch. One similarity included Enoch receiving a vision and being taken up to a hill called Moriah which contained buried treasure of gold and brass plates. Characters on the plates were in Egyptian hieroglyphics. Three attempts were made to secure from the hill the treasure containing not only the plates, but the Urim and Thummim, and a breast plate hidden in a stone box. Hiram Abiff was killed by three men while attempting to secure the treasure but not before he lifted his arms and cried, "Oh Lord, My Lord, is there no help for the widow's son?"[108] Similarities are all too familiar to be coincidental.

At the assassination of Joseph Smith, he stood in the second floor window of the Carthage Jail, his arms lifted in the Masonic signal of distress, and uttered the first four words of the distress signal, "Oh Lord, My God" before a fatal bullet silenced him.[109] From the Masonic ritual Smith also carried the secret names, tokens (handclasps), penalties, signs and phrases into the Mormon Temple ceremonies. Even prominent Masonic symbols such as the beehive and sun face with extending rays were carried over into the Mormon religion.[110] Endowment ceremonies or ordinances in the Mormon temple using Masonic phrases such as

"Pal lay ale"[111] were embellished with Mormon doctrine.

Initially Smith, as indicated, had written anti-Masonic passages into the *Book of Mormon* but by March 12, 1842, Dr. John D. Bennett, having arrived in Nauvoo two years earlier, influenced Smith to establish a Masonic lodge. Bennett rose quickly in the leadership, becoming not only the Commander of the Nauvoo Legion but Mayor of the city. Through his shrewd ability, he was able to obtain a charter of incorporation for Nauvoo but the character of John C. Bennett has further been described by Governor Thomas Ford as "probably the greatest scamp in the western county."[112] "Bennett was a native of Massachusetts by birth, a physician by profession, and an expert politician and demagogue by virtue of predilection and native endowment. Possessed of infinite mental resources, and endowed with great physical energy and superb self-assurance, he assumed a commanding role in whatever circle his lot was cast."[113]

It wasn't long before Smith and Bennett fell out. Bennett apostatized from the Mormons, just before Smith was killed in June 1844, and wrote an exposé of Mormonism which opens with forty-eight pages of letters defending his own character and the rest of the book defaming the character of Smith. Bennett also exposes the Danite lodge, sometimes called Destroying Angels, or Daughter of Zion, patterned after the Masonic lodge, for the very elite Mormons to carry out Smith's clandestine policies.[114] Within two years following his departure from Nauvoo, Bennett joined the Strangite Church and was appointed to its First Presidency. In 1847 both William Smith, brother to Joseph, who had become Patriarch in the Strangite faction and John C. Bennett were expelled from the Strangite Church. A letter to J.J. Strang from Bennett resisting any attempt to bring young Joseph Smith into the church as a patriarch seems to have initiated a rift that ultimately caused his expulsion from the Strangite group.[115]

It was hoped by Smith that a Masonic lodge would curry favor of the Gentiles. Joseph, along with other key leaders of the Mormon church, were introduced almost overnight into the mysteries of the Masonic order, Hyrum having been previously initiated. Before long, most of the adult males in Nauvoo had joined the lodge. This presented a threat to the non-Mormon Masons in Illinois, creating sharp opposition from them, the very opposite of Smith's plan.[116]

There is much discussion concerning the actual time of the inauguration of the endowments into the temple ceremonies. The Reorganized Mormon church insists that Joseph Smith never initiated any such secret ritual, which has no place in their worship. The evidence is, however, against them. Some form of the endowments began early in Kirtland which included anointings, blessings, foot washing, taking of bread and wine, prophesying, and the apparition of angels, although they were neither secret nor selective as to participants at this time.[117] In Nauvoo the endowments took on a definite secret and selective Masonic influence.

In the first visit to the temple, a Mormon receives his "Initiatory Ordinances" which prepares the candidate to receive the endowments. First, the candidate is placed in a loose sheet-like cloth called a "shield" to be washed "clean from the blood and sins of this generation." The temple worker places his hand under running water, touching different parts of the candidates's body, beginning with the top of the head, and, inside the sheet, the shoulders, back, breast, vitals, bowels and loins, pronouncing a blessing on each area. Male temple workers wash males and female temple workers wash females, as would be expected. Two workers then place their hands on the candidate's head, pronouncing the blessing of sealing.

Following the washing is the anointing with oil. The process is repeated with oil, touching each area as a blessing is pronounced. Again, two workers place their hands upon the candidate's head as a final blessing is pronounced over them.[118]

The candidate is then given an undergarment to be worn at all times, called "the garment of the holy priesthood." The temple garment originally had four Masonic emblems embroidered on it. It is worn by both men and women at all times under their clothing. Over the right breast was sewn the figure of a square representing honor and obedience in living up to temple vows. Over the left breast was a figure in the shape of a compass to remind the candidate that all truth may be compressed into one great whole and that appetites must be kept under control. A slit over the navel area indicated a need for physical and spiritual nourishment. A fourth slit over the right knee signified that every knee shall bow to Jesus.[119]

Temple Mormons are very sensitive about any reference to this garment and questions concerning the secret ritual that takes place in the temple. Even though they claim the ritual is not secret but sacred, they are not to discuss it with other temple Mormons and certainly not Gentiles. Because the candidate is told that the garment will protect them as long as they keep their covenants, it becomes a type of magic talisman. At this point they are given a secret new name.

Now the candidate, called a "patron" is prepared to receive the endowments. The first endowments are to secure the patron's own salvation. At this point he is prepared to receive the endowments for others, both the living and the dead. The first endowment, offering limited participation by the couples, is a two-hour video drama enacting the story of creation from the Garden of Eden, up to their reception into the Mormon church.[120]

A second endowment is baptism for the dead. This doctrine, built on the belief that a person must be baptized to be redeemed, teaches that a living individual can stand in by proxy for a deceased person and perform the endowments in his stead. Joseph Smith instituted this doctrine at Far West, Missouri, on July 8, 1838.[121] This teaching is built on a single obscure verse in I Corinthians 15:29 where the Apostle Paul alludes by way of illustration to the fact that the pagan religions baptize for the dead. Paul did not affirm his belief in this practice but merely used it for an illustration of the fact that the pagans believe in immortality, otherwise why would they perform this ritual? Paul used the same kind of argument with the Athenians on Mars Hill when he pointed out their altar to an unknown god. He wasn't affirming his belief in their altar but used it as an illustration to declare the

True and Living God.

A third endowment is a temple marriage for time and eternity. In this ritual the husband and wife are sealed to each other. Having already been married in the local ward for time, they now are married in the temple for eternity. This ceremony may also be performed for deceased couples in order to seal them in marriage for eternity. Only those who have a Temple Recommend may be sealed and those family members who attend must also have a recommend. All are dressed in temple attire. Parents of a bride or groom who are not temple Mormons cannot enter the temple for this or any other ceremony. The couple kneels, facing each other, on an elaborate altar with their right hands joined while resting their heads on the altar.

Children may also be sealed to their parents. They are not allowed to attend their parents' sealing but are brought in afterward, placing their hands, oldest child first, on top of their parents' hands while the sealing is pronounced.[122] The Bible nowhere teaches that marriage continues in heaven. In fact, it teaches the very opposite. Jesus taught that "in the resurrection they neither marry, nor are given in marriage, but are as the angels in heaven" (Matthew 22:30).

The final endowment of the holy Melchizedek Priesthood is often given to young men before they leave on their mission. They pledge to live in obedience to the gospel through chastity and consecrated lives.[123]

One of the most controversial doctrines, excluding the doctrine of polygamy, is the doctrine of blood atonement. While Mormon writer Bruce R. McConkie vehemently denies that involuntary blood atonement was ever taught or practiced by Brigham Young,[124] the evidence proves otherwise. It was certainly practiced with regularity in the early days of Utah. The blood atonement doctrine teaches that under certain circumstances, there are some serious sins for which the cleansing of Christ does not operate, and that men must then have their own blood shed to atone for their sins.[125] This doctrine was kept secret under Joseph Smith but in Utah, away from the eye of established law, it was practiced. Reed Peck, an early Mormon, records in his journal that in 1839, in reaction to dissenters, particularly John Corrill, that Joseph Smith claimed to have talked with the Apostle Peter a few days earlier and that he had told him how Peter had hanged Judas for betraying Jesus.[126] Brigham Young declared, "There is not a man or woman who violated the covenants made with their God, that will not be required to pay the debt. The blood of Christ will never wipe that out, your own blood must atone for it; and the judgments of the Almighty will come, sooner or later, and every man and woman will have to atone for breaking their covenants."[127]

Mormon writer Klaus J. Hansen states that when the Mormons first established themselves in the Utah territory that Brigham Young insisted that there were "plenty of instances where men have been righteously slain in order to atone for their sins."[128] Some of the sins that require blood atonement are murder,[129] adultery,[130] stealing,[131] apostasy,[132] and for condemning Joseph Smith.[133] The Bible is clear that only the blood of Jesus Christ can atone for man's sins. (1 John 1:7,9; Romans 3:25; 1 Peter 1:18-19.)

The Mormon doctrine of heaven is a strange one compared to biblical teaching. Joseph Smith claimed that while he and Sidney Rigdon were "translating" the Bible, it was revealed to them on February 16, 1832, that "the term 'Heaven', as intended for the Saint's eternal home, must include more kingdoms than one."[134] The Mormon concept of heaven is adapted from 1 Corinthians 15:40 which speaks of celestial and terrestrial glory. Smith and Rigdon coined an additional word "telestial" to describe a third dimension of glory. Within the context of 1 Corinthians 15 it is clear that the Apostle Paul is not talking about heaven but the resurrection body which will have a "celestial" (heavenly) and a "terrestrial" (earthly) dimension. Mormons also refer to 1 Corinthians 12:2 where Paul refers to a "third heaven." The reference is not to three separate heavens but three aspects of the one heaven where God dwells. They also use John 14:2 which refers to "many mansions" to teach multiple heavens. This is clearly not the intent of the verse. Heaven simply has many dwellings. They also use Matthew 7:13-14 to teach that the broad road leads to the "terrestrial" heaven but the Bible says explicitly that this road leads to destruction.

The Bible does not teach separation but unification of God's people (John 14:1-3; 1 Thessalonians 4:15-18; 1 Peter 1:3-4). It does not teach exclusiveness but inclusiveness (Ephesians 6:9).

Although Mormon missionaries and apologists have sought to make Mormonism appear Christian, it is by teaching a heretical cult. They deny that Jesus is God, the Holy Spirit is a person, and the biblical doctrine that man is in a fallen state of sin. They do not accept the Bible as the inspired and inerrant Word of God. Orson Hyde said the Bible was "only a history of people 1800 years ago."[135] In the eighth Article of Faith they declare, "We believe the Bible to be the word of God as far as it is translated correctly; we also believe the Book of Mormon to be the word of God."[136] The reader will note that while the *Bible*, which has lasted over two thousand years, is true only as it is correctly translated, that the *Book of Mormon*, which is 168 years old, without any geological, archaeological, or historical evidence, is unqualified as the word of God.

Mormons believe that their church is the only true "restored" church and that all individuals are obliged to acknowledge Joseph Smith to be saved. Bruce R. McConkie has clearly stated: "Thus, in the full sense, the faithful members of the Church of Jesus Christ of Latter-day Saints are the only true believers in the world today . . . ".[137] Brigham Young taught that at the final judgment, mankind will stand before Elohim, Jesus Christ and Joseph Smith. The Prophet Young said, "No man or woman in this dispensation will ever enter the celestial kingdom of God without the consent of Joseph Smith!" McConkie wrote, "Salvation is available to men on earth today because of Joseph Smith." He went on to declare, "If Joseph Smith received power from high, then the Church of Jesus Christ of Latter-day Saints is the kingdom of God on earth and the one place where salvation is found."[138]   In the *Elder's Journal* at Far West, Joseph Smith answered the question, "Will everybody be damned but Mormons?" His printed answer was, "Yes, and a great portion of them unless they repent and work righteousness."[139]   Roy W. Doxey, LDS scholar recently answered the question, "Who is accepted of the Lord?" His answer: " Only those, however, who are sufficiently contrite, or humble enough to accept the truth as taught in the Lord's revelations through the Prophet Joseph Smith and his successors, and who obey the ordinances of water and Spirit baptism are acceptable to him."[140]

Let the Bible speak as to the person and work of our Lord Jesus Christ. Jesus said, "I am the way, the truth, and the life: no man cometh unto the Father, but by me (John 14:6). The Apostle Peter affirmed, "Neither is there salvation in any other: for there is none other name under heaven given among men, whereby we must be saved (Acts 4:12). The Apostle Paul declares, "But though we, or an angel from heaven, preach any other gospel unto you than that ye have received, let him be accursed" (Galatians 1:8). The Apostle John wrote, "These things have I written unto you that believe on the name of the Son of God; that ye may know that ye have eternal life, and that ye may believe on the name of the Son of God (1 John 5:13). Jude warned, "For there are certain men crept in unawares, who were before of old ordained to this condemnation, ungodly men, turning the grace of our God into lasciviousness, and denying the only Lord God, and our Lord Jesus Christ" (Jude 4).

PART FOUR

EXPOSING THE PROBLEMS OF MORMONS

"Yet of all churches in the world only this one has not found it necessary to readjust any part of its doctrine in the last hundred years."

Hugh Nibley
No Ma'am That's Not History
page 46

Chapter Seventeen

THE CHANGING NAME, CHURCH HISTORY, AND DOCTRINE OF GOD

The first problem sincere Mormons must face is the fact that the name of their church has been changed twice since its official organization April 6, 1830. At first Smith called his followers The Church of Christ[1] according to the command of the *Book of Mormon*, (3 Nephi 27:3-9; 26:21; 4 Nephi 1:1). On May 3, 1834 through the influence of Sidney Rigdon, the name of the church was changed from the "Church of Christ" to the "Latter-day Saints."[2]

Several reasons have been suggested for the name change. One writer thinks that Rigdon recommended the change to distance Smith's church from any connection with the Campbellite movement. In a publication, as early as 1825, Campbell was referring to his church as the Church of Christ.[3] Another offers the proposition that the name change was to retain the restoration idea among these Latter-day Saints.[4] Still another maintains that the new name was in response to the millennial theme so prevalent in 1834,[5] but the official reason offered in the church newspaper suggested that it was in response to the negative designations such as "Mormonite" given to the church by outsiders.[6] Yet, the name of the church had nothing to do with the negative designations given to Smith's group. They came from the book he claimed to have translated from the plates inscribed with Egyptian hieroglyphics by the angel Mormon. Changing the name to Latter-day Saints could hardly affect those early designations. The name was likely changed as a result of a combination of all the above suggestions.

The designation "Mormons" has been traditionally rejected until recent years. The church of Joseph prefers to be called the "Saints' Church" or the "Saints," but many of them today accept the name of Mormons as a badge of honor. Yet, it must strike the reader that if Joseph was a true prophet, then why would he not receive a onetime revelation of the church name rather than changing it twice before settling finally on the Church of Jesus Christ of Latter-day Saints?

Warren Parrish, treasurer of the Kirtland Safety Society Bank, along with Oliver Cowdery, had observed Joseph Smith's relationship to a seventeen-year-old girl named Fannie Alger, whom the Smiths had taken into their home to raise. Cowdery was outspoken on the matter of Joseph's polygamous connection with Alger, calling it, in a letter to his brother, "a dirty, nasty, filthy affair." This led to his excommunication from the church.[7] This, along with changing the name of the church, led Parrish and a group of thirty elders to establish a new branch of the church under the original name of "The Church of Christ." Opposition to Smith's leadership became so widespread that Brigham Young had to contact the faithful followers in order to sustain the Prophet at the September 3, 1837, Conference Meeting.[8] This was only one of the many groups that seceded from the original group at Kirtland.

After Sidney Rigdon failed in his attempt to gain the leadership of the Mormon church following the death of Joseph Smith, he gathered some followers and moved to his home area of Pittsburgh where he established a new church called "The Church of Christ," the original name of Joseph's church. The direction the Mormon Church had taken in relation to plural marriages particularly caused him to try to return to the first principles of the Kirtland Church.[9] David Whitmer later rejected the second name because he believed Smith had "gone deep into error" through the polygamy doctrine and cited the fact that the *Book of Commandments* carried the Church of Christ name on the inside cover.[10]

Certainly, Smith became the brunt of criticism from some of his followers for changing the name of the church which carried nothing by way of reference to any name of deity. So on April 26, 1838, at Far West, Missouri, Joseph again changed the name of the church which survives today as the final designation of the followers of Young to Utah as the Church of Jesus Christ of Latter-day Saints.[11] Those who remained in Missouri with the Smith family are called the Reorganized Church of Jesus Christ of Latter-Day Saints.

In 1838, Joseph Smith began dictating the history of the church, which was published in serial form in the church newspaper *Times and Seasons* up to the time the Mormons departed for the Utah Territory. Various secretaries recorded parts of the history but not until Dr. Willard Richards was appointed secretary to Smith was significant progress made in organizing it. Thomas Bullock became Richard's chief scribe, recording the history up to what now appears in Volume 3. The narrative was completed to March 1, 1843, (page 674) when the Mormons pulled out of Nauvoo, heading west on February 4, 1846. Almost seven years later on June 7, 1853, the boxes containing a "duplicate handwritten copy of the History" and the "original manuscript" were unpacked by Willard Richards and Thomas Bullock in the Salt Lake City. On December 1, 1853, Willard Richards entered a single line to continue the history but illness prevented him from writing more. A few months later, March 4, 1854, he died.[12]

George A. Smith, appointed Church Historian to succeed Willard Richards, compiled, corrected and completed the history up to August 8, 1844, which caused him "to suffer much from a nervous headache or inflammation of the brain." In August 1856, seventeen years after it was begun, the history up to Joseph Smith's death at the Carthage Jail was completed.[13]

The history which was completed after Joseph Smith's

death was printed in installments in the *Deseret News* (Utah) and the *Millennial Star* (London). Near the turn of the century, four men, A. Milton Musser, Andrew Jensen, Orson F. Whitney, and B.H. Roberts were employed as assistant Church Historians. In 1901 Roberts was appointed by then President Joseph F. Smith to edit the *Church History* for publication in seven volumes.[14] The history has been revised and reprinted several times since its first publication.

Although the church leaders have consistently stated that the History was written by Joseph Smith, even placing the first six volumes in the first person indicating that Smith wrote it himself, it is in fact from the hand of "over twenty-four scribes and ghostwriters, are known to have assisted him [Smith] during the fifteen years from 1829-1844--the period of his 'writing'."[15] Smith himself wrote, "I am dictating history, I say dictating for I seldom use the pen myself." He also referred to Willard Richards, who was his scribe, as a "failed" historian for not including particulars such as weather during events.[16] Mormon scholar Howard H. Seale further writes, "It is clear from the Prophet's diaries, as well as the journals of the scribes, that he often dictated to his assistants, but it is equally clear that scribes and clerks often composed and recorded information on their own."[17]

When B.H. Roberts edited the *History of the Church* he perpetuated the idea that Joseph had written all of the history by taking the secretarial script, often modified by the secretary, and put it in first person. He also added material and deleted material with no indication. This is easily verified by taking the history in the early Mormon newspapers and comparing it with the published History. Dean C. Jessee, former staff member in the Church Historian's Office, admits that only 40% of the History was written at the time of Smith's death. Of the 2,483 pages of Joseph Smith's history, only 812 were completed at his death.[18] When George W. Robinson, who became Church Recorder when Oliver Cowdery went to Missouri, recorded the "Scriptory Book of Joseph Smith, Jr." from 1837-1838, he did so in the third person. But when B.H. Roberts copied it into the *History of the Church* it was transposed into first person, implying the Prophet had written it.[19]

In the preface of Volume I, Roberts states, "The history of Joseph Smith is now before the world, and we are satisfied that a history more correct in its details than this was never published."[20] Students of Mormon history are indebted to Jerald and Sandra Tanner who have carefully researched the changes in the different printings of the History and reveal that at least 17,000 words have been added and 45,000 words have been deleted from it. In addition to normative changes in spelling, punctuation, grammar, and rearrangement of words, failed prophecies have been deleted or changed, exaggerated or contradictory statements have been adjusted and crude language including profanity by the Prophet has been removed.[21] Numerous references to the "revising" of the History by Brigham Young and scribes may be found in Vol. 7, pp. 389-390, 408, 411, 414, 427-428, 514, 519-520, 532, 533, and 556.[22]

Charles Wesley Wandell, who worked in the Church Historian Office following the death of Smith, recorded in his journal: "I notice the interpolations because of having been employed myself in the Historian's office at Nauvoo by Doctor Richards, and employed, too, in 1845, in compiling this very autobiography, I know that after Joseph's death his memoir was 'doctored' to suit the new order of things, and this, too, by the direct order of Brigham Young to Doctor Richards and systematically by Richards."[23]

Initially, Church Historian B.H. Roberts cited two prophecies of Joseph Smith which he felt authenticated him as a prophet. "The first one was in relation to the removal of the Saints to the valley of the Rocky Mountains; the other was a most remarkable prediction concerning Stephen A. Douglas, just then beginning to become prominent in the politics of Illinois."[24]

A careful research of these two prophecies reveal that they were amended, falsified, or distorted as to the original intended meaning. Rather than authenticating Smith as a prophet, they reveal that historians have fabricated his ability to predict the future. Smith comes off much brighter and certainly more clever, if not immeasurably gifted, when he is quoted in the *History of the Church*.

On August 6, 1842, according to the *History of the Church*, Joseph Smith, along with other Saints, attended a Masonic installation service across the river from Nauvoo in Montrose, Iowa. During the discussion of the "persecution in Missouri," outside the meeting hall, Smith delivered what Roberts called one of his most important prophecies.

"I prophesied that the Saints would continue to suffer much affliction and would be driven to the Rocky Mountains, many would apostatize, others would be put to death by our persecutors or lose their lives in consequence of exposure or disease, and some of you will live to go and assist in making settlements and build cities and see the Saints become a mighty people in the midst of the Rocky Mountains."[25]

Called the "Rocky Mountain Prophecy," Smith is credited with the prediction that the Saints would settle after persecution as a great people in the west. Actually, the prophecy was written into the history after Joseph Smith's death.[26] David Bitton, who served as an assistant Church Historian under Leonard Arrington, in an unpublished paper, indicates that there is no record of the prophecy in the Prophet's own handwriting and that it was referred to generally by the Saints as they traveled west but was added to the history later. Examination of the original handwritten history reveals that the phrase "a mighty people in the midst of the Rocky Mountains" has been squeezed into the original record in a different handwriting.[27]

The other prophecy referred to by B.H. Roberts concerns Judge Stephen A. Douglas Smith, supposedly predicted that Douglas would "aspire to the presidency of the United States." In the *History of the Church* Roberts states that the account was taken from the journal of William Clayton, who was present "with Smith when he dined with Judge Douglas at Carthage." An eighty-six-word entry in Clayton's journal of the event was expanded to 456 words in the *History of the Church*.[28] The short narration in Clayton's journal reads:

"At Carthage we paid some taxes and dined at Backenstos' with Judge [Stephen A.] Douglas who is presiding at Court. After dinner the President and Judge had conversation concerning sundry matters. The President said, 'I prophesy in the name of the Lord God that in a few years this government will be utterly overthrown and wasted so that there will not be a potsherd left' for their wickedness in conniving at the Missouri mobocracy. The Judge appears very friendly and acknowledges the propriety of the President's remarks."[29]

The above brief account was expanded to include, among several other things, this prophecy: "Judge, you will aspire to the presidency of the United States; and if ever you turn your hand against me or the Latter-day Saints, you will feel the weight of the hand of Almighty upon you; and you will live to see and know that I have testified the truth to you; for the conversation this day will stick to you through life."[30] This section was transposed onto the history at least ten years after Smith's death. Additionally, the *Clayton Journal* reveals that Smith predicted "I prophesy in the name of the Lord God that in a few years this government will be overthrown and wasted so that there will not be a potsherd left,"[31] a prophecy that obviously never transpired.

The original History in the *Times and Seasons* records Smith's frank confession that he "frequently fell into many foolish errors and displayed the weaknesses of youth and the corruption of human nature, which I am sorry to say led me into divers temptations, to the gratification of many appetites offensive in the sight of God."[32] The "foolish error" and "temptation" to feign prophecy obviously followed him into adult life. When this original statement appeared in the 1902 revised History, it had been softened, probably fearing reproach upon Smith's character, to read: "I frequently fell into many foolish errors, and displayed the weakness of youth, and the foibles of human nature; which, I am sorry to say, led me into divers temptations, offensive in the sight of God. In making this confession, no one need suppose me guilty of any great or malignant sins. A disposition to commit such was never in my nature."[33]

That there is a changing doctrine of God in Mormonism from its conception to present day is affirmed by key Mormon writers such as Thomas G. Alexander.[34] Some Mormon scholars seek to excuse the changing doctrine of God "which passed clearly through stages of development" by citing reference in *Doctrine and Covenants* to changing revelations (Section 50:40; 42:61; 88:49; 121:28).[35] None of these references have anything to do with "changing revelations." Such an idea of "changing revelation" is completely foreign to biblical prophets. While there is a progressive revelation of God in the Bible, it is neither contradictory nor conflicting. Rather, it is complimentary and developing.

The earliest concept of God in Mormonism, found in the *Book of Mormon*, is Trinitarian. The phrase "the Father, and the Son, and the Holy Ghost, which is one God" occurs throughout the first sacred book of Mormonism (2 Nephi 31:21; Mosiah 15:4; Alma 11:44; 3 Nephi 11:27, 36, 28:10-11; Mormon 7:7). The early *Doctrine and Commandments* also sustained the teaching that the Father and the Son are one God (Section 20:27-28) and that Jesus and the Father are identical. It also taught that Jesus Christ is the Father come in the flesh (Mosiah 7:27; 15:1-5; Ether 4:12).[36]   *A Book of Commandments*, which included the constituting documents of Joseph Smith's church in 1830, declared the "Father and Son and Holy Ghost, is one God, infinite and eternal, without end. Amen".[37] Two years later when the commandments were reprinted and revised it was changed to read the "Father, Son and Holy Ghost *are* one God"[38] to accommodate Smith's changing doctrine of God.

In addition, the earliest presentation of the doctrine of God by Joseph Smith in the *Book of Mormon* was monotheistic, compatible with the teaching of the Bible (Deuteronomy 6:4; Isaiah 44:6,8). In Alma 11:26-28 Zeezroom asked Amulek if there is more than one God. Amulek answered an emphatic "No." The teaching of one God is further confirmed in *The Pearl of Great Price* when God reveals to Moses "there is no God beside me . .

. " (Moses 1:6). But in the later "Book of Abraham," sixty references to "the gods" or "they" or "we" referring to many gods may be found in chapters four and five. Joseph Smith moved from a monotheistic to a polytheistic concept of God.

On March 9, 1844, King Follett, a devoted follower of Joseph Smith from almost the beginning of the new church, was killed when a bucket of rocks fell on him while walling up a well. Smith preached his funeral the next day and some weeks later preached an extended eulogy at the request of the family during the local conference.[39] It was in this final major address that he enumerated, clarified and expanded four major doctrines that he had only hinted to in a veiled way before, doctrines that developed after the *Book of Mormon* and probably were conceived around the time that the "Book of Abraham" came into existence. The sermon taught that men could become gods, there existed many gods, the gods exist one above another innumerably and the God of this universe was once a man.[40]

Finally, the earliest writings of Smith presented God as a Spirit, not as a man with human flesh—an exalted man. The *Book of Mormon* defines God as an infinite personage of Spirit who revealed Himself in the flesh as Jesus Christ. God is called the "Great Spirit" three times in Alma 22:9-11 and He is called the "same yesterday, today and forever . . . " in Mormon 9:9. William A. Cowdery, co-editor along with Frederick G. Williams of the *Messenger and Advocate*, states that "God is immutable in his purposes and unchangeable in his nature."[41] In the 1832 account of Smith's first vision he described the appearance of only one person which he claimed appeared to him in the woods.[42]

Brigham Young added a wrinkle to the doctrine of God when he proclaimed before the conference April 9, 1852, that Adam was God and Eve was one of his wives.[43] It has often been denied by succeeding church leaders that Young taught the Adam-God theory but Young preached the doctrine and continued to proclaim it for twenty-five years of his life.[44]

Chapter Eighteen
REVISING THE REVELATIONS, BLACKS AND THE TEMPLE RITUAL

The revelation on plural marriage was not only fraught with dissension among the Mormons themselves but it brought salient resistance from non-Mormons. It became a constant source of trouble, eventually leading to the Prophet's death. It was this revelation which led to the establishment of the *Nauvoo Expositor* by William Law and his friends. The single issue from the *Expositor* attacked immorality among the Mormons, specifically polygamy, by those within the ranks of Mormonism itself. Smith's fierce reaction to the publication by sending the Nauvoo militia to destroy the press ultimately led to his arrest and death at the Carthage Jail.

When the Mormons moved west, they continued to follow the revelation concerning plural marriages. Brigham Young promoted the practice of polygamy for forty-three years in Utah. It was the threatenings of Young in his famous blood atonement sermon in which he said, "If any miserable scoundrels come here, cut their throats" that led to the famous Mountain Meadow massacre,[45] a sermon directed against government intervention of polygamy. The massacre brought the U.S. government into the affairs of Utah and the ultimate surrender by the Mormon leadership of a revelation that they claimed to be from God through their Prophet Joseph Smith.[46]

Joseph Smith had consistently denied practicing polygamy but had as many as thirty wives.[47] Hyrum Smith vehemently denied the teaching as a lie and a false doctrine.[48] The original revelation, which was suppressed for numerous years, dates back to as early as 1831.[49] Even though the church issued the Manifesto in 1890 calling for an end of polygamy, thirteen years later church officials continued to promote and practice it.[50] There are still Mormons practicing the revelation, particularly in the far Western states. And although the Mormon church officially claims not to sanction these plural marriages, more than one woman may yet be spiritually sealed to a man in the secret temple ceremonies.[51]

Although Mormon leaders declared over and over that the revelation on plural marriages could not be surrendered, that indeed it was a part of the very warp and woof of Mormonism, on October 6, 1890, in an official declaration by President Wilford Woodruff, the Saints were advised that polygamy was forbidden as declared by the laws of the land.[52] How can a revelation of God given to one Prophet be reversed by another? Joseph Smith declared that polygamy was an "everlasting covenant" and failure to abide in it was to be "damned and no one can reject this covenant and be permitted to enter into my glory" (*Doctrine and Covenants*, Section 132:1-4). Some fundamentalist Mormons claim that President John Taylor recorded a revelation rescinding the Manifesto of Wilford Woodruff against polygamy.[53] This is denied by Utah church leaders.

While the Mormons resided at Independence, Missouri, a great controversy arose over the question of blacks migrating to the state. Apparently unknown to the Mormons, there was a Missouri law prohibiting freed blacks from entering the state. Some blacks accepted into the church in other parts of the country considered migrating to Missouri, a state where a large percent of the population was slaves. W.W. Phelps, editor and publisher of the Mormon newspaper *Evening and Morning Star* printed the law concerning "free people of color" considering migrating to western Missouri followed by editorial comments concerning "liberality of opinion." Phelps concluded the article by quoting the Missouri Constitution regarding the rights of all men "to worship Almighty God according to the dictates of their own consciences . . . " and a statement that "much is doing towards abolishing slavery, and colonizing blacks, in Africa." He stated that there was "no special rule in the church, as to people of color . . . ".[54] It was enough, however, to ignite an avalanche of reaction from non-Mormons, who interpreted these remarks as an invitation to free blacks to move to Missouri, culminating in a declaration demanding the expulsion of the Mormons. Although Phelps tried to rescind the article in a subsequent publication, the fires of reaction were already ablaze. A mob stormed the printing office destroying everything in sight.

In the years to follow, blacks were allowed to join the Latter-day Saints but males were refused the normal privilege to serve in the priesthood. Citing the *Book of Abraham* 1:20-27 Mormon Apostle Bruce R. McConkie states "Negroes in this life are denied the priesthood; under no circumstances can they hold this delegation of authority from the Almighty." He further stated: "The Negroes are not equal with other races where the receipt of certain spiritual blessings are concerned, particularly the priesthood and the temple blessings that flow therefrom, but this inequality is not of man's origin."[55] This teaching established by Joseph Smith in the *Book of Mormon* (Moses 5:16-41; 7:8,12,22; Alma 3:6-9; 1 Nephi 12:23; 2 Nephi 5:2) and affirmed by Brigham Young[56] was based upon the belief that blacks are descendants of and under the curse of Cain. The *Book of Mormon* teaches that God favored the white race which was a sign of righteousness and that a black skin is the sign of God's displeasure.

Samuel D. Chambers, born in Alabama one year after the beginning of Smith's new church in 1830, as a thirteen-year-old slave was converted to the Mormon religion. As a free man following the Civil War, and after a failed marriage, Chambers took his son and new wife to Utah. There "in the Eight Ward, where they tithed and donated, received patriarchal blessings," he "was appointed as assistant Deacon" but was never permitted to enter the priesthood. Without the priesthood he sustained no hope of eternal marriage and ultimate exaltation, although a lifetime faithful member of the Mormon Church until his death in 1929 at the age of ninety-eight.[57]

Elijah Abel in the early 1800's became a member of the Mormon church. Abel migrated to Kirtland, Ohio, and was ordained the first black member to the Melchizedek Priesthood and was then appointed to the Quorum of Seventy by 1836. In the patriarchal blessing given by Joseph Smith, Sr., Elijah Abel was not assigned to a particular biblical lineage but was declared "an orphan." The blessing closed with, "Thou shalt be made equal to thy brethren, and thy soul be white in eternity and thy robes glittering."[58] He participated freely in baptisms for the dead when he moved to Nauvoo where he was freely accepted by his fellow Saints. There he served as a carpenter before being appointed undertaker by Joseph Smith. Abel was listed among the men who assembled to rescue Joseph Smith after his arrest near Nauvoo by requisition from the State of Missouri.[59]

In 1842 Abel moved to Cincinnati, Ohio, married and fathered three children before moving to Salt Lake City in 1853. When he arrived in Utah, he discovered that blacks were in disfavor due to the flamboyant and radical behavior of William McCary who was part Indian and part black. McCary's antics had brought the disfavor of Brigham Young and other leaders down upon the approximately 100 black Mormons living in Salt Lake City. In 1849 Young issued statements denying blacks the priesthood rights based on the theory that they were the cursed descendants of Ham. Joseph Smith espoused this view in 1836 through an article rebutting abolitionism.[60] Although Abel was of the Melchizedek Priesthood, he was refused participation in the temple ordinances in Utah, and, therefore, could not receive marriage for eternity or hope for ultimate exaltation.

One hundred years after Brigham Young announced that blacks were ineligible for the Mormon Priesthood, the First Presidency reaffirmed this position. Previously in the Temple endowments, the Devil was described as having "claws like a bear," "roar of a lion" and "a black skin."[61] Lester E. Bush, Jr., in an extensive article five years before the official Declaration rescinding the revelation on blacks, traced the "Mormonism's Negro Doctrine" and concluded with four searching questions. Did Joseph Smith issue any policy excluding blacks from the Priesthood? Was Brigham Young merely reflecting the view of his day in denying the priesthood to blacks? Does the "Book of Abraham" teaching, in *The Pearl of Great Price*, that blacks are the cursed descendants of Cain have anything to do with the black Priesthood question or is this nineteenth century influence? Finally, he asked if present day Prophets have received confirmation of this teaching.[62]

The Mormon Prophet Spencer W. Kimball in June 1987 delivered a "revelation" reversing 130 years of teaching on blacks and permitting them to hold the priesthood. The 1830 edition of the *Book of Mormon* referred to dark-skinned people becoming "white and delightsome" through acceptance of the Mormon teachings. But in the editions after the 1978 Declaration, 2 Nephi 30:6 was changed to "pure and delightsome." Many other major passages in the *Book of Mormon* concerning blacks today remain intact as originally given.

During the 1960's and 70's, demonstrations followed almost every Brigham Young University athletic event. In 1969 Stanford University severed relationship with BYU although the school maintained no policies which prevented blacks from entering the school.[63] Integration and the presence of black athletic students at BYU played a significant part in the new "revelation," but how can a teaching recorded in a book more sacred to the Mormons than the Bible be reversed?

Since their initial introduction into the Mormon religion the endowments of the temple have undergone numerous adjustments and several significant changes. What began as an all inclusive ceremony for every member developed into an exclusive ritual for the elite. From a public ritual developed a private (secret) endowment. An endowment that initially took between six and nine hours was reduced to three hours. Temple garments that were long and bulky were shortened to accommodate more modern styles. The endowments originally produced by a live cast were later filmed for convenience. In addition, the endowments have been severely altered through the years, dropping items that were offensive to non-Mormons, as the contents of the ceremonies became more public.

An early form of an endowment ceremony was introduced by Joseph Smith on October 5, 1835, during the Kirtland years. Smith instructed the Council of the Twelve "concerning duties to come . . . attended to the ordinance of the washing of feet, and to prepare their hearts for the endowment with power from on high . . . ".[64] It later included "washing . . . bodies in pure water," "sealings," receiving the ordinances and seeing "glorious visions." With the exception of the "washings in pure water" these ceremonial rituals were public congregational acts performed during the dedication of the Kirtland Temple.[65]

After the Mormons moved to Nauvoo, these observances prepared the way for a new revelation, permanently fixing the "anointing, and your washings, and your baptisms for the dead".[66] Although Smith claimed that the endowments were divinely revealed on May 4, 1842,[67] it is obvious that they were more progressive in development, drawing deeply on Masonic ritual.[68] But as late as 1988, Ezra Taft Benson claimed, "The endowment was revealed by revelation and can be understood only by revelation . . . "[69] The Nauvoo temple endowment was expanded to include "communication of keys pertaining to the Aaronic Priesthood, and so onto the highest order of the Melchizedek Priesthood . . . and all those plans and principles by which one is enabled to secure the fullness of those blessings which have been prepared for the Church . . . " Further the *History of the Church* reveals that "the weakest of the Saints" were to receive the endowments when the temple was completed. It was, however, specifically for the "spiritually minded" which meant only Mormons.[70]

While the first sacred book to Mormons, the *Book of Mormon*, contains some apparent anti-Masonic passages (Alma

37:21-32 and Ether 8:18-26), it also is clear that the later Mormon Temple endowment is distinctly colored by Masonic ritual. As previously noted, both Joseph and Hyrum Smith along with other key leaders, were Masons. A lodge was established in Nauvoo by the Mormons but the Masons withdrew charter because the Mormons used no discretion in bringing every man into the lodge simply because they were Mormons. Smith carried the penalties, oaths, symbols and signs from the Masonic lodge over into the Mormon temple ritual.[71]

Mormons often argue that the ceremonies in the temple are sacred rather than secret which prevents their discussion, but "they are obviously both."[72] Some scholars claim that "certain key words or symbols that are part of the ceremony" are not to be discussed because they take place upon sacred ground but feel free to deal with the general themes of the endowments.[73] Through the years from inception, portions of the endowments have periodically surfaced in the printed page. The first bit of information concerning the endowments seems to have surfaced in a newspaper account by a letter from a Mormon lady answering erroneous reports of immorality in the ceremony. She told more of the ceremony than officials ever intended concerning washings, anointings and the Garden of Eden drama itself.[74] A year later, a Mormon couple who left the church published the basic elements of the entire ritual.[75] Through the years the ritual has been exposed to the public through the printed page by former Mormons.

The public at large was made aware of certain elements in the temple ritual such as the secret oath of vengeance through the Senate hearings on the confirmation of Senator Reed Smoot of Utah in 1904-1906. Four volumes of discussion and debate, including testimony of a former temple Mormon, make up the report of the hearings.[76] In 1980 a former Mormon and temple worker printed the most accurate and up to date exposé of the secret temple ceremonies.[77] Two years later Chuck Sackett, who served as a guide for the Los Angeles Temple for three years, secretly recorded, as have others, the actual endowment ritual and reproduced it verbatim in a book.[78] John Hyde, Jr., joined the Mormons as a young man in England. He was bright, sincere and gifted. In 1853 he came to America to join the Saints at Salt Lake City and later left the church. He called the view that the secret temple endowments came through revelation a myth.

"There is one thing that is utterly ridiculous, the pretending to claim inspiration as its source. Its signs, tokens, marks and ideas are all plagiarized from masonry. The whole affair is being constantly amended and corrected . . . "[79]

Joseph F. Smith, sixth President of the Latter-day Saints, insisted in an article that it would be a "grievous sin" to even alter the original design of the temple garments.[80] Yet, sometime later the long sleeves were shortened, and the length of the garments were cut off to just below the knee, collars were removed, and buttons replaced the strings.[81] The endowment itself was shortened significantly from the original time of nine to six hours. Today the endowment takes approximately three hours.

In one fell swoop in April of 1990, due to mounting pressure from several sources, the Mormon church made some drastic changes in the temple ceremony, shortening the ceremony again possibly up to one third. A widely circulated dramatic film in evangelical churches depicting a Christian preacher as a hireling of the devil in the temple ceremony, continuous evidence linking the secret oaths, passwords, handshakes and names to Masonic ritual, and the pressure of feminist groups within the Mormon church caused a deletion of the Christian minister scene, much of the Masonic tokens and penalties, and a requirement of women to obey their husbands.[82] The original endowments are claimed to have been given under divine inspiration to the prophet of God. Ezra Taft Benson, President of the Mormon Church, declared, "The endowments was revealed by revelation and can be understood only by revelation . . . ".[83] Yet, they have been changed several times, the accompanying temple garments altered, and the ceremony ultimately reduced in length by almost two-thirds.

PART FIVE

ESTABLISHING THE PRESENTATION TO MORMONS

"If after a rigid examination, it be found an imposition, it should be extensively published to the world as such: the evidences and arguments on which the imposture was detected should be clearly and logically stated that those who continue to publish the delusion may be exposed and silenced by evidences adduced from Scripture and reason."

Apostle Orson Pratt
Divine Authority of the Book of Mormon
Pamphlet printed in 1850 - 1851

Chapter Nineteen
WHY WITNESS TO MORMONS?

E vangelicals need not only be introduced to the prophet of the Mormons, nor simply to understand the philosophy of Mormonism, but to develop a clear, concise, presentation of the true Gospel of Jesus Christ to them. Christians should have a deep compassion for the millions that have been and are being drawn into the maze of Mormonism.

Why is it necessary to witness to Mormons? The answer to that question will be the same reason given for witnessing to any non-Christian group parading under the guise of Christianity. Mormons are a cult. A clear definition of a cult has been provided by Charles Braden, professor of History and Literature of Religions at Northwestern University.

"A cult, as I define it, is any religious group which differs significantly in someone or more respects as to belief or practice, from those religious groups which are regarded as the normative expressions of religion in our total culture."[1]

Mormon teachings differ widely from biblical theology held by mainline evangelicals. They have a different God, a different Holy Spirit, a different Christ, a different scripture, a different plan of salvation, and a different view of the afterlife than the Bible presents.

There are six standard guidelines by which a group may be measured to determine if they are a cult. The areas are an additional prophet, denial of the deity of Christ, claim to an exclusive salvation, added revelational material equal to or superior to the Bible, salvation by works and a non-biblical view of the afterlife as presented in Scripture. The Mormons have all of these.

Joseph Smith is viewed as an additional prophet to Jesus by the Mormons. They deny the deity of Christ, ascribing to Him the position of spirit-brother to Lucifer. Brigham Young set Smith before Jesus by stating that, "No man or woman in this dispensation will enter the celestial kingdom of God without the consent of Joseph."[2]

Mormons claim an exclusive "restored gospel," superior to all other denominations which Smith claimed God told him were "all wrong;...their creeds were an abomination in his sight; that those professors were all corrupt;...having a form of godliness, but they deny the power thereof."[3] Mormons view the *Book of Mormon* as superior to the Bible which, according to their view, is only valuable "as far as it has been translated correctly."[4]

Regarding the Mormon teaching of the afterlife, they believe there are three levels of heaven, the highest level being the celestial glory reserved for the elite Mormons who take endowments in one of their temples. Mormons hold a synergistic view of salvation which incorporates both faith and works. It is definitely a system based upon works as the primary road to godhood. They believe Jesus only saves from the sin of Adam which provides a resurrection[5] but works are necessary to complete the plan. A corrupted translation of Ephesians 2:8 is 2 Nephi 25:23 which states, " . . . for we know by grace that we are saved, after all we can do." The third article in the "Articles of Faith" found in the *Doctrine and Covenants* states, "We believe that through the Atonement of Christ, all mankind may be saved, by obedience to the laws and ordinances of the Gospel." "There is no salvation without accepting Joseph Smith" according to the tenth president of the Mormon church, Joseph Fielding Smith.[6]

Why witness to Mormons? Because the Scripture admonishes true Christians to "reprove the unfruitful works of darkness" (Ephesians 5:11), "go . . . and teach . . . in the name of Father, and the Son, and the Holy Spirit . . . " (Matthew 28:19), and "earnestly contend for the faith once delivered unto the saints" (Jude 3). The Scripture also commands us to " . . . sanctify the Lord God in your hearts: and be ready to give an answer to every man that asketh you a reason of the hope that is in you . . . " (1 Peter 3:15.)

Why witness to Mormons? Joseph Fielding Smith, further challenged Christians: "If Joseph Smith was a deceiver, who willfully attempted to mislead the people, then he should be exposed; his claims should be refuted, and his doctrines shown to be false . . . ".[7]

The Mormons spend millions of dollars each year promoting their public image through television, radio, magazines and newspapers. James Walker, former Mormon, reminds us that, before the Mormons moved to Madison Avenue with their high-tech advertising in order to change their image, everyone knew they were a cult.[8]

TV Guide has carried an ad entitled "Twenty Reasons Why Mormons are Christians." Systematically the Mormons run television spots to promote their image as a family-centered church. No other religion has ever been given the coverage afforded them in the *Sports Illustrated*. Twelve pages were dedicated to promoting the Mormon church under the title "A Season for Spreading the Faith." Two full color pages pictured Scott Peterson, top football player from Brigham Young University on mission, baptizing a convert. The remaining pages were dedicated to reviewing the plaudits of these young missionaries. The primitive living conditions, the difficulties of their assignments, and the personal sacrifices were lauded by the writer. A storytelling photo accompanied each page of the article. A large color picture of the Brigham Young University football squad highlighted those who had gone on mission. The concluding photo pictured two hands holding a copy of the *Book of Mormon* with the caption "BYU missionaries go by the book."[9]

Each year thousands of unsuspecting people are drawn into the Mormon organization only to discover later what they really believe. Many faithful Mormons are confused by the extensive changes in the temple endowments that were claimed as divine revelations. Numerous Mormon scholars have become disillusioned over critical areas of Mormon history such as Joseph Smith's first vision and the extensive changes in their sacred writings. Although new temples are being erected around the country, the number of members attending them is declining.[10]

There is no doubt that there are many sincere, decent and clean-living Mormons. They promote their religion as a family centered faith. Joseph Fielding Smith wrote, "We are notwithstanding our weaknesses, the best people in the world. I do not say this boastingly, for I believe that the truth is evident to all who are willing to observe for themselves. We are morally clean, in every way equal, and in many ways superior to any other people."[11]

Yet, a look at some recent statistics reveal serious problems in the heartland of Mormonism. In a state that boasts of having 74% of its inhabitants as members of one church (Latter-day Saints) and being the most wholesome of people anywhere, the following statistics must be an embarrassment. It is not being suggested that mainline evangelicals are free from problems, but they do not brag to the world that they are the "cleanest people alive" and the "paragon of family life." Neither do mainline denominations claim to be the only true restored church on earth. Certainly, it must acknowledged that there are many good Mormon families.

In September of 1996 the United Way of Greater Salt Lake released a report, which was reviewed by the Mormon Church, identifying critical health and human service concerns in the state of Utah. The following are only some of the facts:

☐ The report identified the need for food, shelter, child protective services, child rape/ abuse services as well as adult protective services of the elderly.

☐ The Utah Division of Family Services investigated 17,125

cases of child abuse in 1994. Of that total 10,430 were confirmed. The Child Welfare League of America reported that Utah had the nations ninth-highest rate of substantiated child-sexual-abuse cases.

☐ Since 1990 victims of domestic violence utilized centers at an increased rate of 42.9%. During this same period the days by victims spent in shelters have increased 209.5%.

☐ In Salt Lake City, violent offences by adults peaked in 1994 with 3,071 arrests. In 1995 it dropped to 2,716, but it still maintained a 62% increase from 1990-1994.

☐ In Salt Lake City, headquarters of the Mormon church, the number of domestic violence-related cases increased from 2,133 to 3,959 since 1995. This represents an 85% increase.

☐ Approximately 32,557 adults in Utah have less than a ninth grade education, and 188,390 adults do not have high school diplomas. In comparison to nationwide statistics, Utah spends less money per pupil than any other state. Utah ranks 50.

☐ In Salt Lake County alone more than 8000 senior citizens are abused, neglected, or exploited each year.

☐ In the largest county in Utah, Salt Lake County, the 1994 divorce rate was 5.4%, well over the national average of 4.6%.

☐ A 1994 report documented that only 49.3% of Utah's children entering kindergarten had been properly immunized before age two.

☐ In excess of 50% of births to women of Utah ages 15-19 occur outside of marriage.

☐ In 1995 the number of gangs increased in Salt Lake County from 75 in 1990 to 288.

All these things are happening in city where the "most moral of peoples' church in all the world" is headquartered. It may be concluded from the above facts that in a state dominated by the Mormons (almost 75% of Utah's population claims membership in the Mormon Church) that they are not morally better than other religions in America today and in some respects the statistics reveal they are worse.[12]

Chapter Twenty
SEVEN SUGGESTIONS IN WITNESSING TO MORMONS

There are some general guidelines that must be mastered before beginning to witness to Mormons. The following helpful points have been gleaned out of the writings and tapes of prominent Christian writers on Mormonism, several of whom are former Mormons themselves.

All researchers of Mormonism are indebted to two former Mormons, Jerald and Sandra Tanner, Sandra being a great-great-grandchild of Brigham Young. They have spent almost thirty-eight years methodically and carefully reproducing important documents, out-of-print books, and exposing the errors of Mormonism. No student of Mormonism should be without their 600 page volume entitled *Mormonism-Shadow or Reality?* and their numerous other important works. In fact, many have given copies of this work to Mormon friends and family members as a means of witnessing with some success.

Jerald Tanner, in a cassette tape entitled "Problems in Winning Mormons," suggests that the first requirement for winning Mormons "is a sincere love for them as a people." This must be our motive for witnessing to them. He rightfully states that many people have "more zeal than love" and reminds us that we are urged by Scripture to "speak the truth in love" (Ephesians 4:15.) Citing the scriptural example of the Good Samaritan, he encourages us to minister to the "spiritually wounded by pouring oil and wine into their wounds for healing."

Tanner's own pilgrimage began by reading a copy of David Whitmer's booklet, *An Address to All Believers in Christ* which charged that revelations of Joseph Smith had been changed. In setting about to disprove this statement he found more than expected, which led to his conversion to Christ. An important approach in witnessing to Mormons is to politely challenge them to prove that certain statements about the church are erroneous. Patient love will often prevail in reaching those holding heretical doctrine. Though he is quick to admit that there is no one pat approach to winning Mormons, his own method is to show the changes in Joseph Smith's first vision and changes made in the *Doctrine and Covenants*. Photocopies or statements in books by Mormons themselves is the best evidence against their error.[13]

A corollary principle is to be kind. Harry L. Ropp, before his untimely death in an airplane crash, offered many helpful suggestions in witnessing to Mormons. Chief among them was kindness. Quoting 2 Timothy 2:24-26, he reminds us that the Lord's servant must not be quarrelsome but kind, patient and able to teach the truth to those ensnared by false teachings. "Enemies, not friends, are made when an encounter turns into an argument," writes Ropp. "A soft answer turneth away wrath: but grievous words stir up anger" (Proverbs 15:1.) Ridicule, sarcasm and insult have no place in a Christian witness. You can win skirmishes and lose the battle in witnessing to Mormons. An unkind approach only leaves them embittered and hardened against the Christian witness. Ropp employed a three-step method in his witnessing which began by showing that the Bible is trustworthy, proving that the sacred books of Mormonism are not God's Word, and exposing a Mormon's faith in the *Book of Mormon* to be purely subjective.[14]

Another important suggestion is be bold. Love and kindness do not prevent us from being bold. John L. Smith, a thirty-five-year veteran missionary to Mormons, considers boldness to be a lost element in witnessing. He reminds us that it was a prominent characteristic of the New Testament apostles.

"One who lacks boldness will almost always be rejected immediately by the Mormon," he writes.[15]

Boldness must be brought under the Holy Spirit's control in order to know when to raise particular questions in the witnessing process. Questions may not bring an immediate conversion but they can plant a seed of doubt which can germinate at some future time. Most people won from Mormonism reveal that the person who planted the original seed of truth was not the one who ultimately brought them to the Lord. This fact should also tell us something about our role in the witnessing process. Harvesting is not always the privilege of the witness. He must be content to be a seed sower. It is Smith's view that Mormon women are easier to win than Mormon men.

A fourth suggestion is the best offensive comes from a good defensive position. In other words, know what you believe. Be ready to show what the Bible teaches. Wally Tope, faithful witness to the Mormons until his fatal injury while witnessing during the Los Angeles riots of 1992, when he was beaten into unconsciousness and later died, suggests that being well prepared defensively is the first preparation for a witness. "Study to show thyself approved unto God, a workman that needeth not to be ashamed, rightly dividing the word of truth" (2 Timothy 2:15)." For instance, if you quoted Ephesians 2:8,9 as proof that we can't earn salvation, you should be ready to deal with James 2:17-20.[16]

A fifth suggestion is to be versed in Mormon beliefs. Ignorance regarding the beliefs and doctrine of a group may be interpreted as a lack of respect. Most people are attracted to the Mormons for non-theological reasons. It is unlikely that anyone is drawn into the Mormon religion by reading the *Book of Mormon*. Theological reasons are almost always secondary. Many youth join the Mormons because they are attracted to the concept of authority or they fell in love with a Mormon.[17]

John R. Farkas, former Elders Quorum President of a Rochester, New York Mormon Ward, came to the Lord after reading 1 Nephi 18:25 which described cows, oxen, horses and goats in the New World.[18] It occurred to him that these animals were brought over by the European settlers and couldn't have existed in the New World before then as the *Book of Mormon* stated. It was the first step toward true faith in the real Jesus of the Bible. Farkas, along with co-writer David A. Reed, begin their book with a brief history, a synopsis of Mormon beliefs and a review of the sacred writings of Mormons. You will likely win respect of the Mormons if you are able in a polite way to cite from their own works and show factual familiarity with their teachings. You will need to obtain and mark key passages in the *Book of Mormon, Doctrines and Covenants,* and *The Pearl of Great Price*. These can usually be obtained free from Mormon missionaries but don't allow them to come back until you have prepared to meet them. All three of these volumes are sometimes bound together. They are not likely to give you a copy of the single volume.

A sixth suggestion is friendship. When it is possible, forming a friendship with the Mormon is the best way to be accepted as a witness. This is a strategy they use in winning their neighbors and friends to Mormonism. Take time to get to know them. They have been taught from childhood to believe their doctrine. What they hold as fact may seem as plausible to them as what you believe. Friendships are not likely possible with the missionary who comes to your door. He has a limited stay in your area and is usually moved around if he raises questions to his superiors that you have presented to him. Witnessing to Mormons takes time.

A seventh suggestion is to be patient. Give time for your guest to share his point of view but don't allow him to dominate the conversation. In order not to get tied up where the Mormon missionaries do all the talking you can say something like this, "I am familiar with the material in your flip chart so it won't be necessary to get it out. Why don't we just share with one another?" Always share your experience with the Lord but do not use the term testimony when witnessing to Mormons as it means something entirely different to them. Listening provides prospective on the best place to raise a sensitive issue concerning his beliefs.

This writer had two Mormon missionaries visit a Wednesday evening worship service at First Baptist. Following the service they were invited to an office to talk, which they cheerfully accepted. After a time of polite discussion, it seemed there was not going to be a good place to raise a pointed question. The discussion was drawing to a close as one of the missionaries boldly declared that his church was the true and restored church. At that point the Holy Spirit provided the proper question. "If it is true that your church is the only true church, may I ask why Joseph Smith found it necessary to change the name of your church twice?" It hit the missionary like a bomb. "That isn't true," the more versed of the pair retorted. "Where did you get that—out of some anti-Mormon book?"

"It is right out of your authorized seven volume history edited by B.H. Roberts."

"Well, that isn't true. The name of our church has always been the Church of Jesus Christ of Latter-day Saints."

The following question was then asked, "If it is true, and it is, where does the authority for your restoration stand?" It was suggested they check with their superiors and come back and resume the discussion. They were reminded that when these questions were raised, they would not be allowed to return. The conversation concluded on friendly grounds. It was hoped they would return. However, they never did, but one of them, while visiting one of the members of First Baptist, stated he considered this writer well versed concerning the Mormon church. It was a seed that is hoped will grow and someday be harvested by another.

It is helpful in getting to know Mormons to discover their level of commitment. Every person is different so it is necessary to discern where each individual stands in relation to their religion. There are five basic categories into which most Mormons fall. The *faithful member* is dedicated to the doctrine of the church, and attends the local ward regularly, and keeps the *Word of Wisdom*. Males go on mission, tithe and participate in the endowments of the temple. It has been estimated, however, that at least 60% of all males have no real testimony prior to going on mission. The faithful will be quick to give his testimony of trust in Joseph Smith as a prophet and the current President as the vehicle of God's revelations, but he nevertheless may have deep reservations. He will be a bold witness for his faith, using his work, his home and his means to bring others into the Mormon faith.

A second category is the *fundamental member* who is not only a zealous defender of his religion, a leader in the local Ward, tithes as well as sacrificially supports the work, declares his church as the only true and restored church but may even continue to practice polygamy. He could be violent if challenged and might physically defend his right to polygamy.

A third category is the *faltering member*. He fails to keep the *Word of Wisdom*, irregularly attends the local ward, doesn't tithe, therefore is not permitted to enter the Temple, and is typed a "jack-Mormon" by faithful members.

A fourth category is the *favorable member*. He has lost his doctrinal reasons for belonging to the church but it fits his social and business needs. Some major Mormon scholars fall into this category, though they may be relatively faithful to the local ward and occasionally attend the temple for endowments. They usually resent non-Mormons attacking the Church, preferring to reform it from within.

A fifth category is the *fallen member*. He has lost faith in Joseph Smith as a prophet, rejects major doctrine of the church, recognizes that the revelations have been changed, and resents the church leadership for keeping important secret documents locked away in the church vault. Although he no longer attends the ward, he has not yet severed ties with the church.

Evaluating the commitment level of the Mormon can be very helpful in deciding the approach to be taken in the witness encounter. For the faithful, only pointed questions may crack his confidence in his prophet and the doctrines of the church. It will take what some call "knocking the polish off" his testimony. The fanatical must be approached with care as he is apt to be hostile, although most Mormons do not fall into this category. The faltering and the favorable may be more difficult to reach since they are only nominal believers and hold little interest in any religion at the time. The fallen, having lost faith in what he once believed was the only true religion and having been taught to believe that all other religions are false, will perhaps be the most difficult to win.

Chapter Twenty-One
TWENTY-FIVE TROUBLING QUESTIONS FOR MORMONS

Once you have discovered something of the commitment level of the Mormon you will be better equipped to use some of the following probing questions to penetrate his confidence. These questions should be handled carefully in a conversational way rather than just blunt attack. An approach may be phrased, "What if I could show you that the *Book of Mormon* and the *Doctrine and Covenants* contradict each other. Would that disturb you?" Or perhaps something like, "Would it disturb you to discover that the *Book of Mormon* teaches that there is and has always been only one God?" Many writers believe that the best place to begin a witnessing encounter is with the Mormon doctrine of God.

1. **Does Mormonism teach that there is more than one God?** Although Mormons believe that our God is one among many gods, the *Book of Mormon* teaches that there is only one true God. In 2 Nephi 31:21 we read " . . . *And now, behold, this is the doctrine of Christ, and the only and true doctrine of the Father, and of the Son, and of the Holy Ghost, which is one God, without end. Amen.*" Later Joseph Smith taught that there are many gods.[19] The Bible teaches, as does the *Book of Mormon*, that there is only one God. *"Thus saith Jehovah . . . I am the first,*

and I am the last; and beside me there is no God" (Isaiah 44:6). The Old Testament clearly declares that there is one God and the Jews defended this teaching in the face of their polytheistic neighbors.[20]

2.   **According to the teachings of your church, do you believe that God is an exalted man?** In Joseph Smith's famous King Follett funeral discourse, he stated, "God Himself who sits enthroned in yonder heavens is a Man like unto one of yourselves . . .".[21] This was Satan's lie to Eve in the Garden of Eden *"Thou shalt be as gods . . . "* (Genesis 3:5). Yet the Bible states: *"God is not a man, that he should lie; neither the son of man that he should repent* (Numbers 23:19.) The Bible distinctly teaches that God is a spirit (John 4:24). The Apostle Paul condemned those who reduced God to a created being: "Professing themselves to be wise, they became fools, And changed the glory of the incorruptible God into an image made like to corruptible man" (Romans 1:22-23). Mormons often point out that the Bible refers to physical features of God such as His eye, hand or face. These are called anthropomorphic terms used to describe certain attributes of God. The Bible also refers to God as having wings (Psalm 91:4). If taken literally, that would make God a bird.

3.   **On the basis of your belief that God was once a man, is it correct to conclude that God has changed sometime in the past?** The *Book of Mormon* teaches that God is "from everlasting to everlasting . . . (Moroni 7:22). That means that God has always existed as God. Mormon 9:9 says that God "is the same yesterday, today and forever . . . " In Moroni 8:18 God is said to be "unchangeable from all eternity to all eternity."

4. **Do you believe that God has a wife with an exalted human body?** Bruce R. McConkie, Mormon scholar of the First Council of Seventy, affirms "This doctrine that there is a Mother in Heaven" as did several of the First Presidency of the Church.[22] Mormons reason that if there is a Father in heaven, there must be a Mother. Although the *Doctrine and Covenants* teaches the concept of a Mother god in heaven, (Section 132: 19-32) it is not found in the *Book of Mormon* nor the *Bible*. It is strictly a pagan concept.

5. **Do Mormons believe that Jesus is a spirit-brother to Lucifer?** Mormons teach that Jesus is the spirit-child of a heavenly Mother and Father God and the brother of Lucifer, another one of their spirit-children. Milton R. Hunter, a Mormon apologist, taught that Lucifer, "spirit-brother of Jesus," contended with Jesus for the position as Savior of the world.[23] The Bible teaches that Jesus was born of the Holy Spirit (Matthew 1:18; Luke 1:35). It also teaches that Jesus is the Creator of "all things," which includes Lucifer (Colossians 1:16-17.)

6. **Did you know that some of your leaders taught that Jesus was a polygamist?** Apostle Orson Pratt taught that both God the Father and Jesus were married.[24] And Orson Hyde, President of the Quorum of twelve Apostles, taught that Mary, Martha and Mary Magdalene were wives of Jesus.[25] Although Mormon leaders have disclaimed this as a doctrine of their church, there are yet Mormon scholars who defend its teaching.[26] Although polygamy was permitted in the Old Testament, it was never sanctioned by God and nowhere in the Bible is there any hint that Jesus was married.

7. **Why in the original 1830 printing of the *Book of Mormon* is Joseph Smith listed as "Author and**

Proprietor" but in succeeding editions it reads, "Translation by Joseph Smith, Jr."?

8. How do you account for the fact that Joseph Smith predicted in the *Doctrine and Covenants* 84:1-4 that during his lifetime a temple would be built in Independence, Missouri which never happened?[27] According to Deuteronomy 18:20-22 a failed prophecy is evidence of a false prophet.

9. Did you know that Joseph Smith predicted in *Doctrine and Covenants* 114:1 that David W. Patten would go on a mission, yet Patten was killed, thus contradicting the prophecy?[28]

10. How do you explain that Joseph Smith predicted the copyright for the *Book of Mormon* would be sold in Toronto, Canada by Hiram Page and Oliver Cowdery but was instead copyrighted in America?[29]

11. Are you aware that Joseph Smith predicted in 1835 that within fifty-six years Christ would come and wind up history as we know it?[30]

12. If you do not practice or plan to practice polygamy, how do you expect to get to glory since Joseph Smith predicted that you cannot enter without it in *Doctrine and Covenants* 132:4?

13. Do you know that Joseph Smith predicted that there were men on the moon, dressed like Quakers, who are nearly 1,000 years old?[31]

14. Who is Oliver Granger? Joseph Smith predicted that he would be known forever and ever in *Doctrine and Covenants*, 117:12.

15. How do you explain that Alma 7:10 states that Jesus was born in Jerusalem but the Bible clearly tells us it was Bethlehem?

16. Are you aware in the *Journal of Discourses*, Volume 13, page 271 that Brigham Young said that the sun was inhabited?

17. Must a person be baptized, according to Mormon belief, before he can baptize or confer the priesthood upon others? According to *The Pearl of Great Price*, the "messenger from heaven" conferred the priesthood upon Joseph Smith and Oliver Cowdery before they baptized each other. Therefore we must conclude that the priesthood was conferred upon unsaved individuals.[32]

18. Why can no city, individuals, nor inscriptions named in the *Book of Mormon* be found by archaeologists? Top Mormon scholars agree that no archaeological proof exists for support of the *Book of Mormon*.[33]

19. How do you account for the fact that animals such as horses are listed in 1 Nephi 18:25 as being on the American continent as early as 600 BC when they were brought here by the Europeans no earlier than the seventeenth century?[34]

20. If the Latter-day Saints are the truly restored church, why was their name changed twice by Joseph Smith?[35]

21. Why have there been over 4,000 changes in the *Book of Mormon* if it is the "most correct of any book on earth?"[36] One of the many changes include the name of King Benjamin on page 200 of the 1830 edition. It was changed to King Mosiah on page 188 of the 1981 edition.

22. *The Doctrine and Covenants* 116; 117:8; 107:53-55 places the Garden of Eden and the area of Adam and Eve's expulsion from the Garden in the area of Jackson/Daviess counties, Missouri, called Adam-ondi-Ahman. The Bible in Genesis 2:14 places Eden in the Middle East and so does *The Pearl of Great Price*.[37] How do you account for this?

23. How do you account for the fact that in the Book of Mormon, translated from plates dating back to 600 BC, you find quotes directly from the King James version of the Bible translated in A.D. 1611?

24. Since your church has always taught that blacks are the cursed race of Ham, according to the "Book of Abraham" 1:20-27, how, after 150 years, can such a revelation be reversed?

25. How can the Aaronic priesthood be held by men today who are not of the Levitical line of Aaron as the Bible teaches was required (Exodus 28:1-4; Leviticus 6:19-23)? Mormons often use evasive phrases to sidetrack the witness when they are unable to answer a question. Phrases such as "That is only his opinion," "That is a mistranslation," "Where do you get your authority," "We have a modern day prophet to guide us,"[38] "That's just your interpretation," "You have the spirit of contention" and "You are persecuting me" are common responses to avoid addressing issues.[39]

A strategy most often used by a Mormon is to bear his testimony when faced with evidence against his church. Unlike a Christian testimony, it is subjectively based on his "inner feeling" or a "burning in his bosom" (*Doctrine and Covenants*, 9:7-8). A Christian testimony declares new life in Christ based on the cross and resurrection of Jesus. The Latter-day Saint will bear witness that the *Book of Mormon* is true, Joseph Smith was a prophet of God and the Mormon Church is the restored church of Jesus Christ. A good question to ask is, "Since our eternal destiny is dependent on where we put our trust now, shouldn't there be something more trustworthy than feelings?"[40] The Bible teaches us to "search the Scriptures daily . . . " (Acts 17:11) and to "Try the spirits whether they are of God: because false prophets are gone out into the world" (I John 4:1). If the Mormon offers James 1:5 as a proof test for a testimony, show him that the text does not teach that one may receive an "inner feeling" or a "burning in the bosom." God promises knowledge, not a feeling. Another strategy often used by Mormons is to ask why Christians do not view Mormons as fellow Christians. Charles M. Larson, once a very dedicated Latter-day Saint, writes of a young Mormon who asked if he considered the Mormon church to be Christian, based on the same criteria that he considered his own church to be Christian. After considering the question he responded that he "felt the proportion of orthodox Christians who considered Mormonism to be Christian was probably about the same as that of Latter-day Saints who considered orthodox Christianity acceptable in God's sight."[41] It is a response worth remembering.

Sometimes Mormons will ask in derision, "How can you believe in the Trinity?" James R. Spencer, former Mormon elder, rightfully warns against glib answers like "You can't understand the Trinity; you just have to take it by faith." Of course we can't know everything about the Trinity but we certainly can know that God is one, infinite and eternal, Jesus is one with the Father, and that the Holy Spirit is a person who can be grieved, resisted and quenched. "Christians believe that there is only one God, and within the nature of that one God are three eternal persons who exist without confusion and without separation."[42] At the conclusion of "The Testimony of Three Witnesses" found in every *Book of Mormon* we read, "And the honor be to the Father, and to the Son, and to the Holy Ghost, which is one God. Amen." This is a clear teaching of the Christian doctrine of the Trinity.

In defense of the Mormon belief that there are many gods

they often state, "The Bible says there are gods many and lords many." A fundamental principle in interpreting Scripture is to understand the verse within the context of what goes before and what comes after a verse. The verse, I Corinthians 8:5, cited by some Mormons on many gods has to do with pagan gods. The question Paul is raising is whether it is right for Christians to eat meat sacrificed to idols. The verses before and after this verse refute the idea of many gods, and teaches that there is only one true God. You might also ask where the idea of many gods appears in the *Book of Mormon*. Such teachings, although contrary, are found in the *Doctrine and Covenants*. *The Book of Mormon* never teaches this or any other major Mormon doctrine. These are some of the more frequently used Mormon responses.

In order to throw you off, Mormons will often say that they believe in both the Bible and the *Book of Mormon*, which they claim are the two sticks of Ezekiel 37:15-17. They teach the "stick of Judah" represents the Bible because it was written by the Jews as the descendants of Judah. The "stick of Ephraim" represents the *Book of Mormon* written by the Nephites as descendants of Ephraim (*Doctrine and Covenants* 27:5). Orson Pratt argues that Jeremiah kept sacred records "rolled around a stick and called a book; therefore these two sticks represent two records.[43] The Hebrew word translated "stick" means a piece of wood and the Hebrew word "scroll" means entirely something else. They are never used interchangeably in the Bible. Ezekiel 37 has to do with the restoration of Israel and not two sacred writings on scrolls. In the context of Ezekiel 37 it is clearly stated that the two kingdoms of Israel would be brought together as one nation. Furthermore, since the passage states that Ezekiel wrote upon both the sticks, may we conclude then that Ezekiel wrote both the *Bible* and the *Book of Mormon*?[44]

A prophecy that is cited by Mormons as proof that Joseph Smith had ability to tell the future is his prediction concerning the Civil War. On December 25, 1832, Joseph Smith predicted a civil war between the North and the South would spread to all the nations of the world (*Doctrine and Covenants*, Section 87). That the war would "be poured out upon all nations," of course, never happened. James J. Stewart, Mormon scholar, admits that the revelation was given during a time close to the beginning of the Civil War and that Smith had access to information concerning the problems in South Carolina.[45] The so-called prophecy was not even printed until 1851, seven years after Smith's death.[46]

Every day literally hundreds of people are drawn into what Leland Jamison called " . . . an irreconcilable Christian heresy and the most typically American theology yet formulated on this continent."[47] The Mormons preach a different gospel about which the Apostle Paul warned, "But though we, or an angel from heaven, preach any other gospel unto you than that which we have preached unto you, let him be accursed" (Galatians 1:8). They have a different God, a different Jesus and a different Holy Spirit than found in the Bible. However sincere, they are lost to the Christian gospel and therefore a Christless eternity. It is hoped that what has been presented in these pages will create effective tools for witnessing to Mormons.

Appendix A
KEY TO MORMON TERMS

It is important to understand Mormon terminology. They have adapted many Christian terms to express their teachings, which differ significantly from the historic use by Christians through the centuries. In Mormon usage they take on new meaning. The following list will acquaint the reader with Mormon terms as they define them:

Atonement	by Christ assures resurrection and places one in a position to work out his salvation.
Apostle	one of twelve men who serves different responsibilities within the Mormon church under the First Presidency.
Apostate	one who has rejected the teachings of Mormonism, usually a former member of the Mormon church.
Aaronic Priesthood	entered by most male members at the age of twelve.
Bible	true only as correctly translated by Joseph Smith.

Baptism	by immersion from LDS priests and considered essential for salvation.
Baptism for the dead	is baptism by proxy for a deceased relative of any age for remission of sins.
Bishop	the closest in comparison to a minister in a Christian congregation.
Blessing	pronounced by a faithful elderly male leader in a local ward over an individual.
Blood Atonement	the shedding of an individual's blood to atone for sin not covered by the general atonement of Christ.
Branch	congregation in embryo.
Celestial Kingdom	the highest level of three spheres of heaven, granted only to Mormons baptized while living on earth.
Conference	for the LDS is a general, worldwide meeting held twice a year in Salt Lake City.
Deacon	an office held by Mormon boys beginning at the age of twelve years old, who have entered the Aaronic priesthood.
Elder	lowest of three offices given to males in the Melchizedek Priesthood.
Endowments	secret ceremonies performed in the Mormon Temples investing power upon the priesthood going on mission or in

preparation of those for celestial (eternal) marriage.

Exaltation   attaining the position of godhood through celestial marriage, priesthood and obedience to the Mormon gospel.

Fall of Man   presented man through death an opportunity for resurrection but denies the inheritance of a fallen nature found in the Christian view.

First Presidency   President of the Mormon church who functions as a prophet aided by a First and Second Counselor.

General Twelve   includes President, Two Counselors and
Authorities   Twelve Apostles.

Gentile   a non-Mormon, including Jews.

God   a man with resurrected human body who attained Godhood in a prior time, one of many Gods in the universe.

Gospel   doctrine of salvation by works as defined by the Mormon Church.

Heaven   comprised of three separate levels of existence.

Hell   abode of evil spirits and extremely wicked individuals who can escape by debt payment.

Holy Ghost   distinguished from the Holy Spirit by

Mormons to mean a separate God to the Father and Jesus.

Holy Spirit	seen only as a non-personal influence.
"Jack Mormons"	designation given to LDS Mormons who are inactive and break the *Word of Wisdom.*
Jaredites	descendants of Jared - builders of the Tower of Babel, ancestors of Jewish American Indians.
Jehovah	another name for God as distinguished from the Father.
Jesus Christ	resurrected man with a human body, a god before us in time.
Kingdom of God	refers only to the Celestial Kingdom where the presence of God resides.
Lamanite	wicked descendant of Laman, black-skinned people (1 Nephi 12:23) Jews who became American Indians, also any person who rejects the Mormon gospel.
LDS	designation of the Church of Jesus Christ of Latter-day Saints - Utah branch.
Melchizedek Priesthood	entered by males at the age of nineteen.
Nephite	white-skinned people who became dark-skinned Indians.

Polygamy	the practice of taking more than one wife, also known as plural marriages, in opposition to the Christian view of monogamy, the taking of one wife. Introduced by Joseph Smith officially through a revelation July 12, 1843 and abolished in 1890 by President Wilford Woodruff under pressure by the United States Congress.
Priesthood	a representative of God in the Mormon church (see Aaronic and Melchizedek Priesthoods.)
Redeemed	refers to redemption only from the power of death, not a sinful condition or state.
RLDS	Reorganized Church of Jesus Christ of Latter-Day Saints established largely by Joseph Smith's family after Brigham Young led a large body of the Mormons west to the Utah territory in 1846. RLDS, until recently, claimed apostolic succession through Joseph's son.
Repentance	is from individual acts only - not from a fallen nature.
Saints	short term for Mormons.
Sin	specific acts of sin, not as designation of a fallen nature.
Spirit-child	produced by a Father and Mother god in Celestial heaven who have physical bodies.

Stake	a district building composed of wards and branches
Stake President	presiding high priest in the stake.
Telestial Kingdom	lowest sphere of heaven granted to servants of God.
Temple	where secret ceremonies are performed such as endowments, eternal marriage and baptism for the dead.
Temple Mormon	one who performs Temple endowments.
Temple Recommend	by the local Bishop and Stake President that admits the most dedicated of Mormons to the Temple.
Terrestrial Kingdom	second realm of heaven granted to those who accept Mormon gospel in spirit world.
Undergarment	is underwear worn by Temple Mormons intended to remind them of their commitment to Mormon teachings.
Ward	a local Mormon church building.
Word of Wisdom	revelation of Joseph Smith in Kirtland, Ohio, in 1833 forbidding the use of "hot drinks," coffee, tea, tobacco, and alcoholic drinks by Mormons.
Zion	specifically refers to the temple lot in Independence, Missouri - generally Mormonism worldwide.

Appendix B
CHRONOLOGY OF MORMON HISTORY

1805   Joseph Smith Jr., born in Sharon, Vermont. Third son and fourth child to Joe and Lucy Mack Smith.

1816   Move to Palmyra, New York.

1820   First vision in the woods of Palmyra.

1823   Angel Moroni visits Smith to reveal where the golden plates containing the ancient history of America are buried.

1826   Arrest and trial of Smith in South Bainbridge (Chennago County) N.Y. as a "glass looker."

1827   Smith weds Emma Hale; permitted after four years by Angel Moroni to take and translate the plates; meets Martin Harris.

1828   Martin Harris becomes Smith's first scribe.

1829   Oliver Cowdery comes to Smith's home in Harmony, Pennsylvania, (April 5); Cowdery becomes second scribe; appearance of John the Baptist to Smith and Cowdery, conferring upon them the Aaronic Priesthood (May 15).

1830   *Book of Mormon* published by Egbert B. Grandlin Printing in Palmyra; the Church of Christ organized (April 6) at Fayette, N.Y.; Smith arrested and tried a second time at South Bainbridge as a "disorderly person and imposter" in treasure digging (July 4); Sidney Rigdon brings his church into Mormonism.

1831   Kirtland, Ohio, revealed to be the new center of Mormon population; Independence, Missouri named "Zion" of Christ's return; first endowment given.

1832   Brigham Young's conversion to Mormonism; degrees in glory revelation by Smith and Rigdon.

1833   First Temple begun in Kirtland and dedicated in March 1836; *Word of Wisdom* is recorded.

1834   Name of church changed from "Church of Christ" to "Latter-day Saints."

1835   Purchase of Chandler papyri which becomes the *Pearl of Great Price*; *Book of Commandments* (*Doctrine and Covenants*) compiled; organization of "Council of Twelve Apostles" and the "Quorum of Seventy"; Smith sealed to Fannie Alger at Kirtland as first known plural wife.

1836   Kirtland Temple dedicated; established Kirtland Safety Society Bank.

1837   Martin Harris is excommunicated.

1838	Kirtland Bank fails; Smith and Rigdon flee Kirtland for Missouri at night; Danites organized; Oliver Cowdery excommunicated; name of church is changed for the second time to "The Church of Jesus Christ of Latter-day Saints"; David Whitmer withdraws from church.
1839	Smith moves to Commerce (Nauvoo), Illinois; Mormons driven from Missouri into Illinois.
1840	"Baptism for the dead" doctrine revelation; Commerce, Illinois becomes Nauvoo.
1841	Cornerstone for Nauvoo Temple lain.
1842	Record account of First vision; publishes the *Book of Abraham*; baptizes for the dead in the Mississippi river; John C. Bennett is excommunicated and publishes articles against the church; Smith is initiated into the Masonic order by receiving the first three degrees.
1843	"Eternal Marriage" (plural marriage) revelation publicly declared.
1844	*Nauvoo Expositor* published by William Law exposing polygamy among the Mormon officials; Smith commands *Expositor* destroyed; Smith arrested and jailed at Carthage; death of Joseph and Hyrum Smith in a shootout with mob descending on jail.
1845	Young chosen as prophet of the church.
1846	Mormons migrate west under Young's leadership, first stop Council Bluff, Iowa.

1847	First migration arrives at Salt Lake Valley; Young takes position as president.
1848	Sea gulls save crops in Utah.
1849	Provisional state of Deseret is organized.
1850	Young becomes governor of Utah territory.
1851	Tabernacle built in Salt Lake City.
1853	Temple cornerstone lain.
1857	Mountain Meadows Massacre.
1877	Young dies (August).
1880	John Taylor becomes president.
1882	Edmunds Act passed by Congress making polygamy illegal.
1887	Taylor dies; Edmund-Tucker Act passed by Congress divesting the Mormon Church of its corporation.
1889	Wilford Woodruff becomes president.
1890	"Declaration" rescinding polygamy issued by Woodruff.
1896	Utah admitted to the Union; receives statehood.

Appendix C
MAJOR MORMON SOURCES

1.   The *Book of Mormon* is the first published work of
      Joseph Smith, Jr., printed in Palmyra, New York in 1830
      by E. B. Grandin Printing.

2.   *The Book of Commandments* contained revelations of
      Joseph Smith, Jr. to his church.   It was printed in
      Independence, Missouri in 1833. When a mob descended
      on the press, destroying most of the copies, it was later
      reprinted under the title *The Book of Doctrine &
      Covenants.*

3.   The *Doctrine and Covenants*, third publication by Joseph
      Smith, Jr., contained additional revelations for the church
      including the "Lectures on Faith" used in the School of
      Prophets at the Kirtland Temple and was printed at
      Kirtland in 1835.

4.   In recent years the original *Book of Commandments*
      (1833) and later revelations in the *Doctrine and
      Covenants* (1835) were revised and combined into one
      volume in the *Doctrine and Covenants.*

5.   *The Pearl of Great Price*, containing the early history of
      Joseph Smith, was first printed in Liverpool, England, in
      1851.

6.   The *Evening and Morning Star*, church newspaper, was issued at Independence, Missouri, June 1832-January 1835. In 1835 it was reprinted in Kirtland, Ohio, with revisions of the revelations of Joseph Smith to conform to the printing of the *Doctrine and Covenants*, also printed in 1835.

7.   The *Messenger and Advocate* was printed in Kirtland, Ohio, October 1834-September 1837.

8.   The *Elder's Journal* had only four issues, October & November 1837 issued at Kirtland, Ohio and July & August 1838 issued in Far West, Missouri.

9.   The *Times and Seasons*, church newspaper, was originally printed in Commerce, Illinois, and ultimately at Nauvoo, in November 1839-February 1846.

10. The *Latter-day Saints Millennial Star*, church newspaper for the British branch of the Mormon church, was printed respectively in Manchester and Liverpool, England. The paper was edited by Parley P. Pratt May 1840-April 1843 and by Thomas Ward May 1843-June 1846.

11. *The Wasp*, Nauvoo, Illinois newspaper, was printed April 16, 1842-April 26, 1843.

12. The *Nauvoo Neighbor*, was issued May 3, 1843-October 29, 1845.

13. The single issue of the *Nauvoo Expositor* edited by William Law, disillusioned member of the church, was printed June 7, 1844. The destruction of this paper by Joseph Smith led to his ultimate arrest and death in the Carthage Jail.

14. *History of the Church*, Volume 1, (LDS) was produced under Joseph Smith's name with subsequent volumes edited by B.H. Roberts, Church Historian.

15. *A Comprehensive History of the Church of Jesus Christ of Latter-day Saints*, (LDS) a more objective six volumes and factually correct history, was edited by B.H. Roberts in 1930 at Salt Lake City.

16. *History of The Church of Jesus Christ of Latter-Day Saints* (RLDS), four volumes was edited by Herman C. Smith.

17. *Journal of Discourses* by Brigham Young and the Prophets was printed in Liverpool, England, 1854-1886, 26 volumes.

18. *Brigham Young University Studies* is published quarterly by the Brigham Young University in Provo, Utah.

19. *Dialogue: A Journal of Mormon Thought* published at Stanford, California, 1966-1977, Los Angeles, California, 1971-1975, and Washington, D.C. is a scholarly publication that deals with current and controversial issues within Mormonism, 1976- .

20. *Journal of Mormon History* is published annually by the Mormon History Association, 1965- .

21. *Sunstone*, an issue-oriented publication produced six times a year, is printed by the Sunstone Foundation in Salt Lake City, Utah, 1977- .

22. *The Return*, monthly newspaper edited by Ebenezer Robinson, formerly Joseph Smith's printer, Davis City, Iowa: 1889-1890.

ENDNOTES

INTRODUCTION

1. Jan Shipps, "The Prophet Puzzle: Suggestions Leading Toward a More Comprehensive Interpretation of Joseph Smith" *Journal of Mormon History* Volume 1, 1974, 3.
2. Milton R. Hunter, *The Gospel Through the Ages* (Salt Lake City: Stevens and Wallace Inc., 1945), 38.
3. LeGrand Richards, *A Marvelous Work and A Wonder* (Salt Lake City: Deseret Book Company, 1979), 32, 37, 82, 146-147, 149-150, 136, 266.
4. Mark E. Peterson, "Which Church Is Right?" (Salt Lake City, Utah: Deseret News Press, n.d.) 15-16.
5. Jim Kjelgarrd, *The Coming of the Mormons* (New York: Random House, 1953), 19-21.
6. Leonard J. Arrington & Davis Bitton, *The Mormon Experience* (New York: Alfred A. Knopf, 1979), 100-101, 103.
7. Maurice Whipple, *This Is The Place: Utah* (New York: Alfred A. Knopf, 1945), 14.
8. J.H. Beadle, *Life in Utah* (Cincinnati: National Publishing Co., 1870), 428-429.
9. No author, "Who Are the Saints?" (Independence, Missouri: Herald Publishing House, 1985), 5.
10. John Doyle Lee, *The Mormon Menace* (New York: Home Protection Publishing Co., 1905), 199.

11. Steven L. Shields, *Latter-Day Saint Beliefs* (Independence, Missouri: Herald Publishing House, 1986), 17, 19-20.

12. Steven L. Shields, *Divergent Paths of the Restoration* (Los Angeles: Restoration Research, 1990), listed in the Table of Contents.

13. William Edwin Berrett, *The Restored Church* (Salt Lake City, Utah: Deseret Book Company, 1961), 207-210.

14. Gordon H. Fraser, *Is Mormonism Christian?* (Chicago: Moody Press, 1977), 152.

15. Donald P. Shoemaker, "Why Your Neighbor Joined the Mormon Church," *Christianity Today*, (October 11, 1974), 111-116.

16. William Alexander Linn, *The Story of the Mormons* (New York: Russell & Russell Inc., 1963), 2.

17. J.K. Van Baalen, *The Chaos of the Cults* (Grand Rapids: William B. Eerdman's Publishing Company, 1967), 190.

PART ONE

CHAPTER ONE

1. Joseph Smith, *The Pearl of Great Price* (Salt Lake City: Church of Jesus Christ of Latter-day Saints, 1982), 47.

2. John Phillip Walker, Editor, *Dale Morgan on Early Days of Mormonism* (Salt Lake City: Signature Books, 1986), 219. There is little doubt that Morgan during his lifetime was the most exacting historian on early Mormonism. This posthumous printing contains a rich treasure of correspondence with leading Mormon writers, as well as others, which reveal that he became a sifting and filtering sieve for documentation and certification of Mormon sources.

3.   Herbert Spencer Salisbury, "The Mormon War in Hancock County" *Journal of the Illinois State Historical Society*, July 1915, 281-282. Salisbury, grandnephew of Joseph Smith maintained that polygamy was established by Brigham Young.

4.   William J. Whalen, *The Latter-day Saints in the Modern Day World* (New York: The John Day Company, 1964), 23.

5.   J.H. Kennedy, *The Early Days of Mormonism* (New York: Charles Scribner's Sons, 1888), 8, as quoted from *The Historical Magazine*, 1870, 316.

6.   Donna Hill, *Joseph Smith - The First Mormon* (New York: Doubleday and Company, 1977), 25-26.

7.   Fawn Brodie, *No Man Knows My History* (New York: Alfred A. Knopf, 1985), 5, as quoted by John M. Mecklin in *The Story of American Dissent*, 37, 123.

8.   Pomeroy Tucker, *Origin, Rise and Progress of Mormonism* (New York: D. Appleton and Company, 1867), 12. Tucker was personally acquainted with the Smiths, Harris and Cowdery. He worked in Grandin Printing in Palmyra where he proofread much of the original *Book of Mormon* as it was printed. He was a key witness to the early days of Mormonism.

9.   Mrs. Dr. Horace Eaton, *The Origin of Mormonism* (New York: Board of Home Missions of Presbyterian Church, 1881), 1.

10. Lucy Mack Smith, *Biographical Sketches of Joseph Smith The Prophet and His Progenitors For Many Generations* (Liverpool, England: Published for Orson Pratt by S.W. Richards, 1853), 54-55. The first edition was recommended by the *Deseret News* and rejected in 1865 by Brigham Young who noted some errors that needed to be corrected. Changes have been made in later versions.

11. Kennedy, *Early Days of Mormonism*, 2.

12. Roger I. Anderson, *Joseph Smith's New York Reputation Reexamined* (Salt Lake City: Signature Press, 1990), 116.

13.   Dale Morgan Walker on *Early Days of Mormonism*, 221.

14.   Daniel P. Kidder, *Mormonism and the Mormons: A Historical View of the Rise and Progress of the Sect Self-styled Latter-day Saints* (New York: Carlton and Lanhan, 1842), 20-21.

15.   Smith, *History of the Church*, Volume 2, 340-343.

16.   Smith, *Pearl of Great Price*, "Joseph Smith History," Section 1:8, 48.

17.   Thomas F. O'Dea, *The Mormons* (Chicago: The University of Chicago Press, 1975), 11.

18.   Brodie, *No Man Knows My History*, 12.

19.   Walker, *Dale Morgan on Early Days of Mormonism*, 226, as cited from *Wayne Sentinel*, May 26, 1826, and *Woodstock Vermont Chronicle*, June 24, 1831.

20.   O'Dea, *The* Mormons, 15.

21.   *The Reflector*, June 1, 1830; Thomas D. Clark and F. Gerald Ham, *Pleasant Hill and Its Shakers* (Lexington, Kentucky: Keystone Printery, Inc., 1987), 7.

22.   *The Reflector*, June 1, 1830, 51.

23.   Kennedy, *The Early Days of Mormonism*, 113; *History of the Church*, Volume 1, 409.

24.   Smith, *Doctrine and Covenants*, section 109:36, 225.

25.   J.W. Gunnison, *The Mormons* (Philadelphia: J.B. Lippincott & Company, 1856), 102-103.

26.   Bruce R. McConkie, *Mormon Doctrine* (Salt Lake City: Bookcraft, 1966), 799-801; Lee Copeland, "Speaking in Tongues in the Restoration Churches," *Dialogue*, Volume 24, Number 1, Spring 1991, 13.

27.   *The Latter-day Saints Millennial Star*, Volume 8, 124-128.

28.   Clark and Ham, *Pleasant Hill and Its Shakers*, 50.

29.   Smith, *Doctrine and Covenants*, section 89, 175-176.

30.   McConkie, *Mormon Doctrine*, 845.

31.   Herbert A. Wisbey, Jr., *Pioneer Prophetess Jemima Wilkinson the Publick Universal Friend* (Ithaca, New York: Cornell Union Press, 1964), 13, 141, 174-175.

32.   William Alexander Linn, *The Story of the Mormons* (New York: Russell & Russell, 1902), 9.

33.   Leroy Edwin Froom, *The Prophetic Faith of Our Fathers*, (Tokoma Park, Washington, DC, *Review and* Herald, Volume 4, Publishing Association, 1954), 462-465.

34.   Smith, *History of the Church of Jesus Christ of Latter-day Saints*, Volume 2, 182.

35.   Smith, *Doctrine and Covenants* (Salt Lake City: The Church of Jesus Christ of Latter-day Saints, 1984), Section 84:1-4, 153-154.

36.   *The Reflector*, March 16, 1830.

37.   Tucker, *Origin, Rise and Progress of Mormonism*, 28, 38.

38.   *The Reflector*, June 12, July 7, 1830; February 28, 1831.

39.   Wesley P. Walters, *Joseph Smith's Bainbridge, New York Court Trials* (Salt Lake City: Reprinted by Utah Lighthouse Ministry, (no date), 123, 128-129, 134-135.

40.   Smith, *History of the Church*, Volume 1, 17, 89-91.

41.   Lucy Mack Smith, *Biographical Sketches of Joseph Smith The Prophet and His Progenitors for many Generations*, 91-92.

42.   David Whitmer, *An Address to All Believers in Christ* (Concord, California: Pacific Publishing Co., 1960), 30.

43.   Susquehanna Register, May 1, 1834.

44.   Jerald and Sandra Tanner, *Mormonism, Magic and Masonry* (Salt Lake City: Utah Lighthouse Ministry, 1988), 2-5.

45.   D. Michael Quinn, *Early Mormonism and the Magic World View* (Salt Lake City: Signature Press, 1987), 27-28.

CHAPTER TWO

46.   Berrett, *The Restored Church*, 61, footnote.

47.   B.H. Roberts, *Mormonism, It's Origin and History* (Independence, MO: Zion's Publishing Co., 1925), 15.

48. Lucy Mack Smith, *Biographical Sketches of Joseph Smith The Prophet and His Progenitors for many Generations* 85.

49. B.H. Roberts, *Studies In The Book of Mormon*, edited by Brigham D. Masden, (Urbana, Illinois: University of Chicago Press, 1985), 155. Robert's manuscript was unpublished at his death and remained in the possession of his family until a grandson permitted some Mormon scholars to review it.

50. Alexander Campbell, *Millennial Harbinger*, Volume 2, February 1831, 85.

51. "Statement Regarding the Book of Mormon," prepared by the Department of Anthropology Smithsonian Institution, Point 2.

52. Smith, *Elder's Journal*, August 1838, 56.

53. Smith, *History of the Church*, Volume 6, 408-409.

54. Charlotte Haven, "A Girl's Letter from Nauvoo," *Overland Monthly Magazine* December 1890, 621.

55. Smith, *History of Church*, Volume 5, 316, 524.

56. Peter H. Burnett, *Recollections and Opinions of an Old Pioneer* (New York: D. Appleton and Company, 1880), 66.

57. Berrett, *The Restored Church*, 5.

58. Kidder, *Mormonism and the Mormons* (New York: Carlton and Lanahan, 1842), 4 of preface.

59. I. Woodbridge Riley, *The Founder of Mormonism* (New York: Dodd, Mead & Company, 1902), 3, 73. Riley, though not a psychiatrist was nevertheless a bright scholar who completed his Ph.D. at Yale University in 1901. His work was reviewed by some of the best academicians of his day.

60. Brodie, *No Man Knows My History*, 417.

61. Orson Pratt, "Remarkable Visions," (Liverpool, England: Richard James Printer, 1848), 1 of pamphlet.

62. David Whitmer, *An Address to All Believers in Christ*, 31.

63. Tucker, *Origin, Rise, and Progress of Mormonism*, 16.

64. *Journal of Discourses*, Volume 2, 326.
65. Frank S. Mead, *Handbook of Denominations in the United States* (Nashville: Abingdon Press, 1975), 80.
66. Robert Patterson, *Who Wrote the Book of Mormon?* (Philadelphia: L.H. Everts, 1882), 13.
67. F. Mark McKiernan, *The Voice of One Crying in the Wilderness: Sidney Rigdon Religious Reformer 1793-1876* (Lawrence, Kansas: Coronado Press, 1977), 25.
68. A.S. Hayed, *Early History of Disciples in the Western Reserve* (Cincinnati: Chase and Hall Publishers, 1876), 209.
69. F. Mark McKiernan, "The Conversion of Sidney Rigdon", *Dialogue*, Volume 2, Summer 1970, 75-76; *Alexander Campbell, Millennial Harbinger*, Volume 2, 100.
70. Pearson H. Corbett, *Hyrum Smith Patriarch* (Salt Lake City, Utah: Deseret Book Co., 1971), 67-68.
71. Leonard J. Arrington and Davis Bitton, *The Mormon Experience* (New York: Alfred A. Knopf, 1979), 27.
72. Milton R. Hunter, *The Gospel Through the Ages* (Salt Lake City, Utah: Stevens and Wallis, 1945), 93-95.
73. Gordon H. Fraser, *Is Mormonism Christian?* (Chicago: Moody Press, 1977), 163.
74. John Hyde, Jr., *Mormonism: Its Leaders and Designs* (New York: W.P. Fetridge & Co., 1857), 152-153.
75. Smith, *Doctrine and Covenants*, Section 76, 141-142.
76. Smith, *History of the Church*, Volume 1, 245.
77. Whitmer, *An Address to All Believers In Christ*, 64.
78. James B. Allen and Glen M. Leonard, *The Story of The Latter-day Saints*, (Salt Lake City, Utah: Deseret Book Co., 1976), 123-124.
79. William Mulder & A. Russell Mortensen, *Among the Mormons* (New York: Alfred A. Knopf, 1958), 94-95.
80. Hill, *Joseph Smith - The First Mormon*, 374.
81. Kennedy, *The Early Days of Mormonism*, 254.

CHAPTER THREE

82. Riley, *The Founder of Mormonism*, 178.
83. Lamar Peterson, *Problems in the Mormon Text* (Salt Lake City, Utah: printed by the author, 1976), 6-7; Roberts, *A Comprehensive History of the Church of Jesus Christ of Latter-Day Saints*, Volume 1, 183; Richard L. Bushman, *Joseph Smith and the Beginnings of Mormonism* (Chicago, Illinois: University of Illinois Press, 1984), 163; Joseph Smith III and Herman C, Smith, *History of the Church of Jesus Christ of Latter-Day Saints*, Volume 1, (Lamoni, Iowa: Reorganized Church of Jesus Christ of Latter-Day Saints, 1922), 64-65.
84. *Doctrine and Covenants*, Section 6:1-2, 10-11.
85. *Doctrine and Covenants*, Section 84:1-4, 153-154.
86. Roberts, *Comprehensive History*, Volume 1, 431-432.
87. Klaus J. Hansen, *Quest for Empire* (East Lansing, Michigan: Michigan State University Press, 1967) 4.
88. *Millennial Star*, Volume 1, May 1840, 8.
89. *Journal of Discourses*, Volume 3, 1856, 71-73.
90. John Heinerman and Anson Shupe, *The Mormon Corporate Empire* (Boston: Beacon Press, 1985), 28.
91. Anson Shupe, *The Darker Side of Virtue* (Buffalo: New York: Prometheus Books, 1991), 158.
92. Smith, *History of Church*, Volume 6, 322.
93. Smith, *Doctrine And Covenants*, 1982, Section 132:52-53, pp. 271-272; Richard S. Van Wagoner, *Mormon Polygamy: A History* (Salt Lake City, Utah: Signature Books, 1989), 6.
94. Smith, *History of the Church*, Volume 5, 380; Lamar Peterson, *Hearts Made Glad* (Salt Lake City, Utah: Lamar Peterson Publisher, 1975). A thorough examination of Joseph Smith's frequent indulgences with the fruit of the vine is examined by Peterson.
95. Howe, *Mormonism Unveiled*, (Painesville, Ohio: published by the author, 1834), 261-262.

96.   Smith, *History of the Church*, Volume 2, 471.
97.   *Millennial Star*, Volume 21, 283.
98.   Smith, *Doctrine and Covenants*, Section 117:12, 237.
99.   Smith, *History of the Church*, Volume 6, 448.
100. J.H. Kennedy, *Early Days of Mormonism*, 19-20.
101. Thomas Gregg, *The Prophet of Palmyra* (New York: John B. Alden Publisher, 1890), 408.
102. Henry Caswell, *The City of the Mormons* (London, England: J.G.F. & J. Rivington, 1842), 36.
103. Smith, *Doctrine and Covenants*, Section 89, 175-176.
104. *Journal of Discourses*, Volume 12, 158.
105. Smith, *History of the Church*, Volume 2, 252.
106. Smith, *History of the Church*, Volume 2, 378.
107. Smith, *History of the Church*, Volume 4, 483.
108. Smith, *History of the Church*, Volume 2, 524.
109. Smith, *History of the Church*, Volume 4, 120.
110. Smith, *History of the Church*, Volume 5, 380.
111. Smith, *History of the Church*, Volume 6, 111.
112. Joseph Smith, "The Memoirs of President Joseph Smith, (1832-1914)," *Saints Herald*, January 22, 1935, 109-110.
113. Linda King Newell and Valeen Tippetts Avery, *Mormon Enigma: Emma Hale Smith* (New York: Doubleday, 1984), 179.
114. Smith, *History of the Church*, Volume 6, 616.
115. Howe, *Mormonism Unveiled*, 261.
116. Richard L. Anderson, "Joseph Smith's New York Reputation Reappraised," Brigham Young University Studies, Spring, 1970, 299.
117. Rodger I. Anderson, *Joseph Smith's New York Reputation Reexamined* (Salt Lake City, Utah: Signature Press, 1990), 113-115.
118. B.H. Roberts also records the Bill of Particulars from the paper in his *Comprehensive History*, Volume 2, 539, as cited in *Nauvoo Neighbour*, October 29, 1845.

PART TWO

CHAPTER FOUR

1.   Smith, *Pearl of Great Price*, Section 1:1-19, 48-49.
2.   Scott H. Fauling, ed., *An American Prophet's Record Diaries and Journals of Joseph Smith* (Salt Lake City, Utah: 1989), 5.
3.   Ibid, 51,59.
4.   *History of the Church*, Volume 3, 375; *Times and Seasons*, Volume 3, March 1, 1842, 707.
5.   Fauling, *An American Prophet's Record Diaries and Journals of Joseph Smith*, 5.
6.   *Times and Seasons*, Volume 3, March 15, 1842, 727; *Messenger and Advocate*, Volume 1, February 1835, 78.
7.   Fauling, *An American Prophet's Record Diaries and Journals of Joseph Smith*, 51,59.
8.   Ibid, 51.
9.   Smith, *Pearl of Great Price*, "History," Section 1:15, 49.
10.   *Journal of Discourses*, Volume 2, 171; Volume 12, 333-334; Volume 13, 77-78; Volume 18, 239; Volume 20, 167.
11.   Joseph Fielding Smith, *Gospel Doctrine* (Salt Lake City, Utah: The Deseret News, 1919), 495.
12.   David O. McKay, *Gospel Ideals* (Salt Lake City, Utah: An Improvement Era Publication, 1953), 85.
13.   John A. Widtsoe, *Joseph Smith - Seeker of Truth* (Salt Lake City, Utah: Bookcraft, 1951), 19.
14.   Jerald and Sandra Tanner, *Major Problems of Mormons* (Salt Lake City, Utah: Utah Lighthouse Ministry, 1989), 55.
15.   Joel Tiffany, *Tiffany's Monthly*, (New York: Published by Joel Tiffany, 1859), 163-170.
16.   Wesley P. Walters, *New Light on Mormon Origins*

(Printed by the author, 1990), 7-8.

17. Smith, *Doctrines and Covenants*, Section 84:21-22, 155.
18. Roberts, *A Comprehensive History of the Church*, Volume 1, 180.
19. Allen and Leonard, *The Story of the Saints*, 44.
20. Lewis A. Drummond, *The Awakening That Must Come* (Nashville: Broadman Press, 1978), 18.
21. Garth M. Rosell and Richard A.G. Dupuis, editors, *The Memoirs of Charles G. Finney* (Grand Rapids, Michigan: Academic Books, 1989), 306. The editors cite "The Second Great Awakening in the Urban Centers: An Examination of Methodism and the 'New Measures,'" *Journal of American History* Volume 59, Number 2, September 1972, 338-339.
22. Frederick Morgan Davenport, *Primitive Traits in Religious Revivals*, (New York: The MacMillan Company, 1905), 191-192.
23. *The New York Evangelist*, February 26, 1831. The *Rochester Observer*, November 12, 1830, reported the wide-reaching effects of the Finney Revival. The *Western Recorder*, a Presbyterian newspaper, had a regular column that reported revival efforts in different parts of the nation and reported the early Finney revivals. The years of 1828 and 1832 are missing from the Utica library. One can speculate that Finney's conversion experience may have been published in one of those years. A Rev. A.E. Campbell, pastor of the Palmyra Presbyterian Church (1828-1830), is listed as an agent for the *Western Recorder* in the February 3, 1829 issue. Joseph Smith's mother, Lucy, Samuel Harrison, Hyrum, and Sophronia were members of the Presbyterian church in Palmyra up to September in 1828 (Brodie, 410.) Orson Parker, a lawyer in Adams, New York, in 1831 recorded an account of a young man who prayed, with no immediate results, at the same log where Finney was converted. This seems to indicate that Finney's conversion experience was well

known in the Adams area and could have been known in the Palmyra area. Orson Parker, *The Fire and the Hammer*(Boston: James H. Earle, 1877), p. 257 as cited by Rosell and Dupuis in *The Memoirs of Charles G. Finney*, 36.

24. Finney, *Memoirs* 8-9, 12, 15-16, 19-20; Scott H. Faulring, *An American Prophet's Record Diaries and Journals of Joseph Smith*, 4-6, 50-51.

25. Dale Morgan Walker *On Early Mormonism*, 260.

26. Walters, *New Light on Mormon Origins*, 18.

27. Roberts, *A Comprehensive History of the Church*, Volume 1, 164-165. In this revelation Smith claimed that the copyright of the *Book of Mormon* would be sold in Canada, which, of course, never happened. Whitmer, *An Address To All Believers In Christ*, 30-31. He received a corrected revelation.

28. Tucker, *Origin, Rise and Progress of Mormonism*, 19.

29. Howe, *Mormonism Unveiled*, 240-241, 244-245, 263.

30. Lucy Mack Smith, *Biographical Sketches of Joseph Smith and His Progenitors for Many Generations*, 91-92.

31. *Millennial Star*, Volume 3, May 1842, 100-101.

32. Roberts, *A Comprehensive History of the Church*, Volume 1, 82.

33. Howe, *Mormonism Unveiled*, 234-237.

34. Tiffany, *Tiffany Monthly*, 165.

35. Smith, *Pearl of Great Price*, "History," Section 1:35, 52.

36. Walters, *Joseph Smith's South Bainbridge Trails*, 129.

37. Smith, *History of the Church*, Volume 1, 17.

38. *Times and Seasons*, Volume 3, April 15, 1842, 753;

39. Smith, *The Pearl of Great Price* (Salt Lake City, Utah: The Church of Jesus Christ of Latter-day Saints, 1982), "History", Section 1:33, 52.

40. Ibid, "History", Section 1:59, 56.

41. Lucy Mack Smith, *Biographical Sketches*, 104-105.

42. John H. Hyde, Jr., *Mormonism: Its Leaders And Designs* (New York: W.P. Fetridge & Co., 1857), 244.

CHAPTER FIVE

43. Smith, *The Pearl of Great Price*, "History", Section 1, 55.
44. Ibid, "History", Section 1:55, 55.
45. Howe, *Manuscript Unveiled*, 254.
46. Joel Tiffany, *Tiffany's Monthly*, 164.
47. Howe, *Mormonism Unveiled*, 261.
48. John A. Clark, *Gleanings Along The Way*, (Philadelphia: W.J. and J.K. Simmons, 1842), 229.
49. Tucker, *Origin, Rise and Progress of Mormonism*, 40-45.
50. Kennedy, *The Early Days of Mormonism*, 47.
51. Smith, *The Pearl of Great Price*, "History", Section 1: 68-72, 57.
52. Joseph Fielding Smith, *Essentials in Church History* (Salt Lake City, Utah: Deseret News Press, 1953), 69.
53. Pomeroy Tucker, *Origin, Rise and Progress of Mormonism*, 51-53.
54. H. Michael Marquardt, "An Appraisal of Manchester As Location For The Organization Of The Church," *Sunstone*, February 1992, 49-57. Marquardt, in a carefully documented paper shows clearly that the weight of evidence is in favor of the Manchester location for the organization of the new church. He maintains that Joseph and David Whitmer were incorrect in their records of the events.
55. Smith, *History of the Church*, Volume 1, 61.
56. *Doctrine and Covenants*, Section 20:3, 34.
57. John A. Clark, *Gleanings By The Way*, 256-257.
58. Ibid, 258; Howe, *Mormonism Unveiled*, 14.
59. *Times and Seasons*, Volume 6, August 15, 1845, 992.
60. Lucy Mack Smith, *Biographical Sketches*, 211-212.
61. *Deseret News*, July 28, 1875.
62. *Doctrine and Covenants*, Section 28:2-11, 46-47.
63. Roberts, *A Comprehensive History of the Church*, Volume 1, 218-219; Smith, *History of the Church*, Volume 1, 115.

64. Smith, *Doctrine and Covenants*, Section 32:1-5, 56.

65. John W. Rigdon, *Dialogue* "The Life and Testimony of Sidney Rigdon", Karl Keller, ed., Winter 1966, 22-24.

66. Rodger I. Anderson, *Joseph Smith's New York Reputation Reexamined*, 2.

CHAPTER SIX

67. *Doctrine and Covenants*, Section 37:3, 62; John Whitmer, *The Book of John Whitmer, Kept By Commandment*, 2. Whitmer's history resides in the library of the Reorganized Church and has been reproduced by the Utah Lighthouse Ministry.

68. Howe, *Mormonism Unveiled*, 110-111.

69. John Corrill, *A Brief History of the Church of Jesus Christ of Latter-Day Saints*, 48.

70. John Whitmer, *The Book of John Whitmer, Kept by Commandment*, Gunnison, The Mormons, 102-103.

71. Roberts, *A Comprehensive History of the Church*, Volume 1, 250.

72. *Times and Seasons*, vol. 5, December 1, 1844, 723.

73. Berrett, *The Restored Church*, 100.

74. Shields, *Latter-day Saint Beliefs*, 28.

75. *Journal of Discourses*, vol. 7 (Liverpool: 1854-1886), 333-335.

76. Smith, *Pearl of Great Price*, "Book of Moses", Section 8:23-24, 27.

77. Kennedy, *Early Days of Mormonism*, 104.

78. *Times and Seasons*, Volume 5, August 15, 1844, 611-612.

79. Hayden, *Early History of the Disciples Church in the Western Reserve*, 221.

80. W.R. Werner, *Brigham Young* (New York: Harcourt, Brace and Company, 1925), 74.

81. Ibid., p. 10.

82. Leonard J. Arrington, *Brigham Young: American Moses* (Urbana and Chicago: University of Illinois Press, 1986), 19.

83. Werner, *Brigham Young*, 14.

84. Smith, *History of the Church*, Volume 1, 297.

85. Smith, *History of the Church*, Volume 1, (Independence, Missouri: Reorganized Church of Jesus Christ of Latter-Day Saints, 1922), 294.

86. Hyde, Jr., *Mormonism: Its Leaders and Designs*, 203.

87. Smith, *History of the Church*, Volume 2, 412-414,428.

88. Russell R. Rich, *Those Who Would Be Leaders - Offshoots of Mormonism*, (Provo, Utah: Extension Department of Brigham Young University, 1967), 3-4.

89. Joseph Smith, *Elder's Journal*, August 1838, 56.

90. James H. Snowden, *The Truth About Mormonism*, (New York: George H. Doran Company, 1926), 149.

91. Smith, *History of the Church*, Volume 2, 468.

92. *Messenger and Advocate*, Volume 3, January 1837, 441, 443.

93. Kennedy, *Early Days of Mormonism*, 161.

94. Roberts, *A Comprehensive History of the Church*, Volume 1, 405.

95. Lucy Mack Smith, *Biographical Sketches of Joseph Smith The Prophet and His Progenitors for Many Generations*, 210.

CHAPTER SEVEN

96. *Doctrine and Covenants*, Section 52:1-3, 95-96; Smith, *History of the Church*, Volume 1, 175, 196.

97. Roberts, *A Comprehensive History of the Church*, Volume 1, 322.

98. John Corrill, *A Brief History of the Church of Jesus Christ of Latter-day Saints, (Commonly Called Mormons), Including An Account Of Their Doctrines and Discipline*

With The Reasons Of The Author For Leaving The Church (St. Louis, Missouri: Printed by the Author, 1839), 18-19; Roberts, *A Comprehensive History of the Church*, Volume 2, 243-244, 287, 328, 333; *The Evening and Morning Star*, Volume 1, July 1832, 13; Volume 2, July 1833, 209.

99. *Evening and Morning Star*, Volume 2, July 1833, 109.

100. Roberts, *A Comprehensive History of the Church*, Volume 2, 40.

101. Wilhelm Wyl, *Mormon Portraits Or The Truths About The Mormon Leaders From 1830 to 1886* (Salt Lake City, Utah: Tribune Printing and Publishing Company, 1886), 54.

102. *Times and Seasons*, Volume 4, September 15, 1843, 320.

103. Ibid, 114-115.

104. *History of Caldwell and Livingston Counties* (St. Louis, Missouri: National Historical Co., 1886), 104-105.

105. Smith, *History of the Church* (RLDS) Volume 2, 178-179.

106. Dean Hughes, *The Mormon Church A Basic History* (Salt Lake City, Utah: Deseret Book Company, 1986), 83.

107. Smith, *History of the Church*, Volume 3, 34.

108. Ibid, 35, 45.

109. Corrill, *A Brief History of the Church of Christ of Latter-day Saints*, 28.

110. Smith, *History of the Church* (RLDS), Volume 2, 111-112.

111. *Millennial Star*, Volume 16, March 4, 1854, 133.

112. Roberts, *A Comprehensive History of the Church*, Volume 1, 434-436.

113. Ebenezer Robinson, ed., "Items of Personal History of the Editor," Volume 1, Number 11, *The Return*, (Davis City, Iowa: Robinson Publishing Company), November, 1889, 170.

114. Roberts, *A Comprehensive History of the Church*, Volume 1, 448-450.

115. Whitmer, *An Address to all Believers in Christ*, 35.
116. John Ahmanson, *Secret History*, translated by Gleanson L. Archer (Chicago: Moody Press, 1984), 143-146.
117. John Doyle Lee, *The Mormon Menace* (New York: Home Protection Publishing Company, 1905) 185: Stanley P. Hirshson, *The Lion of the Lord*, (New York: Alfred A. Knopf, 1969), 157-158.
118. J.H. Beadle, *Life in Utah* (Cincinnati, Ohio: National Publishing Company, 1904), 167-171.
119. Affidavit of Thomas B. Marsh, *Documents* (Published by the Missouri Legislature, October 1838), 57-59.
120. Smith, *History of the Church*, Volume 3, 169-170.
121. *History of Caldwell and Livingston County*, 129-130.
122. B.H. Roberts, *Missouri Persecutions*, (Salt Lake City: GQ Cannon and Sons Co. Publishing, 1900), 228-229.
123. Linn, *The Story of the Mormons*, 203-204.
124. Roberts, *Missouri Persecutions*, 233.
125. *History of Caldwell and Livingston County*, 151.
126. Smith, *History of the Church*, Volume 3, 423.

CHAPTER EIGHT

127. Roberts, *Missouri Persecutions*, 264.
128. William G. Hartley, "Almost Too Intolerable A Burden: The Winter Exodus from Missouri, 1838-39" *Journal of Mormon History* (Provo, Utah: Mormon History Association, Fall 1992), 21.
129. Ford, *History of Illinois* (Chicago: S.C. Griggs and Company Publishers, 1854), 263.
130. Henry Mayhew, *The Mormons or The Latter-day Saints: A Contemporary History* (London, England: Office of the National Illustrated Library, 1851), 108.
131. *Times and Seasons*, Volume 2, January 15, 1841, 275.
132. Roberts, *A Comprehensive History of the Church*, Volume 2, 9.

133. *Times and Seasons*, Volume 2, January 1, 1841, 259-260.
134. *Times and Seasons*, Volume 3, October 1, 1842, 936.
135. *Times and Seasons*, Volume 2, May 1, 1841, 399; July 1, 1841, 459.
136. Smith, *History of the Church*, Volume 5, 501.
137. Roberts, *A Comprehensive History of the Church*, Volume 2, 106.
138. *Doctrine and Covenants*, Section 132, 266.
139. George D. Smith, ed., *An Intimate Chronicle: The Journals of William Clayton* (Salt Lake City: Signature Press Books, 1991), 25 of the Introduction.
140. Smith, *Elder's Journal*, July 1838, 43.
141. *Times and Seasons*, Volume 3, October 1, 1842, 939.
142. Smith, *Book of Mormon*, Jacob 2:24-28, 121; Ether 10:5, 505.
143. Herbert Spencer Salisbury, "The Mormon War in Hancock County," *Journal of the Illinois State Historical Society*, Volume 8, (Springfield, Illinois: Illinois State Historical Society July 1915), 285-286, as cited from *Lutheran Women's Work*, July, 1913.
144. Gregg, The Prophet of Palmyra, 173.
145. Ford, *History of Illinois*, 263.
146. Kennedy, *Early Days of Mormonism*, 211, 213.
147. *Times and Seasons*, Volume 5, September 15, 1844, 655.
148. *Times and Seasons*, Volume 3, July 1, 1842, 839-840.
149. Smith, *Doctrine and Covenants*, Section 132, 267.
150. Sidney Rigdon, *Latter-day Saints Messenger and Advocate*, June 15, 1845, 220.
151. Smith, *History of the Church*, Volume 1, (RLDS), 541.
152. Wyl, *Mormon Portraits*, 311, as cited from a letter of a Mr. Traughber.
153. Ibid, 57.
154. Roberts, *A Comprehensive History of the Church*, Volume 2, 443.
155. Smith, *Doctrine and Covenants*, Section 66:10, 123.

156. Richard Turley, Jr., *Victims: The LDS Church and the Mark Hoffman Case* (Urbana: University of Illinois, 1992), 248.

157. *Times and Seasons*, Volume 5, January 1, 1844, 393-396; June 1, 1844, 548-549.

158. Ford, *History of Illinois*, 321-322; Grover C. Loud, *Evangelized America* (New York: The Dial Press, 1928), 156.

159. *Times and Seasons*, Volume 5, May 15, 1844, 532.

160. *Times and Seasons*, vol. 4, September 15, 1843, 330.

161. Ford, *History of Illinois*, 321.

162. Roberts, A Comprehensive History of the Church, Volume 2, 207.

163. *Millennial Star*, Volume 21, January 15, 1859, 40.

164. Wyl, *Mormon Portraits*, 207-208.

165. *Ensign*, August 1981, 66-67 (Monthly LDS Magazine).

CHAPTER NINE

166. Brodie, *No Man Knows My History*, 288, as cited from *The Wasp*, April 16 & 23, 1842.

167. Ford, *History of Illinois*, 322.

168. John D. Lee, *Mormonism Unveiled*, (New York: Bryan, Brand and Company, 1877), 147; *The Nauvoo Expositor*, Volume 1, Number 1, June 7, 1844, 1.

169. Richard F. Burton, *The City of The Saints And Across The Rocky Mountains To California*, (Niwot, Colorado: University Press of Colorado, 1990), 521.

170. Paul Bailey, *The Armies of God* (Garden City, New York: Doubleday, Inc., 1968), 126.

171. Roberts, *A Comprehensive History of the Church*, Volume 2, 247.

172. Smith, *History of the Church*, Volume 6, 547-548.

173. Roberts, *A Comprehensive History of the Church*, Volume 2, 247.

174. Smith, *History of the Church*, Volume 6, 533, 537.

175. Bailey, *The Armies of God*, 127-128.

176. Linn, *The Story of the Mormons*, 298.

177. Ford, *History of Illinois*, 337; Smith, *History of the Church*, Volume 6, 568.

178. Smith, *History of the Church*, Volume 6, 607-608.

179. *Times and Seasons*, Volume 5, August 15, 1844, 620.

180. Ford, *History of Illinois*, 339-340, 344.

181. Smith, *History of the Church*, Volume 6, 623.

182. Smith, *History of the Church*, Volume 7, 101.

183. Charles J. Scofield, *Historical Encyclopedia and History of Hancock County*, Volume 2, (Chicago: Munsell Publishing Company, 1921), 845.

184. *Times and Seasons*, Volume 5, August 1, 1844, 598-599.

185. John Hay, "The Mormon Prophet's Tragedy" *Atlantic Monthly*, Volume 24, December 1869, 676.

186. Smith, *History of the Church*, Volume 2 (RLDS), 744.

187. Roberts, *Comprehensive History of the Church*, Volume 2, 293.

CHAPTER TEN

188. Shields, *Divergent Paths of the Restoration*, 3-11.

189. Berrett, *The Restored Church*, 207-210.

190. Russell R. Rich, *Those Who Would Be Leaders Offshoots of Mormonism* (Provo, Utah: Brigham Young University Press, 1967), 18.

191. Shields, *Divergent Paths of the Restoration*, 37.

192. McKierman, *The Voice of One Crying in the Wilderness: Sidney Rigdon Religious Reformer 1793-1876*, 143, 145.

193. Milo M. Quaife, *The Kingdom of Saint James* (New Haven, Connecticut: Yale University Press, 1930), 2-3.

194. Riegel, *Crown of Glory* (New Haven, Connecticut: Yale University Press, 1935), 12.

195. Rich, *Those Who Would Be Leaders*, 20-21.

196. Quaife, *The Kingdom of Saint James*, 9-10.
197. Roberts, *Comprehensive History of the Church*, Volume 2, 429.
198. James J. Strang, "The Diamond Being the Law of Prophetic Succession and a Defense of the Calling of James J. Strang as Successor to Joseph Smith" (Voree, Wisconsin: Church of Latter-day Saints of Voree, Wisconsin, 1848), Pamphlet, 3-5.
199. Riegel, *Crown of Glory*, 49-50.
200. Quaife, *The Kingdom of Saint James*, Footnote bottom of 93.
201. Riegel, *Crown of Glory*, 174.
202. Rich, *Those Who Would Be Leaders*, 24.
203. Roberts, *Comprehensive History of the Church*, Volume 2, 431.
204. Quaife, *The Kingdom of Saint James*, 164.
205. Sheilds, *Divergent Paths of the Restoration*, 53-54.
206. Rich, *Those Who Would Be Leaders*, 40-41.
207. Brodie, *No Man Knows My History*, 164.
208. Shields, *Divergent Paths of the Restoration*, 54.
209. Roberts, *Comprehensive History of the Church*, Volume 2, 434-435.
210. Rich, *Those Who Would Be Leaders*, 35-36.
211. Shields, *Divergent Paths of the Restoration*, 65-66.
212. Mulder and Mortensen, *Among the Mormons*, 155.

CHAPTER ELEVEN

213. *Nauvoo Neighbor*, April 23, 1845.
214. Oaks and Hill, *Carthage Conspiracy*, 70, 160, 184.
215. Smith, *History of the Church*, Volume 7, 417-418.
216. Roberts, *A Comprehensive History of The Church*, Volume 2, 474-475.
217. Arrington, *Brigham Young: American Moses*, 123.

218. Roberts, *A Comprehensive History of the Church*, Volume 2, 468-469.

219. Allen and Leonard, *The Story of the Latter-day Saints*, 220.

220. Roberts, *A Comprehensive History of the Church*, Volume 2, 540.

221. Hill, *Joseph Smith: The First Mormon*, 435.

222. Wallace Stegner, *The Gathering of Zion* (New York: McGraw-Hill Book Company, 1964) 43.

223. Roberts, *A Comprehensive History of the Church*, Volume 2, 541.

224. Stegner, *The Gathering of Zion*, 49.

225. Mulder and Mortensen, *Among the Mormons*, 184; *Times and Seasons*, Volume 6, February 15, 1846, 1126.

226. Eliza R. Snow Smith, *Biography of Lorenzo Snow* (Salt Lake City, Utah: Deseret News Co., 1884), 86.

227. Mulder and Mortensen, *Among the Mormons*, 175.

228. Arrington and Bitton, *The Mormon Experience*, 99.

229. Howard Stansbury, *Exploration and Survey of the Valley of the Great Salt Lake of Utah, Including a Reconnaissance of a New Route Through the Rocky Mountains* (Washington: Robert Armstrong Public Printer, 1853), 125.

230. Ibid, 125-126; Arthur Conan Doyle, *A Study In Scarlet* (Middlesex, England: Penguin Books, 1987), 75.

231. Allen and Leonard, *The Story of the Latter-day Saints*, 250-251; Thomas G. Alexander, "A Mixed - Generally Open - Bag," *Sunstone*, Volume 16, Number 6, November 1993, 40.

232. Roberts, *A Comprehensive History of the Church*, Volume 4, 21; Volume 6, 235.

233. T.B.H. Stenhouse, *The Rocky Mountain Saints*, (New York: D. Appleton and Company, 1873), 320-322, 324.

234. Arrington and Bitton, *The Mormon Experience*, 199.

235. *Journal of Discourses*, Volume 1, 361.

236. Orson Pratt, *The Seer*, (Salt Lake City: Publishers Press, 1990), 158.

237. Ibid, 159.

238. *Journal of Discourses*, Volume 2, 82.

239. Wyl, *Mormon Portraits*, 93, as cited in *Deseret News*, November 23, 1878.

240. *Millennial Star*, Volume 16, 133.

241. Fanny Stenhouse, *Tell It All* (Hartford: A.D. Worthington and Company, 1875), 620.

242. Jennie Anderson Froiseth, *The Women of Mormonism or the Story of Polygamy* (Detroit, Michigan: C.G.G.Paine, 1883); Maria Ward, *Female Life Among the Mormons* (New York: Derby and Jackson, 1856); Mrs. T.B.H. Stenhouse, *Tell It All*, (Hartford, Connecticut: A.D. Worthington and Company, 1875); Mrs. A.G. Paddock, *The Fate of Madame La Tour* (New York: Fords, Howard, and Hulbert, 1881.)

243. Marshall Wingfield, "Tennessee's Mormon Massacre" *Tennessee Historical Quarterly*, (Nashville: The Tennessee Historical Quarterly, March 1958), 34.

244. Arrington and Bitton, *The Mormon Experience*, 180.

245. Charles A. Shook, *The True Origin of Mormon Polygamy* (Cincinnati: The Standard Publishing Company, 1914), 203.

246. Jan Shipps, "The Principle Revoked: A Closer Look at the Demise of Plural Marriage", *Journal of Mormon History*, Volume 11, (Salt Lake City, Utah: The Mormon History Association, 1984) 65-66.

247. Fred C. Collier, compiler, *Unpublished Revelations*, (Salt Lake City, Utah: Collier Publishing Co., 1981), Section 88, 180-183.

248. Mark 12:18-25 NASB.

249. Hill, *Joseph Smith: The First Mormon*, 223.

250. Klaus J. Hansen, *Quest For Empire*, 57.

251. John Corrill, *Brief History of the Church*, 31-32.

252.   *Reed Peck Manuscript*, (Salt Lake City, Utah: Utah Lighthouse Ministry, no date), 13.

253.   J.H. Beadle, *Life In Utah: Mysteries and Crimes of Mormonism*(Philadelphia: National Publishing Company, 1870), 177-179; T.B.H. Stenhouse, *Rocky Mountain Saints*, 299.

254.   C.P. Lyford, *The Mormon Problem*, (New York: Phillips and Hunt, 1886), 214-215.

255.   Bill Hickman, *Brigham's Destroying Angel* (Salt Lake City, Utah: Shepard Publishing Company, 1904), 97-98.

256.   Lee, *Mormonism Unveiled*, 240-243.

CHAPTER TWELVE

257.   J.H. Carleton, *Special Report of the Mountain Meadow Massacre* (Washington: Government Printing Office, 1902), 7. Second printing of the report, the first report being made to Congress February 1859 and printed in 1860.

258.   Lyford, *The Mormon Problem*, 295-302.

259.   Juanita Brooks, *The Mountain Meadows Massacre* (Stanford, California: Stanford University Press, 1950) 52. Brooks, a Mormon historian, objectively chronicled the events of the crime, but assigns no blame; Lee, *Mormonism Unveiled*, 240.

260.   William Wise, *The Massacre at Mountain Meadows* (New York: Thomas Y. Crowell Co., 1976), 238-239. Wise superseded Brooks' work in that he discovered eyewitness accounts, previously unseen documents, and a "missing witness" that had traveled with the Fancher party shortly before the massacre.

261.   Carleton, *Special Report of the Mountain Meadow Massacre*, 11.

262.   Lee, *Mormonism Unveiled or the Life and Confession of John D. Lee*, 243.

263. William J. Whalen, *The Latter-day Saints in the Modern World* (New York: The John Day Company, 1964), 81.
264. Norman F. Furniss, *The Mormon Conflict* (New Haven, Connecticut: Yale University Press, 1960), 228.
265. Lee, *Mormonism Unveiled*, 388.
266. Brooks, *The Mountain Meadows Massacre*, 21.
267. Hyde, *Mormonism: Its Leaders and Designs*, 151.
268. Roberts, *A Comprehensive History of the Church*, Volume 4, 154-155.
269. Carleton, *Special Report of the Mountain Meadows Massacre*, 9.
270. Wise, *The Massacre of Mountain Meadows*, 175-176, quote from jacket cover.
271. Arrington, *Brigham Young: American Moses*, title page.
272. Wyl, *Mormon Portraits*, 53.
273. H. Lorenzo Reid, *Brigham Young's Dixie of the Desert* (Zion National Park, Utah: Zion Natural History Association, 1964), 55.
274. Fritz Hugh Ludlow "Among the Mormons", *Atlantic Monthly*, April 1864, 488.
275. Sir Richard Francis Burton, *The City of the Saints and Across the Rocky Mountains to California* (New York: Harper and Brothers, 1862), 240.
276. Arrington, *Brigham Young: American Moses*, 420-421.
277. Werner, *Brigham Young*, 459,462; Lester E. Bush, Jr., "Brigham Young in Life and Death: A Medical Overview," *Journal of Mormon History*, Volume 5, 1978, 92-103.
278. Malcolm C. Duncan, *Duncan's Masonic Ritual and Monitor* (New York: David McKay Company), 128; Allen Roberts "Where Are All the All-Seeing Eyes?", *Sunstone*, Volume 10, (Salt Lake City, Utah: Sunstone Foundation, May 1985), 38, 42-44.
279. Fred C. Collier, ed., *The Teachings of President Brigham Young* (Salt Lake City, Utah: Collier Publishing Co., 1987), 29 of preface.

280. Ezra Taft Benson, "Our Divine Constitution", *Ensign* (Salt Lake City, Utah: The Church of Jesus Christ of Latter-day Saints, November 1987), 6.

281. Eugene England, "The Hosea Shout in Washington, D.C.", Volume 9, Number 2, *Dialogue: A Journal of Mormon Thought* (Los Angeles, California: Dialogue Foundation, Summer 1974), 66.

282. Ibid, "Hanging By A Thread: Mormons and Watergate", 10.

PART THREE

CHAPTER THIRTEEN

1. Smith, *History of the Church*, Volume 6, 289.
2. *Millennial Star*, Volume 3, August 1842, 69.
3. Thomas F. O'Dea, *The Mormons*, 160-161.
4. Clark, Gleanings By The Way, 258; Howe, *Mormonism Unveiled*, 14.
5. *Doctrine and Covenants*, Section 23:1, 42.
6. Ibid, Section 28:2-3, 48.
7. Roberts, *Comprehensive History of the Church*, Volume 1, 197.
8. *Doctrine and Covenants*, Section 65:1-6, 122.
9. Ibid, Section 134:1-12, 279-280.
10. *Times and Seasons*, Volume 3, Number 22, Sept. 15, 1842, 919-920.
11. O'Dea, *The Mormons*, 184.
12. Whalen, *The Latter-day Saints in the Modern Day World*, 143.
13. Vernal Holley, *Book of Mormon Authorship: A Closer Look* (Roy, Utah: published by the author, 1989), 42.
14. Roberts, *A Comprehensive History of the Church*, Volume 1, 41; Smith, *History of the Church*, Volume 1, 352.

15. Brodie, *No Man Knows My History*, 145.

16. Charles A. Shook, *The True Origin of the Book of Mormon* (Cincinnati, Ohio: The Standard Publishing Company, 1914), 129-136; 155-166.

17. Holley, *Book of Mormon Authorship: A Closer Look.* (Roy, Utah: published by the author, 1989), 26-37.

18. Howe, *Mormonism Unveiled*, 283.

19. George Arbaugh, *Revelation in Mormonism* (Chicago: University of Chicago Press, 1932), 9, 10.

20. Lucy Mack Smith, *Biographical Sketches of Joseph Smith*, 85.

21. Harry L. Ropp, *Are the Mormon Scriptures Reliable?* (Downers Grove, Illinois: 1987), 41.

22. *Times and Seasons*, Volume 3, June 1, 1842, 813-814.

23. Brodie, *No Man Knows My History*, 47.

24. B.H. Roberts, *Studies in the Book of Mormon*, edited by Brigham D. Madsen, (Chicago: University of Illinois Press, 1985), 22-24 of introduction.

25. Mark Twain, *Roughing It* (Hartford, Connecticut: American Publishing Co., 1872), 127.

26. *Messenger and Advocate*, Volume 2, December 1835, 229.

27. Fraser, *Is Mormonism Christian?*, 131; *Times and Seasons*, Volume 3, June 1, 1842, 813.

28. Brodie, *No Man Knows My History*, 45.

29. John Codman, "Mormonism", *The International Review*, Volume 1, (New York: A.S. Barnes and Company, September 1881), 225.

30. Smith, *History of the Church*, Volume 4, 461.

31. Oliver B. Huntington III, *Journal, Utah State Historical Society*, 168.

32. Jerald and Sandra Tanner, *3,913 Changes in the Book of Mormon* (Salt Lake City, Utah: Utah Lighthouse Ministry, no date).

33. Ropp, *Are the Mormon Scriptures Reliable?*, 43.

34. *The Improvement Era*, Joseph Fielding Smith, Volume 64, Number 12, December 1961, 924-925.

35. B.H. Roberts, *Defense of the Faith And The Saints*, Volume 2, (Salt Lake City, Utah: *The Deseret News*, 1912), 279.

36. Raymond T. Matheny, unpublished manuscript in the Harold B. Lee Library of Brigham Young University, 29. This lecture was originally delivered at the Sunstone Symposium, August 25, 1984.

37. Finney, *Memoirs of the Rev. Charles G. Finney*, 136.

38. M.T. Lamb, *The Golden Bible* (New York: Ward and Drummond, 1887), 234.

39. Ibid, 235.

40. Fraser, *Is Mormonism Christian?*, 134.

41. *Book of Mormon*, (Salt Lake City, Utah: George Q. Cannon and Sons Company, 1891) footnote 47.

42. John L. Sorenson, *An Ancient American Setting for the Book of Mormon* (Salt Lake City, Utah: Deseret Books, 1985), 1-3.

CHAPTER FOURTEEN

43. John A. Widtsoe, *The Message of the Doctrine and Covenants* (Salt Lake City, Utah: Bookcraft, 1969), 1.

44. *Evening and Morning Star*, Volume 2, Number 15, December 1833, 114.

45. Karl F. Best, "Changes In The Revelations 1833 to 1835", *Dialogue*, Volume 25, Number 1, March 1992, 97,111.

46. *Doctrine and Covenants*, "Articles of Faith", (Kirtland, Ohio: F.G. Williams and Sons, 1835), 12.

47. Milton R. Hunter, *The Gospel Through the Ages*, 104.

48. Ibid, 105.

49. Ropp, *Are the Mormon Scriptures Reliable?*, 65.

50. Jerald and Sandra Tanner, *Mormonism: Shadow or Reality?*, 23, 26.
51. Joseph F. Smith, *Answers To Gospel Questions*, Volume 4, (Salt Lake City, Utah: Deseret Book Co., 1963), 112-113.
52. David Whitmer, *An Address To All Believers In Christ*, 31.
53. *Doctrine and Covenants*, Section 35:20, 61.
54. *The Holy Scriptures, Inspired Version* (Independence, MO: Herald Publishing House of the Reorganized Church of Jesus Christ of Latter-Day Saints, 1867), 699-700.
55. Ibid, 79.
56. Wyl, *Mormon Portraits*, 124.
57. Linn, *The Story of the Mormons*, 118.
58. Osborne J.P. Widtsoe, *The Reformation of the Gospel* (Salt Lake City, Utah: Deseret Book Company, 1925), 116; *Messenger and Advocate*, Volume 2, Number 3, December 1835, 233-237.
59. Josiah Quincy, *Figures of the Past From the Leaves of Old Journals* (Boston: Roberts Brothers, 1883), 386.
60. Smith, *History of the Church*, Volume 2, 236; David H. Ludlow, ed., *Encyclopedia of Mormonism*, Volume 1, "Book of Abraham - Origins of the Book of Abraham", 132.
61. K.A. Kitchen, "Rosetta Stone", *The Zondervan Pictorial Encyclopedia of the Bible* (Grand Rapids, Michigan: 1975), 172-173; Joseph Ward Swain; "Rosetta Stone", *The World Book Encyclopedia*, Volume 16, (Chicago: Field Enterprises Educational Corporation, 1973), 442.
62. H. Michael Marquardt, *The Book of Abraham Revisited* (Salt Lake City, Utah: Utah Lighthouse Ministry, 1982), 104.
63. Hugh W. Nibley, *B.Y.U. Studies*, Volume 8, Number 2, "Prolegomena to Any Study of the Book of Abraham", Winter 1968, 171.

64. Thomas Stuart Ferguson, *One Fold and One Shepherd* (San Francisco, California: *Book of California*, 1958, 263.

65. Thomas Stuart Ferguson, "Written Symposium on *Book of Mormon* Geography", *Ferguson's Manuscript Unveiled* (Salt Lake City, Utah: Utah Lighthouse Ministry, 1988), 4.

66. Charles M. Larson, *By His Own Hand Upon Papyrus* (Grand Rapids, Michigan: Institute of Religious Research, 1992), 31.

67. Stan Larson, "The Odyssey of Stuart Ferguson", *Dialogue: A Journal of Mormon Thought* (Logan, Utah: Dialogue Foundation, Spring, 1990), 86.

CHAPTER FIFTEEN

68. *Times and Seasons*, Volume 5, August 15, 1844, 613; Milton R. Hunter, *The Gospel Through the Ages*, 12.

69. Lorenzo Snow, *The Instructor*, Volume 73, 1938, 574; Hunter, *The Gospel Through the Ages*, 105-106 as cited in *Millennial Star*, Volume 54, 404.

70. Linda Wilcox, "The Mormon Concept of a Mother in Heaven", *Sunstone*, September-October 1980, 10.

71. Milton R. Hunter, *The Gospel Through the Ages*, 98.

72. Joseph Fielding Smith, *Answers to Gospel Questions*, Volume 3, (Salt Lake City, Utah: Deseret Book Company, 1960), 142.

73. Carl F.H. Henry, *God, Revelation and Authority*, Volume 5, (Waco, Texas: Word Publishing Company, 1976), 159.

74. Bruce R. McConkie, *Mormon Doctrine* (Salt Lake City, Utah: Bookcraft, 1966), 750-751.

75. *Millennial Star*, Volume 23, 247.

76. Gleason L. Archer, *Encyclopedia of Bible Difficulties* (Grand Rapids, Michigan: Zondervan Publishing House, 1982), 373-374.

77. *Journal of Discourses*, Volume 1, 50-51.
78. *Millennial Star*, Volume 15, November 26, 1853, 769-770.
79. Juanita Brooks, *On the Mormon Frontier: The Diary of Hosea Stout*, Volume 2, (Salt Lake City, Utah: University of Utah Press, 1982), 435.
80. Jerald and Sandra Tanner, *LDS Apostle Confesses Brigham Young Taught Adam-God Doctrine* (Salt Lake City, Utah: Utah Lighthouse Ministry, 1982), 6, 9 of reproduced letter.
81. *Conference Report of the Church of Jesus Christ of Latter-day Saints* October 2, 1976, 115.
82. McConkie, *Mormon Doctrines*, 278.
83. Milton R. Hunter, *The Gospel Through the Ages*, 15.
84. John A. Widtsoe, *Evidences and Reconciliations*, 76-77.
85. Bruce R. McConkie, "Spirit of the Lord", *Discourses on the Holy Ghost*, compiled by N.B. Lundwall (Salt Lake City, Utah: Bookcraft, 1959), 59.
86. James E. Talmage, "The Holy Ghost", *Discourses on the Holy Ghost*, compiled by N.B. Lundwall (Salt Lake City, Utah: Bookcraft, 1959), 16-18.
87. Gordon H. Fraser, *Is Mormonism Christian?*, 72.
88. Joseph F. Smith, *The Way to Perfection* (Independence, Missouri: Zion Publishing Company, 1945), 57.
89. Joseph F. Smith, *Doctrines of Salvation*, Volume 1 (Salt Lake City, Utah: Bookcraft, 1954), 134.
90. McConkie, *Mormon Doctrine*, 62, 669.
91. James E. Talmage, *Articles of Faith* (Salt Lake City, Utah: Deseret Book Company, 1942), 61, 410.
92. *Doctrine and Covenants*, Section 76:36-38, 139; Smith, *The Way to Perfection*, 212, 213.
93. McConkie, *Mormon Doctrine*, 70.
94. *Pearl of Great Price*, "Article of Faith", Number 3, 60.
95. McConkie, *Mormon Doctrine*, 92.
96. Joseph F. Smith, *Doctrines of Salvation*, Volume 1, 189-190.

97.   Talmage, *Articles of Faith*, 124.
98.   *Doctrine and Covenants*, Section 20:41, 56, 68, 37-38;
       Talmage, *The Hand of the Lord*, 78.
99.   Matthias F. Cowley, *Wilford Woodruff, History of His Life and Labors* (Salt Lake City, Utah: Bookcraft, 1964), 65; Smith, *History of the Church*, Volume 2, 480.
100.   James B. Allen and Glen M. Leonard, *The Story of the Latter-day Saints*, 323.
101.   Boyd K. Packer, *The Holy Temple*, (Salt Lake City, Utah: The Church of Jesus Christ of Latter-day Saints, 1982), 2.
102.   James E. Talmage, *The House of the Lord* (Salt Lake City, Utah: Deseret Book Company, 1971), 67, 72.
103.   Ibid, Preface.

CHAPTER SIXTEEN

104.   *Journal of Discourses*, Volume 2, 203.
105.   Whitney R. Cross, *The Burned-Over District* (New York: Hippocrene Books, 1981), 114-120.
106.   Klaus J. Hansen, *Quest for Empire*, 55.
107.   Reed C. Durham, Jr., *No Help For the Widow's Son* (Nauvoo, Illinois: Martin Publishing Company, 1980), 15-16, as cited from Rob Morris.
108.   Ibid, 25-27.
109.   Roberts, *Comprehensive History of the Church*, Volume 2, 286.
110.   Bob Witte and Gordon H. Fraser, *What's Going On In Here?* (Eugene, Oregon: Gordon Fraser Publishing, no date), 7.
111.   Chuck Sackett, *What's Going On In There?* (Thousand Oaks, California: Sword of the Shepherd Ministries, Inc., 1982), 45.
112.   Thomas Ford, *A History of Illinois*, 263.
113.   Milo M. Quaife, *The Kingdom of St. James*, 34.

114. John C. Bennett, *The History of the Saints* (Boston: Leland and Whiting Publishing Company, 1842), 268, 271-272.
115. Quaife, *The Kingdom of St. James*, 61-62.
116. E. Cecil McGavin, *Mormonism and Masonry* (Salt Lake City, Utah: 1956), 91-92.
117. Wyl, *Mormon Portraits*, 269.
118. Sackett, *What's Going On In There?*, 6-7.
119. Witte and Fraser, *What's Going On In Here?*, 6.
120. Sackett, *What's Going On In There?*, 7-10.
121. *Doctrine and Covenants*, Section 124:28-36, 248; Section 119:1-7, 238-239.
122. Sackett, *What's Going On In There?*, 54-55.
123. McConkie, *Mormon Doctrine*, 226-227; Whalen, *The Latter-day Saints in the Modern Day World*, 142.
124. McConkie, *Mormon Doctrine*, 92.
125. *Doctrine and Covenants*, Section 132:19-27, 268-269; Joseph F. Smith, *Doctrines of Salvation*, Volume 1, 133-134.
126. *Reed Peck Manuscript*, University of Utah Library, 13.
127. *Deseret News*, October 19, 1963.
128. Hansen, *Quest For Empire*, 70.
129. Joseph F. Smith, *Doctrines of Salvation*, Volume 1, 136.
130. Orson Pratt, *The Seer*, 223; *Journal of Discourses*, Volume 3, 247.
131. Smith, *History of the Church*, Volume 7, 597.
132. *Journal of Discourses*, Volume 6, 34-35.
133. Hansen, *Quest For Empire*, 127.
134. *Doctrine and Covenants*, Section 76: Introduction by Smith, 136.
135. *Journal of Discourses*, Volume 2, 75.
136. *Pearl of Great Price*, "Articles of Faith", 60.
137. McConkie, *Mormon Doctrine*, 81, 138, 670.
138. *Journal of Discourses*, Volume 7, 289; Bruce R. McConkie, *A New Witness for the Articles of Faith* (Salt Lake City, Utah: Deseret Book Co., 1985), 1, 13.

139. *Elder's Journal*, July 1838, 42.

140. Roy W. Doxey, *Doctrine and Covenants Speaks* (Salt Lake City, Utah: Deseret Book Company, 1964), 362.

PART FOUR

CHAPTER SEVENTEEN

1. *Doctrines and Covenants*, Section 20:1, 34.
2. Smith, *History of the Church*, Volume 2, 63; Robinson, *The Return*, Volume 1, Number 1, January 18, 1889, 11.
3. Tanners, *Mormonism: Shadow or Reality?*, 67.
4. Arrington and Bitton, *The Mormon Experience*, 21.
5. Linn, *The Story of the Mormons*, 108-109.
6. *The Evening and the Morning Star*, Volume 2, Number 20, (May 1834), 158.
7. Brodie, *No Man Knows My History*, 182.
8. Rich, *Those Who Would Be Leaders*, 3.
9. *The Latter-day Saint's Messenger and Advocate*, Volume 1, Number 1, (October 15, 1844), 220.
10. Whitmer, *An Address to All Believers in Christ*, 27, 73-74.
11. *Doctrine and Covenants*, Section 15:4, 235.
12. Dean C. Jessee, "The Writing of Joseph Smith's History", *Brigham Young University Studies*, Volume 11, Number 4 (Summer 1971), 469-470.
13. Ibid, 47-472.
14. James B. Allen and Glen M. Leonard, *The Story of the Latter-day Saints*, 447.
15. Howard A. Seale "Authorship of the History of Joseph Smith: A Review Essay", *Brigham Young University Studies*, Volume 21, Number 1 (Winter 1981) 103.

16. Joseph Smith, *History of the Church*, Volume 4, 1; Volume 5, 298.
17. Seale, "Authorship of the History of Joseph Smith: A Review Essay", 105.
18. Jesse, "The Writing of Joseph Smith's History", 441, 469.
19. Seale, "Authorship of the History of Joseph Smith: A Review Essay", 105.
20. Joseph Smith, *History of the Church*, Volume 1, p.v. of introduction.
21. Jerald and Sandra Tanner, *Changes In Joseph Smith's History* (Salt Lake City, Utah: Utah Lighthouse Ministry, no copyright date) 2-3.
22. Jerald and Sandra Tanner, *Falsification of Joseph Smith's History* (Salt Lake City, Utah: Utah Lighthouse Ministry, 1971) 2.
23. James F. Mintun, "A History of Presidents of Seventy", *Journal History*, Volume 8, (Lamoni, Iowa: January 1915), 75, 76, as cited in *Deseret News*, 1855.
24. Roberts, *A Comprehensive History of the Church of Jesus Christ of Latter-day Saints*, Volume 2, 181.
25. Joseph Smith, *History of the Church*, Volume 5, 85.
26. Jessee, "The Writing of Joseph Smith's History", 441.
27. Davis Bitton, "Joseph Smith in the Mormon Folk Memory", *Restoration Studies*, Volume 1, Sesquicentennial Edition, (Independence, Missouri: RLDS Church, 1980), 85.
28. Smith, *History of the Church*, Volume 5, 395-398.
29. George D. Smith, ed., *An Intimate Chronicle The Journal of William Clayton* (Salt Lake City, Utah: Signature Books in association with Smith Research Associates, 1991), 104.
30. Smith, *History of the Church*, Volume 5, 393-394.
31. Smith, *An Intimate Journal*, 104.
32. *Times and Seasons*, Volume 3, Number 11 (April 1842), 749.
33. Smith, *History of the Church*, Volume 1, 9.

34. Thomas G. Alexander, "The Earliest Mormon Concept of God"; Gary James Bergera, ed., *Line Upon Line*, (Salt Lake City, Utah: Signature Books, 1989), 53.

35. Ibid, Van Hale, "Defining the Contemporary Mormon Concept of God", 8.

36. Ibid, Van Hale, 9.

37. *A Book of Commandments for the Government of the Church of Christ* (Zion: W.W. Phelps, 1833), Section 24:18, 50.

38. *Doctrine and Covenants*, Section 20:28, 36.

39. Donald Q. Cannon, "The King Follett Discourse: Joseph Smith's Greatest Sermon in Historical Prospective", *Brigham Young University Studies*, Volume 18, Number 2 (Winter 1978), 180.

40. Ibid, Van Hale, "The Doctrinal Impact of the King Follett Discourse", 213.

41. *Messenger and Advocate*, Volume 1, May 1835, 113, 8th reflection.

42. Thomas G. Alexander, "The Reconstruction of Mormon Doctrine", Gary James Bergera, ed., *Line Upon Line*, 54.

43. David John Buerger, *Dialogue*, Volume 15, Number 1, Spring 1982, "The Adam-God Doctrine", 14.

44. D. Michael Quinn, "New Mormon Hysteria", *Sunstone* Volume 16, Number 4 (March 1993) 5.

CHAPTER EIGHTEEN

45. *Journal of Discourses*, Volume 2, 311.

46. *Doctrine and Covenants*, Section 132:1-7,61-62, 226-227, 272.

47. D. Michael Quinn, "LDS Church Authority And New Plural Marriages, 1890-1904", *Dialogue*, Volume 18, Number 1 (Spring 1985), 9, 21.

48. *Times and Seasons*, Volume 5, (March 15, 1844), 474.

49. Brodie, *No Man Knows My History*, 184 footnote; *Doctrine and Covenants*, see introductory paragraph for section 132 of the 1982 version.

50. Quinn, "LDS Church Authority And New Plural Marriages, 1890-1904", 56.

51. *Millennial Star*, Volume 15, (April 9, 1853), 226.

52. *Doctrine and Covenants*, Official Declaration 1, 291-292.

53. Fred C. Collier, *Unpublished Revelations* (Salt Lake City, Utah: Collier Publishing Company), 145-146.

54. *Evening and Morning Star*, Volume 2, Number 14 (July 1833), 109-110.

55. Bruce R. McConkie, *Mormon Doctrine*, 527.

56. *Journal of Discourses*, Volume 2, 142-143; Volume 7, 290-291; Volume 10, 110.

57. Mary Lythgoe Bradford and Lester E. Bush, Jr., "Saint Without Priesthood: The Collected Testimonies of Ex-Slave Samuel D. Chambers", *Dialogue*, Volume 12, Number 2, (Summer 1979), 13, 16.

58. Newell G. Bringhurst, "Elijah Abel and the Changing Status of Blacks Within Mormonism", *Dialogue*, Volume 12, Number 2, (Summer 1979) 24, blessing quoted from copy of original in the LDS Church Archives.

59. Joseph Smith, *History of the Church*, Volume 4, 365.

60. *Messenger and Advocate*, Volume 2, (April 1836), 289-290.

61. Witte and Fraser *What's Going On In Here?*, 23.

62. Lester E. Bush, Jr., "Mormonism's Negro Doctrine: An Historical Overview", *Dialogue*, Volume 8, Number 1, (Spring 1973) 49.

63. Brian Walton, "A University's Dilemma: B.Y.U. and Blacks", *Dialogue*, Volume 6, Number 1 (Spring 1971), 31.

64. Smith, *History of the Church*, Volume 2, 287.

65. Ibid, 430.

66. *Doctrine and Covenants*, Section 124:39, 249.

67. Smith, *History of the Church*, Volume 5, 1.

68. Davis John Buerger, "The Development of the Mormon Temple Endowment Ceremony", *Dialogue: A Journal of Mormon Thought*, Volume 20, Number 4 (Winter 1987) 43-44.

69. Ezra Taft Benson, *The Teachings of Ezra Taft Benson* (Salt Lake City, Utah: Bookcraft, 1988), 250.

70. Smith, *History of the Church*, Volume 5, 2.

71. Buerger, "The Development of the Mormon Temple Endowment Ceremony", 45-46.

72. Armand L. Mauss, "Culture, Charisma, and Change: Reflections on Mormon Temple Worship", *Dialogue: A Journal of Mormon Thought*, Volume 20, Number 4 (Winter 1987), 77.

73. Buerger, 33.

74. *Warsaw Signal*, (April 15, 1846).

75. Increase Mcgee Van Deusen, *The Mormon Endowment; A Sacred Drama, or Conspiracy, in the Nauvoo-Temple in 1846,* (Syracuse, New York: N.M.D. Lathnot, Printer, 1847).

76. Reed Smoot Hearings, Proceedings Before the Committee on Privileges and Elections of the United States Senate in the Matter of the Protests Against the Right of Hon. Reed Smoot, A Senator from the State of Utah, to Hold His Seat, 4 volumes, (Washington: Government Printing Office, 1906).

77. Bob Witte and Gordon H. Fraser, *What's Going On In Here?,* 1980.

78. Chuck Sackett, *What's Going On In There?,* 1982.

79. John Hyde, Jr., *Mormonism: Its Leaders and Designs,* 100.

80. Joseph F. Smith, *The Improvement Era*, Volume 9, 813.

81. Thomas G. Alexander, *Mormonism In Transition: A History of the Latter-day Saints, 1890-1930.* (Chicago: University of Illinois Press, 1986), 300-301.

82. Buerger, "The Development of the Mormon Temple Endowment Ceremony", 67-68; *Salt Lake Tribune*, April 29, 1990 reveals that the oath of obedience has been changed.

83. Ezra Taft Benson, *The Teachings of Ezra Taft Benson* (Salt Lake City, Utah: Bookcraft, Inc., 1988) 250.

PART FIVE

CHAPTER NINETEEN

1. Charles Braden, *These Also Believe* (New York: Macmillan, 1951), xii.
2. *Journal of Discourses*, Volume 6, 229.
3. Smith, *The Pearl Of Great Price*, "Joseph Smith-History", 49.
4. Ibid, "Articles of Faith", 60.
5. Hunter, *The Gospel Through the Ages*, 14.
6. Smith, *Doctrines of Salvation*, Volume 1, 189.
7. Ibid, Volume 1, 188.
8. James Walker, "Truths that Transform", May 23, 1990, 1.
9. Gary Smith, "A Season for Spreading the Faith", *Sports Illustrated*, December 1985, 84-101.
10. "The Development of the Mormon Temple Endowment Ceremony", *Dialogue* Volume 20, Number 4 (Winter 1987), 65-66.
11. Smith, *Doctrines of Salvation*, Volume 1, 236.
12. "The Greater Salt Lake City State of the Community," United Way of The Great Salt Lake Area (September 1996.)

CHAPTER TWENTY

13. Jerald Tanner, "Problems In Winning Mormons", Salt Lake City, Utah: Utah Lighthouse Ministry, July 1987 (tape).
14. Harry L. Ropp, *Are The Mormon Scriptures Reliable?* (Downers Grove, Illinois: InterVarsity Press, 1987), 98, 101.
15. John L. Smith, *Witnessing Effectively To Mormons*, (Marlow, Oklahoma: Utah Missions, Inc., 1975), 31.
16. Wally Tope, *On the Frontline Witnessing To Mormons* (La Canada Flintridge, California: Frontline Ministries, 1988), preface.
17. Ronald Enroth, "How Can You Reach a Cultist?" (Chicago: *Moody Monthly Magazine*, November 1987, 68.
18. David A. Reed and John R. Farkas, *Mormons Answered Verse by Verse* (Grand Rapids: Baker Book House, 1992).

CHAPTER TWENTY-ONE

19. Smith, *History of the Church*, Volume 6, 308.
20. Anthony A. Hoekema, "Ten Questions to Ask the Mormons" *Christianity Today*, January 19, 1968, 11.
21. Stan Larson, "The King Follett Discourse: A Newly Amalgamated Text", *Brigham Young University Studies*, Volume 18, Number 2, (Winter 1978), 200.
22. McConkie, *Mormon Doctrine*, 516.
23. Hunter, *The Gospel Through the Ages*, 15.
24. Pratt, *The Seer*, 172.
25. *Journal of Discourses*, Volume 4, 259.
26. William E. Phipps, "The Case For A Married Jesus", *Dialogue*, Volume 7, Number 4, (Winter 1972) 44.
27. Tanners, *Mormonism-Shadow or Reality?*, 188-190.

28. Floyd C. McElveen, *From Mormon Illusion To God's Love*, (Issaquah, Washington: Saints Alive In Jesus, no cc), 19.

29. Whitmer, *An Address to All Believers In Christ*, 31.

30. Smith, *History of the Church*, Volume 2, 182.

31. *The Young Women's Journal*, Volume 3, (Salt Lake City, Utah: Zion's Young Ladies Mutual Improvement Associations, 1892), 263; Oliver B. Huntington Diary, typed copy in Utah Historical Society, 166.

32. Hal Hougey, *Where Did You Get Your Authority?* (Concord, California: Pacific Publishing Company, 1981), 2-3.

33. Stan Larson, "The Odyssey of Thomas Stuart Ferguson", 77, 80.

34. John R. Farkas, *Mormons Answered Verse By Verse* (Grand Rapids, Michigan: Baker Book House, 1992), 129.

35. Smith, *History of the Church*, Volume 2, 63; *Doctrines and Covenants*, Section 15:4, 235.

36. Smith, *History of the Church*, Volume 4, 461.

37. Smith, *The Pearl Of Great Price*, Book of Moses 3:10-16, 8.

38. *Witnessing to Mormons*, (La Mesa, California: Utah Christian Tract Society, no cc), 6.

39. "Pointers For Proselyting For Mormon Missionaries", (Saint Louis, Missouri: Personal Freedom Outreach, 1990), pamphlet.

40. Jerry and Dianna Benson, *How To Witness To A Mormon* (Chicago: Moody Press, 1986), 20-21.

41. Charles M. Larson, *By His Own Hand Upon Papyrus* (Grand Rapids, Michigan: Institute for Religious Research, 1992), 188.

42. James R. Spencer, *Have You Witnessed to a Mormon Lately?* (Old Tappen, New Jersey: Fleming H. Revell Co., 1986), 90,136.

43. Pratt, *Journal of Discourses*, Volume 2, 290-291.

44. Marvin W. Cowan, *Mormon Claims Answered* (Salt Lake City, Utah: Utah Christian Publications, 1989), 36.

45. John J. Stewart, *Joseph Smith: the Mormon Prophet* (Salt Lake City, Utah: Mercury Publishing Company, 1966), 88.

46. Roberts, *Comprehensive History of the Church*, Volume 1, 294.

47. James Ward Smith, ed. *A Leland Jamison: The Shaping of American Religion* (Princeton, New Jersey: 1961), 214.

BIBLIOGRAPHY

PRIMARY MORMON SOURCES

Alexander, Thomas G. *Mormonism in Transition.* Urbana, Illinois: University of Illinois Press, 1986.

Alexander, Thomas G. and James B. Allen. *Mormons & Gentiles.* Boulder, Colorado: Pruett Publishing Company, 1984.

Allen, James B. and Glen M. Leonard. *The Story of the Latter-day Saints.* Salt Lake City, Utah: Deseret Book Company, 1976.

Arrington, Leonard J. *Brigham Young: American Moses.* Urbana, Illinois: University of Illinois Press, 1986.

_____. *Great Basin Kingdom.* University of Nebraska Press, 1958.

Arrington, Leonard J. & Davis Bitton. *The Mormon Experience: A History of the Latter-day Saints.* New York: Alfred A. Knopf, 1979.

Bailey, Paul. *The Armies of God.* Garden City, New York: Doubleday & Company, 1968.

Bergera, Gary James, ed. *Line Upon Line Essays Upon Mormon Doctrine*. Salt Lake City, Utah: Signature Books, 1989.

Berrett, William E. *Teachings of the Book of Mormon*. Salt Lake City: Deseret News Press, 1952.

Brodie, Fawn M. *No Man Knows My History*. New York: Alfred A. Knopf, 1985.

Brooks, Juanita. *The Mountain Meadows Massacre*. Stanford, California: Stanford University Press, 1950.

_____. *On The Mormon Frontier: The Diary of Hosea Stout 1844-1848*. Volume 1. Salt Lake City, Utah: University of Utah Press, 1982 reprint.

_____. *On The Mormon Frontier: The Diary of Hosea Stout 1848-1861*. Volume 2. Salt Lake City, Utah: University of Utah Press, 1982 reprint.

Bushman, Richard L. *Joseph Smith And The Beginnings of Mormonism*. Urbana, Illinois: University of Illinois Press, 1984.

Cleland, Robert Glass and Juanita Brooks. *A Mormon Chronicle: The Diaries of John D. Lee 1848-1876*. Volume 1. Salt Lake City, Utah: University of Utah Press, 1983 reprint.

_____. *A Mormon Chronicle: The Diaries of John D. Lee 1848-1876*. Volume 2. Salt Lake City, Utah: University of Utah Press, 1983 reprint.

Collier, Fred C., comp. *The Teachings of President Brigham Young*. Salt Lake City, Utah: Collier's Publishing Company, 1987.

_____. comp. *Unpublished Revelations of the Prophets And Presidents of The Church Of Latter-day Saints.* Salt Lake City, Utah: Collier's Publishing Company, 1979.

Corbett, Pearson H. *Hyrum Smith Patriarch.* Salt Lake City, Utah: Deseret Book Comp., 1971.

Crowley, M.F. *Crowley's Talks on Doctrines.* Chicago: E.O. Etten Press.

Davis, Inez Smith. *The Story of the Church.* Independence, Missouri: Herald Publishing House, 1964.

Dryer, Alvin A. *The Refiner's Fire: The Significance of Events Transpiring in Missouri.* Salt Lake City, Utah: Deseret Book Company, 1972.

Evans, John Henry. *Joseph Smith: An American Prophet.* Salt Lake City, Utah: Deseret Book Company, 1989.

Faulring, Scott H., ed. *An American Prophet's Record The Diaries and Journals of Joseph Smith.* Salt Lake City, Utah: Signature Books, 1989.

Fisher, Vardis. *Children of God.* New York: Harper and Brothers, 1939.

Flint, B.C. *An Outline History of the Church of Christ (Temple Lot).* Independence, Missouri: The Board of Publications The Church of Christ (Temple Lot), 1953.

Gibbons, Francis M. *Joseph Smith: Martyr-Prophet of God.* Salt Lake City, Utah: Deseret Book Company, 1977.

Gospel Ideals Selections From The Discourses of David O. McKay. Salt Lake City, Utah: Deseret Book Company, 1976.

Grant, Heber J. *Gospel Standards Selections from the Sermons and writings of Heber J. Grant.* Salt Lake City, Utah: The Improvement Era Publication, 1943.

Graw, Stewart L. *A Tabernacle In The Desert.* Salt Lake City, Utah: Deseret Book Company, 1958.

Hafen, LeRoy R. and Ann W. Hafen. *Handcarts to Zion the story of a Unique Western Migration 1856-1860 with Contemporary Journals, Accounts, Reports; and Rosters of Members of the Ten Handcart Companies.* Glendale, California: The Arthur H. Clark Company, 1960.

Hajicek, John J., copier. *Newsclippings From Iowa and Illinois 1841-1849.* Burlington, Wisconsin: 1992.

Hansen, Klaus J. *Mormonism and the American Experience.* Chicago: University of Chicago Press, 1981.

_____. *Quest For Empire.* East Lansing, Michigan: Michigan State University Press, 1967.

Hill, Donna. *Joseph Smith: The First Mormon.* Garden City, New York: Doubleday & Comany, 1977.

History of the Reorganized Church of Jesus Christ of Latter-Day Saints (RLDS) Volumes 1 - 8. Independence, Missouri: 1922, 1929, 1969, 1970-1973, 1976.

Hunter, Milton R. *The Gospel Through the Ages.* Salt Lake City, Utah: Stevens and Wallis, 1945.

Jessee, Dean C., ed. *The Papers of Joseph Smith*. Volume 1. Salt Lake City, Utah: Deseret Book Company, 1989.

_____. ed. *The Papers of Joseph Smith*. Volume 2. Salt Lake City, Utah: Deseret Book Company, 1992.

_____. comp. *The Personal Writings of Joseph Smith*. Salt Lake City, Utah: Deseret Book Company, 1984.

Kirkham, Francis W. *A New Witness for Christ in America The Book of Mormon*. Volumes 1 & 2. Salt Lake City, Utah: Utah Printing Company, 1960.

Kjelgard, Jim. *The Coming Of The Mormons*. New York: Random House, 1953.

Lundwall, N.B., comp. *Masterpieces of Latter-day Saint Leaders*. Salt Lake City, Utah: Deseret Book Company, 1953.

McConkie, Bruce R., compiler. *Doctrines of Salvation. The Sermons and Writings of Joseph Fielding Smith*. Volumes 1-3. Salt Lake City: Bookcraft, 1966.

_____. *Mormon Doctrines*. Salt Lake City: Bookcraft, 1966.

McGavin, E. Cecil. *Mormonism and Masonry*. Salt Lake City, Utah: Bookcraft Publishers, 1956.

_____. *The Mormon Pioneers*. Salt Lake City, Utah: Stevens & Wallis, 1947.

_____. *Nauvoo The Beautiful*. Salt Lake City, Utah: Stevens & Wallis, 1946.

McKierman, F. Mark. *The Voice of One Crying in theWilderness: Sidney Rigdon, Religious Reformer 1793-1876.*

Madsen, Brigham D., ed. *B.H. Roberts Studies Of The Book of Mormon.* Urbana, Illinois: University of Illinois Press, 1985.

Matheny, Ray T. *Book of Mormon Archeology - What Does The Evidence Show?* Salt Lake City, Utah: The Sunstone Foundation, 1984.

Mulder, William & A. Russell Mortenson, ed. *Among the Mormons Historic Accounts by Contemporary Observers.* New York: Alfred A. Knopf, 1958.

Mullen, Robert. *The Latter-day Saints: The Mormons Yesterday andToday.* New York: Doubleday & Company, 1966.

Newell, Linda King and Valeen Tippetts Avery. *Mormon Enigma: Emma Hale Smith Prophet's Wife, "Elect Lady," Polygamy's Foe, 1804-1879.* New York: Doubleday, 1984.

Nibley, Hugh. *Lehi In The Desert. The World of the Jaredites. There Were Jaredites.* Salt Lake City, Utah: Deseret Book Company, 1988.

Oaks Dallin H. and Marvin S. Hill. *Carthage Conspiracy TheTrial of the Accused Assassins of Joseph Smith.* Urbana, Illinois: University of Illinois Press, 1975.

Pratt, Orson. *Pamphlets By Orson Pratt.* Salt Lake City, Utah: Utah Lighthouse Ministry, reprint of originals.

Quaife, Mil M. *The Kingdom of Saint James: A Narrative of the Mormons.* New Haven, Connecticut: Yale University Press, 1930.

Quinn, D. Michael. *Early Mormonism and the Magic World View.* Salt Lake City: Signature Books, 1987.

_____. *On Being A Mormon Historian.* Salt Lake City: Utah Lighthouse Ministry, 1982.

Reynolds, George and Janne M. Sjodahl. *Commentary on the Pearl of Great Price.* Salt Lake City, Utah: Deseret Book Company, 1980.

Richards, LeGrand. *A Marvelous Work and a Wonder.* Salt Lake City: Deseret Book Company, 1976.

Riegel, O.W. *Crown of Glory: The Life Of James J. Strang: Moses Of The Mormons.* New Haven, Connecticut, Yale University Press, 1935.

Roberts, B.H. *The Missouri Persecutions.* Salt Lake City, Utah: G.Q. Cannon and Sons Company Publishers, 1900.

Robinson, Ebenezer., ed. "Items of Personal History of the Editor." *The Return.* Davis City, Iowa: 1889-1890.

Scrow, Ron, Wayne Scrow & Marybeth Raynes, editors. *PeculiarPeople: Mormons And Same-Sex Orientation.* Salt Lake City, Utah: Signature Books, 1991.

Shields, Steven L. *Divergent Paths of the Restoration A History of the Latter-day Saint Movement.* Los Angeles, California: Restoration Research, 1990.

_____. *Latter-Day Saint Beliefs*. (RDLS) Independence, Missouri: Herald Publishing House, 1986.

Smith, George D., ed. *An Intimate Chronicle The Journals of William Clayton*. Salt Lake City, Utah: Signature Books,1991.

Smith, Joseph. *History Of The Church Of Jesus Christ Of Latter-day Saints (LDS) Volumes 1-7*. Salt Lake City: The Deseret Book Company, 1946.

_____. *Book of Mormon*. Palmyra: E.B. Grandin Printers, 1830.

_____. *The Doctrines and Covenant*. Salt Lake City: The Church of Latter-day Saints Publishers, 1982.

_____. *The Holy Scriptures Inspired Version*. Independence, Missouri: Herald Publishing House, 1974.

Smith, Joseph Fielding. *Answers to Gospel Questions*. Volumes 1-5. Salt Lake City, Utah: Deseret Book Co., 1966.

_____. *Gospel Doctrine*. Salt Lake City, Utah: Deseret Book Company, 1939.

_____. *Life of Joseph F. Smith Sixth President of The Churchof Jesus Christ of Latter-day Saints*. Salt Lake City, Utah: The Deseret News Press, 1938.

_____. comp. *Teachings of the Prophet Joseph Smith*. Salt Lake City: Deseret Book Company, 1977.

_____. *The Way to Perfection*. Salt Lake City, Utah: Press of Zion Printing and Publishing Company, 1945.

Smith, Lucy. *Biographical Sketches of Joseph Smith: The Prophet and His Progenitors For Many Generations.* Liverpool, England: S.W. Richards, 1853.

Sorenson, John L. *An Ancient American Setting For The Book of Mormon.* Provo, Utah: Foundation for Ancient Research and Mormon Studies, 1985.

Stewart, John J. *Joseph Smith: The Mormon Prophet.* Salt Lake City, Utah: Mercury Publishing Company, 1966.

Talmage, James E. *A Study of the Articles of Faith.* Salt LakeCity, Utah: The Church of Jesus Christ of Latter-day Saints, 1924.

_____. *Jesus The Christ A Study of the Messiah and HisMission according to Holy Scripture both Ancient and Modern.* London, England: Church of Jesus Christ of Latter-day Saints, 1962.

_____. *The House Of The Lord.* Salt Lake City, Utah: Deseret Book Company, 1971.

Walker, John Phillip, ed., *Dale Morgan On Early Mormonism Correspondence & A New History.* Salt Lake City, Utah: Signature Books, 1986.

West, Jr., Ray B. *Kingdom Of The Saints.* New York: The Viking Press, 1957.

Whipple, Maurine. *This Is The Place: Utah.* New York: Alfred A. Knopf, 1945.

Whitmer, John. *John Whitmer's History.* Salt Lake City, Utah:Utah Lighthouse Ministry, no cc.

Widtsoe, John A. *Evidences And Reconciliations*. Salt lake City, Utah: Bookcraft , 1960.

_____. *The Message of the Doctrine and Covenants*. Salt Lake City: Bookcraft, 1969.

Winn, Kenneth H. *Exiles in a Land of Liberty Mormons in America 1830-1846*. Chapel Hill, North Carolina: The University of North Carolina Press, 1989.

Woodruff, Wilford C. *Joseph Smith Begins His Work*. Volumes 1 & 2. Salt Lake City: Publishers Press, 1958.

MORMON PAMPHLETS

"Contributions of Joseph Smith." Salt Lake City: Deseret Press, 1958.

"Joseph Smith Tells His Own Story...". Salt Lake City, Utah:Church of Jesus Christ of Latter-day Saints, no cc.

Morgan, John. "The Plan of Salvation". Salt Lake City, Utah:Missions of the Church of Jesus Christ of Latter-day Saints, no cc.

"Plan of Salvation." Salt Lake City: The Church of Jesus Christ of Latter-day Saints, 1983.

Rich, Ben E. "A Friendly Discussion." Salt Lake City, Utah:Missions of the Church of Jesus Christ of Latter-day Saints, no cc.

"The Family Registry." Salt Lake City: The Church of Jesus Christ of Latter-day Saints, 1983.

"The Historic Grandin Building." Salt Lake City: The Church of Jesus Christ of Latter-day Saints, 1983.

"The Prophet Joseph Smith's Testimony." Salt Lake City: The Church of Jesus Christ of Latter-day Saints, 1984.

"The Purpose of Life." Salt Lake City: The Church of Jesus Christ of Latter-day Saints, 1983.

"The Purpose of the Temple." Salt Lake City: The Church of Jesus Christ of Latter-day Saints, 1980.

"The Traveler's Guide to Mormon Points of Interest." Salt Lake City: The Church of Jesus Christ of Latter-day Saints, 1981.

"30 Minutes for Your Family." Salt Lake City: The Church of Jesus Christ of Latter-day Saints, 1976.

"Welcome to Historic Mormon Country." Rochester: The Church of Jesus Christ of Latter-day Saints.

"Why Genealogy?" Salt Lake City: The Church of Jesus Christ of Latter-day Saints, 1982.

"Witnesses to the Book of Mormon." Salt Lake City: The Church of Jesus Christ of Latter-day Saints, 1977.

PRIMARY NON-MORMON SOURCES

Adair, James R. and Ted Miller, ed. *We Found Our Way.* Grand Rapids: Baker Book House, 1974. pp. 11-18.

Adams, Quincy. *The Birth of Mormonism*. Boston: The Gotham Press, 1916.

Adamson, Jack and Reed C. Durham, Jr. *No Help For The Widow's Son*. Nauvoo, Illinois: Martin Publishing Company, 1980.

Ahmanson, John. *Secret History*. Translated by Gleason Archer.Chicago: Moody Press, 1984.

Anderson, Einar. *History and Beliefs of Mormonism*. Grand Rapids, Michigan: Kregel Publications, 1981.

_____. *I Was A Mormon*. Grand Rapids, Michigan: Zondervan Publishing House, 1964.

Ankerberg, John and John Weldon. *The Facts On The Mormon Church*. Eugene, Oregon: Harvest House Publishers, 1991.

Arbaugh, George Bartholomew. *Revelation In Mormonism Its Character and Changing Form*. Chicago, Illinois: University of Chicago Press, 1932.

Bales, James D. *Apostles or Apostates*. Concord, California: Pacific Publishing Company, 1976.

Bankcroft, Hubert H. *History of Utah*. San Francisco, California: The History Company, Publishers, 1890.

Barnett, Maurice. *Mormonism Against Itself* 2 vols. Cullman, Alabama: Printing Service, 1980.

Baskin, R.N. *Reminiscences of Early Utah*. Salt Lake City: Baskin Publisher, 1914.

Beadle, J.H. *Mysteries and Crimes of Mormonism*. Cincinnati, Ohio: National Publishing Company., 1904.

Beardsley, Harry M. *Joseph Smith And His Mormon Empire*. Boston, Massachusetts: Houghton Mifflin Company, 1931.

Bennett, John C. *The History of the Saints; or, an Exposé of Joe Smith and Mormonism*. Boston: Leland & Whiting Publishing Company, 1842.

Benson, Jerry and Dianna. *How To Witness To A Mormon*. Chicago: Moody Press, 1986.

Berry, Harold J. *Examining the Cults*. Lincoln: Back to the Bible, 1979.

Birney, Hoffman. *Zealots of Zion*. Philadelphia: The Penn Publishing Company, 1931.

Bjornstad, James. *Counterfeits at Your Door*. Ventura: Regal Books, 1975.

Branch, Rick comp., *How Shaky A Foundation*. Arlington, Texas: Watchman Fellowship, no cc.

Briggs, Michael. *An Index To Mormonism - Shadow or Reality?* Salt Lake City, Utah: Utah Lighthouse Ministry 1984.

Burton, Sir Richard F. *The City Of The Saints And Across The Rocky Mountains To California*. Niwot, Colorado: University Press of Colorado, 1990.

By The Wife Of A Mormon Elder. *Female Life Among The Mormons A Narrative Of Many Years' Personal Experience*. Cincinnati: Derby & Jackson, 1856.

Call, Lamoni. *2000 Changes In The Book Of Mormon*. Bountiful, Utah: Published by the Author, 1898.

Cannon, Frank J. *Under The Prophet in Utah*. New York: Harper and Brothers, Publishers, 1854.

Carlton, J.H. *Special Report Of The Mountain Meadows Massacre*. Washington: Government Printing Office, 1902.

Clapp, Rodney. "Fighting Mormonism in Utah". *Christianity Today*. July, 1982, 30-48.

Clark, John A. *Gleanings By The Way*. Philadelphia: W.J. & J.K. Simon, 1842.

Coates, James. *In Mormon Circles*. New York: Addison-Wesley Publishing Company, 1991.

Coe, Jolene and Greg Cole. *The Mormon Experience*. Eugene: Harvest House Publishers, 1985.

Cowan, Marvin W. *Mormon Claims Answered*. Salt Lake City, Utah: Utah Christian Publications, 1989.

Davis, Howard A., Donald Scales, and Wayne L. Cowdery with Gretchen Passantino. *Who Really Wrote The Book ofMormon?*. Santa Ana, California: Vision House Publishers, 1980.

Doyle, Sir Arthur Conan. *A Study in Scarlet*. Penguin Books, New York, 1987.

Duncan, Malcolm C. *Duncan's Masonic Ritual and Monitor Or Guide to Three Symbolic Masonic Degrees Of The Ancient York Rite And To The Degrees of Mark Master,*

Past Master, Most Excellent Master, And The Royal Arch by Malcolm C. Duncan Explained And Interpreted By Copious Notes And Numerous Engravings. New York: David McKay Co., Inc., no cc.

Farkas, John R. *Does The Mormon Church Attack Orthodox Christianity?*. St. Louis, Missouri: Personal Freedom Outreach, 1988.

Ferris, Benjamin G. *Utah and the Mormons*. New York: Harper and Brothers, Publishers, 1854.

Finney, Charles Garrison. *Memoirs of Rev. Charles G. Finney*. New York: Fleming H. Revell Co., 1903.

Ford, Thomas. *A History of Illinois, From Its Commencement As a State In 1818 To 1847*. Chicago: S.C. Griggs & Company, 1854.

Fraser, Gordon H. *Is Mormonism Christian?*. Chicago: Moody Press, 1977.

_____. *Joseph and the Golden Plates -- A Close Look at The Book of Mormon*. Gordon H. Fraser Publisher, 1978.

_____. *Sects of the Church of the Latter-day Saints*. Eugene: Industrial Litho, Inc., 1978.

Froiseth, Jennie Anderson, ed. *The Women Of Mormonism Or The Story Of Polygamy As Told by the Victims Themselves*. Detroit, Michigan: C.G.G. Paine Company, 1882.

Gatewood, Otis and Kenneth E. Farnsworth. *Gatewood Farnsworth Debate on "Mormonism"*. Abilene, Texas: Published by Otis Gatewood, 1942.

Geer, Thelma. *Mormonism, Mama and Me.* Tucson: Calvary Missionary Press, 1984.

Gerstner, John H. *The Teachings of Mormonism.* Grand Rapids, Michigan: Baker Book House, 1987.

Gibbs, Josiah F. *The Mountain Meadows Massacre.* Salt Lake City, Utah: Salt Lake City Tribune Publishing Company, 1910.

Green, Nelson Winch. *Fifteen Years Among the Mormons: Being The Narrative Of Mrs. Mary Ettie V. Smith, Late Of Great Salt Lake City: A Sister Of One Of The Mormon High Priest She Having Been Personally Acquainted With Most Of The Mormon Leaders, And Long In The Confidence Of The "Prophet," Brigham Young.* New York: H. Dayton, Publisher, 1859.

Green, N.W. *Mormonism: Its Rise, Progress, And Present Condition.* Hartford: Belknak & Bliss, 1870.

Gregg, Thomas. *The Prophet of Palmyra.* New York: The John B. Alden, Publisher, 1890.

Gruss, Edmond C. *What Every Mormon Should Know.* Denver: Accent Books, 1975.

Gunnison, Lieut. J.W. *The Mormons, (A History of).* Philadelphia: J.B. Lippincott and Co., 1856.

Hall, Howard. *Tennessee Historical Quarterly.* Volume 17, Number 1. "Tennessee Mormon Massacre", Nashville: Tennessee Historical Society, March, 1958.

Heinerman, John and Anson Shupe. *The Mormon Corporate Empire.* Boston: Beacon Press, 1985.

Hickman, Bill. *Brigham's Destroying Angel: Being The Life Confession, and Startling Disclosures of the Notorious Bill Hickman, The Danite Chief of Utah.* Salt Lake City: Utah, Shepherd Publishing Company, 1904.

Holley, Vernal. *Book of Mormon Authorship: A Closer Look.* Roy, Utah: Vernal Holley, 1989.

Hougey, Hal. *Archeology and the Book of Mormon.* Concord, California: Pacific Publishing Company, 1980.

_____. *Latter-day Saints-Where Did You Get Your Authority?* Concord, California: Pacific Publishing Company, 1981.

Howe, E.D. *Mormonism Unveiled.* Painesville, Ohio: E.D. Howe Publisher, 1834.

Hyde, John Jr. *Mormonism: Its Leaders and Designs.* New York: W.P. Fetridge-N-Company, 1857.

Hymns. Salt Lake City: Deseret Book Co., 1972.

Joseph Smith's Egyptian Alphabet and Grammar. Salt Lake City, Utah: Utah Lighthouse Ministry.

Kennedy, J.H. *Early Days of Mormonism.* New York: Addison-Wesley Publishing Co., 1888.

Kidder, Daniel P. *Mormonism and the Mormons.* New York: Carlton and Lanahan, 1842.

Kinney, Bruce. *Mormonism: The Islam of America.* London and Edinburgh: Fleming H. Revell Co., 1912.

Lamb, M.T. *The Golden Bible; Or, The Book of Mormon. Is it From God?*. New York: Published by Ward & Drummond, 1887.

Larson, Charles M. *By His Own Hand Upon Papyrus: A New Look At The Joseph Smith Papyri*. Grand Rapids, Michigan: Institute for Religious Research, 1992.

Lewis, Alfred Henry. *The Mormon Menace*. New York: Home Protection Publishing Company, 1905.

Lindsey, Robert. *A Gathering of Saints*. New York: Dell Publishing Company, 1988.

Lyford, C.P. *The Mormon Problem*. New York: Phillips and Hunt, 1886.

Lynn, William A. *The Story Of The Mormons*. New York: Russell and Russell, Inc., 1963.

McElveen, Floyd C. *The Mormon Illusion*. Ventura, California: Regal Books, 1985.

_____. *From Mormon Illusion To God's Love*. Issaquah, Washington: Saints Alive In Jesus, no cc.

Marquardt, H. Michael. *The Book of Abraham Papyrus Found*. Salt Lake City, Utah: Utah Lighthouse Ministry, 1975.

_____. Marquardt, H. Michael. *The Book of Abraham Revisited*. Salt Lake City, Utah: Utah Lighthouse Ministry, 1982.

Mayhew, Henry. *The Mormons Or Latter-day Saints*. London, England: Office of the National Illustrated Library, 1858.

Mead, Frank. *Handbook of Denominations in the United States.* Nashville: Abingdon Press, 1975.

Morgan, William. *Illustrations Of Masonry By One Of The Fraternity Who has devoted Thirty Years to the Subject.* Chicago: Charles T. Powner, 1827.

No author. *Document Containing The Correspondence, Orders, & C. In Relation To The Disturbances With The Mormons; And The Evidence Given Before the Hon. Austin A. King, Judge Of The Fifth Judicial Circuit Of The State Of Missouri, At The Court-House In Richmond, In A Criminal Court Of Inquiry, Begun November 12, 1838, On The Trial of Joseph Smith, Jr., And Others, For High Treason And Other Crimes Against The State.* Fayette, Missouri: Boon's Lick Democrat, 1841.

No author. *History of Caldwell And Livingston Counties, Missouri, Written and Compiled From The Most Authentic Official And Private Sources, Including A History Of Their Townships, Towns and Villages, Together With A Condensed History of Missouri; A Reliable And Detailed History Of Sources, Biographical Sketches Of Prominent Citizens; General And Local Statistics Of Great Value; Incidents And Reminiscences.* St. Louis: National Historical Co., 1886.

O'Dea, Thomas F. *The Mormons.* Chicago: The University of Chicago Press, 1957.

Paddock, Mrs. A.G. *The Fate of Madame La Tour.* New York: Fords, Howard, and Hulbert, 1881.

Petersen, LaMar. *Hearts Made Glad: The Charges of Intemperance Against Joseph Smith the Mormon Prophet (and Folks that Dronken ben of Ale).* Salt Lake City, Utah: Printed by the Author, 1975.

_____. *Problems In Mormon Text.* Salt Lake City, Utah: Printed by the author, 1957.

Reed, David A. and John R. Farkas. *Mormons Answered Verse by Verse.* Grand Rapids, Michigan: Baker Book House, 1992.

Richardson, Jabez. *Richardson's Monitor Of Free-Masonry; Being A Practical Guide To The Ceremonies In All The Degrees Conferred In Masonic Lodges, Chapters, Encampments, &c. Explaining The Signs, Tokens And Grips, And Giving All The Words, Pass-Words, Sacred Words, Oaths, Hieroglyphics Used By Masons.* New York: Published by Lawrence Fitzgerald, no cc.

Riley, I. Woodbridge. *The Founder Of Mormonism A Psychological Study of Joseph Smith, Jr.* New York:Dodd, Mead, & Company, 1902.

Ropp, Harry L. *The Mormon Papers -- Are the Mormon Scriptures Reliable?.* Downers Grove: InterVarsity Press, 1977.

Sackett, Charles. *What's Going On In There?.* Thousand Oaks, California: Sword of the Shepherd Ministries, 1982.

Senate Document 189. Richmond, Missouri: Senate of State of Missouri, 1841.

Sheldon, Henry C. *A Forefold Test of Mormonism.* New York: The Abingdon Press, 1914.

Shoemaker, Donald P. "Why Your Neighbor Joined the Mormon Church". *Christianity Today*. October 11, 1974.

Shook, Charles A. *Cumorah Revisited*. Cincinnati: Standard Publishing Company, 1910.

_____. *The True Origin of Mormon Polygamy*. Cincinnati: The Standard Publishing Company, 1914.

_____. *The True Origin of the Book of Mormon*. Cincinnati, Ohio: The Standard Publishing Company, 1914.

Shupe, Anson D. *The Darker Side of Virtue*. Buffalo, New York: Prometheus Books, 1991.

Smith, Ethan. *View Of The Hebrews; or the Tribes Of Israel In America*. Poultney, Vermont: Smith and Smith Publishers, 1835.

Smith, John L. *Hope or Despair?*. Marlow, Oklahoma: Utah Missions Inc., 1959.

_____. *Witnessing Effectively to Mormons*. Marlow, Oklahoma: Utah Missions Inc., 1975.

Smucker, Samuel M. *Life Among The Mormons, Or The Religious, Social, And Political History Of The Mormons, From Their Origin To The Present Time; Containing Full Statements Of Their Doctrines, Government and Condition, And Memoirs Of Their Founder, Joseph Smith*. New York: Hurst and Company, Publishers, 1884.

Snowden, James H. *The Truth About Mormonism*. New York: George H. Doran Company, 1926.

Spencer, James R. *Beyond Mormonism*. Old Tappan: Chosen Books, 1984.

_____. *Have You Witnessed to a Mormon Lately?*. Old Tappan: Chosen Books, 1986.

Stansbury, Howard. *Exploration And Survey Of The Valley Of The Great Salt Lake of Utah, Including A Reconnaissance Of A New Route Through The Rocky Mountains.* Washington: Robert Armstrong Public Printer, 1853.

Stegner, Wallace. *The Gathering Of Zion The Story of the Mormon Trail.* New York: McGraw-Hill Book Company, 1964.

Stenhouse, T.B.H. *The Rocky Mountain Saints: A Full And Complete History Of The Mormons, From The First Vision Of Joseph Smith To The Last Courtship of Brigham Young; Including The Story Of The Hand Cart Emigration-The Mormon War-The Mountain-Meadows Massacre -The Reign Of Terror In Utah-The Doctrine Of Human Sacrifice-The Political, Domestic, Social, And Theological Influences Of The Saints-The Facts Of Polygamy-The Colonization Of The Rocky Mountains, And The Development Of The Great Mineral Wealth Of The Territory Of Utah.* New York: D. Appleton and Company, 1873.

Stenhouse, Mrs. T.B.H. *Tell It All.* Hartford: A.D. Worthingston and Company, 1974.

Swartzell, William. *Mormonism Exposed, Being A Journal of AResidence In Missouri from the 28th of May to the 20th of August, 1838.* Perkin, Ohio: Published by the Author, 1840.

Tanner, Jerald. "Problems In Winning Mormons", Salt Lake City, Utah: Utah Lighthouse Ministry. (tape)

_____. "Salt Lake City Messenger". Volumes. 58-63. Salt Lake City, Utah: Utah Lighthouse Ministry Publication, 1985-87.

Tanner, Jerald and Sandra. *Changes in Joseph Smith's History.* Salt Lake City, Utah: Utah Lighthouse Ministry, no cc.

_____. *Changes in the Key to Theology.* Salt Lake City, Utah: Utah Lighthouse Ministry, 1855.

_____. *Clayton's Secret Writings Uncovered.* Salt Lake City, Utah: Utah Lighthouse Ministry, no cc.

_____. *Evolution of the Mormon Temple Ceremony: 1842-1990.* Salt Lake City, Utah: Utah Lighthouse Ministry, 1990.

_____. *Falsification of Joseph Smith's History.* Salt Lake City, Utah: Utah Lighthouse Ministry, 1971.

_____. *Ferguson's Manuscript Unveiled.* Salt Lake City, Utah: Utah Lighthouse Ministry, 1988.

_____. *LDS Apostle Confesses Brigham Young Taught Adam-God Doctrine.* Salt Lake City, Utah: Utah Lighthouse Ministry, 1982.

_____. *Mormonism, Magic and Masonry.* Salt Lake City, Utah: Utah Lighthouse Ministry, 1988.

_____. *Mormonism -- Shadow or Reality?.* Salt Lake City, Utah: Utah Lighthouse Ministry, 1982.

_____. *The Lucifer-God Doctrine*. Salt Lake City, Utah: Utah Lighthouse Ministry, no cc.

_____. *3,913 Changes in The Book of Mormon*. Salt Lake City, Utah: Utah Lighthouse Ministry.

_____. *Unmasking A Mormon Spy*. Salt Lake City, Utah: Utah Lighthouse Ministry, 1980.

Tanner, Sandra. *The Bible and Mormon Doctrine*. Salt Lake City, Utah: Utah Lighthouse Ministry, 1986.

Taylor, Samuel W. *Rocky Mountain Empire The Latter-day Saints Today*. New York: Macmillan Publishing Company, Inc., 1978.

Thacker, James, ed. *Mormonism versus the Bible*. Great Bend: Golden Belt Printing, 1984.

The Reed Peck Manuscript. Salt Lake City, Utah: Utah Lighthouse Ministry.

Tingle, Donald S. *Mormonism*. Downers Grove, Illinois: InterVarsity Press, 1987.

Tope, Wallace W. *On the Frontlines: Practical Help for Witnessing to Mormons*. La Canada Flintridge: Wallace W.Tope, 1980.

Tucker, Pomeroy. *Origin, Rise, And Progress of Mormonism*. New York: D. Appleton And Company, 1867.

Turner, Wallace. *The Mormon Establishment*. Boston, Massachusetts: Houghton Mifflin Company, 1966.

Twain, Mark. *Roughing It*. Hartford, Connecticut: American Publishing Company, 1872.

Vellinga, M.C. *Mormon Mysteries Revealed*. Los Angeles: West Coast Publishing Comany, 1927.

Waite, Mrs. C.V. *The Mormon Prophet And His Harem; Or An Authentic History Of Brigham Young, His Numerous Wives And Children*. Cambridge, Massachusetts: Riverside Press, 1867.

Walker, James K. *Witnessing with the Book of Mormon*. Arlington, Texas: Watchman Fellowship, no cc.

Walker, John Phillip, ed. *Dale Morgan on Early Mormonism*. Salt Lake City, Utah: Signature Books, 1986.

Wallace, Irving. *The Twenty-Seventh Wife*. New York: Simon and Schuster, 1961.

Walters, Wesley P., ed. *An Examination of B.H. Roberts' Secret Manuscript*. Bainbridge, no cc.

_____. *Joseph Smith Among The Egyptians*. Salt Lake City, Utah: Utah Lighthouse Ministry, 1973.

_____. *Joseph Smith's Bainbridge, N.Y., Court Trials*. Salt Lake City, Utah: Utah Lighthouse Ministry, 1977.

_____. *New Light On Mormon Origins From The Palmyra (N.Y.) Revival*. La Mesa, California: Utah Christian Tract Society, 1967.

_____. *The Use of the Old Testament in the Book of Mormon*. Salt Lake City, Utah: Utah Lighthouse Ministry, 1990.

Ward, Austin N. *Male Life Among the Mormons*. New York: Derby & Jackson, 1859.

Ward, Mrs. Austin N. *Female Life Among The Mormons*. New York: Derby and Jackson, 1856.

Werner, M.R. *Brigham Young*. New York: Harcourt, Brace and Company, 1925.

Whalen, William J. *The Latter-day Saints in the Modern Day World An Account of Contemporary Mormonism*. New York: The John Day Company, 1964.

Whitmer, David. *An Address to All Believers in Christ*. Richmond, Missouri, 1887.

Winn, William Alexander. *The Story Of The Mormons: From the Date of their Origin to the Year 1901*. New York: Russell & Russell, Inc., 1963.

Wise, William. *Massacre at Mountain Meadows An American Legend and a Monumental Crime*. New York: Thomas Y. Crowell Company, 1976.

Witte, Bob & Gordon H. Fraser. *What's Going On In Here?* Eugene, Oregon: Gordon Fraser Publishing, 1980.

_____. comp., *Where Does It Say That?*. Grand Rapids, Michigan: Gospel Truths, no cc.

Wyl, William. *Mormon Portraits Or The Truth About The Mormon Leaders From 1830 To 1886*. Salt Lake City, Utah: Salt Lake City Tribune Printing And Publishing Co., 1886.

Young, Kimball. *Isn't One Wife Enough? The Story of Mormon Polygamy*. New York: Henry Holt and Company, 1954.

NON-MORMON PAMPHLETS

"Here They Come.....30,000 of Them." Issaquah: Saints Alive in Jesus.

"I Bear You My Witness." Garland: American Tract Society, 1985.

"I Was a Mormon." Grand Rapids: Grace Mission, Inc.

"Mormonism." Oradell: American Tract Society.

"Mormonism: Christian or Cult?" Issaquah: Saints Alive in Jesus.

"Mormons -- Belief Bulletin." Atlanta: North American Mission Board, Southern Baptist Convention, 1983.

"My Defense Before the Mormon Court." Grand Rapids: Grace Ministries International, Inc.

"My Experience in Mormonism." Grand Rapids: Grace Publications, Inc.

"My Testimony of the Gospel of the Grace of God." Phoenix: The American Desert Mission, 1944.

"Ten Reasons Why I Cannot Be a Mormon (Latter-day Saint)." Great Bend: Golden Belt Printing, Inc.

"The Pearl of Great Price." Issaquah: Saints Alive in Jesus.

"The Testimony of a Convert from Mormonism." La Mesa: Utah Christian Tract Society.

"The Testimony of Three Witnesses." Issaquah: Saints Alive in Jesus.

"Three Reasons Not to Become a Mormon." Alta Loma: Religious Research Center.

"True Archeological Data versus Book of Mormon." La Mesa: Utah Christian Tract Society.

"Was the Virgin Mary Really a Virgin?" The Mormon Church Says No!. Issaquah: Saints Alive in Jesus.

"Who's That Knocking at Your Door?." Issaquah: Saints Alive in Jesus.

"Who Is This Man....Why Did He Have 19 Wives and 64 Children?." Tucson: Calvary Missionary Press.

INDEX

B Babbitt, Almon W., 12, 31, 43, 45, 215, 216, 227

Bainbridge, (New York), 234, 289

baptism, 22, 23, 27, 53, 59, 76, 77, 129, 130, 134, 147, 148, 149, 151, 154, 161, 178, 180, 209, 210, 214, 217

baptismal regeneration, 59, 130, 148

baptism for the dead, 77, 134, 151, 157, 210, 214, 217

Baptists, 21, 22, 50, 55, 70, 95, 103, 291

Bateman, William, 112

Beaver Island, (Michigan), 96, 97

beehive symbol, 115, 154

Bennett, Dr. John C., 78, 79, 82, 96, 155, 217, 255, 277

Benson, Ezra Taft, 115, 180, 182, 248, 260, 261

Bidamon, Major L.C., Emma's second husband, 13

bishop, 56, 67, 120, 150, 210, 214

Bitton, David, 23, 170, 223, 229, 244, 255, 256, 257, 265

Black, Justice Adam, 70

black race, 134, 175, 176, 177, 178, 179, 204, 212, 259

blessing, patriarchal, 177, 178

blood atonement, 109, 158, 159, 175

Bogart, Captain Samuel, 71

Boggs, Lilburn, Governor of Missouri, 71

Book of Abraham, 139, 140, 141, 142, 144, 173, 177, 179, 204, 217, 251, 282

Book of Commandments, 62, 133, 135, 136, 167, 172, 216, 219, 258

Book of Mormon, 6, 9, 12, 14, 15, 16, 19, 20, 39, 42, 44, 50, 52, 53, 54, 55, 58, 59, 61, 69, 78, 83, 93, 98, 110, 120, 122, 123, 124, 125, 126, 127, 128, 129, 130, 131, 134, 136, 137, 138, 139, 140, 141, 143, 144, 145, 146, 147, 150, 153, 154, 155, 160, 165, 172, 173, 177, 179, 180, 183, 186, 187, 192, 193, 194, 199, 200, 201, 202, 203, 204, 205, 206, 216, 219, 225, 228, 229, 234, 240, 248, 249, 250, 252, 266, 269, 270, 272, 273, 275, 278, 279, 281, 282, 285, 288, 289, 292

Book of the Law of the Lord, The, 96

Booth, Ezra, 59

Boudinot, Elias, 127
Boynton, John F., 31, 63
breastplate, 45, 46
Brodie, Fawn, M., 19, 124, 225, 226, 228, 233, 241, 243, 249, 256, 259, 266
Bullard, Isaac, 7
Bullock, Thomas, 167
Bushman, Richard L., 28, 230, 266
Butterfield, Josiah, 18

Ccaldwell County, (Missouri), 25, 67, 71
Calhoun, John C., 81
Campbell, Alexander, 16, 21, 22, 23, 55, 59, 93, 165, 228, 229
Campbellite movement, 21, 23, 165
Cannon, George Q., 107
Carlin, Governor Thomas, (Illinois), 75, 82
Carleton, Major J.H., 114, 246
Carthage Greys, 89
Carthage Jail, (Illinois), 32, 88, 89, 95, 154, 167, 175, 220
celestial glory, 149, 186
celestial marriage, 77, 109, 211
celibacy, 9
Chamberlain, Judge Joseph, 12
Chambers, Samuel D., 177, 259
Champollion, Jean Francis, 141
Chandler, Michael H., 19, 140, 216
Chase, Willard, 42, 43
Church of Christ, Smith's first church, 32m 53m 62m 69, 94, 165, 166, 167, 216
Church of Christ (Temple Lot), 98
Church of Jesus Christ of Latter-day Saints(LDS), 23, 28, 94, 117, 160, 166, 167, 195

Church of Jesus Christ of Latter-Day Saints (RLDS),83,120,125,

128,228

Clark, General John B., 71, 124

Clay County, (Missouri), 67

Clay, Henry, 81

Clayton, William, secretary to Smith, 77, 170

coffee, (*Word of Wisdom*), 9, 30, 31, 33, 214

cola, (*Word of Wisdom*), 9

Commerce, (Illinois), 75, 76, 217

communal living, 9, 22, 55, 93

Corrill, John, 57, 72, 109, 159

Council Bluff, Iowa, 103, 104, 218

Council of Fifty, 29, 102, 121

Council of Seventy, 120, 201

Counselors, 120, 211

Cowdery, Oliver, 16, 28, 39, 52, 53, 56, 62, 126, 168

    accuses Smith of adultery, 106

    baptizes Joseph Smith, 27

    baptized by Joseph Smith, 27

    charged by council, 68

    chosen by John the Baptist, 27

    claimed revelatory powers, 120

    conflict with Smith, 28, 55

    leaves church, 69, 166

    moves to New York, 124

    revelation concerning, 134

    secretary to Smith, 215

    sent on mission to Indians, 55, 64

    sent to Canada for copyright, 20

    sent to Philadelphia for plates, 63

Cradlebaugh, Judge John, 113

Crawford, Charles, 126

Cumorah, hill of, 45, 122, 131

D danites, (Destroying Angels), 70, 71, 109, 217

  Daughters of Zion (Danites), 109

Daviess County, (Missouri), 68, 70
deacon, 121, 177, 210
Deming, Minor, 101
Deseret News, 168
"divining rod", 14
doctrine of God, 165, 172, 173, 199
doctrine of heaven, 24, 159, 160, 214
doctrine of hell, 149, 153, 211
doctrine of the Holy Ghost, 27, 138, 145, 146, 147, 149, 172,
    199, 205, 211
doctrine of Jesus Christ, 23, 172, 173, 186, 201, 212
doctrine of salvation, 1, 23, 28, 77, 80, 148, 149, 157, 160, 185,
    186, 209, 211
Douglas, Stephen A., 169, 170
dreams, 4, 5, 10, 19, 81, 154
Durham, Reed, 13, 154

E edmunds bill, 107, 218
Edmunds-Tucker Act, 107
    Edwards, Jonathan, 127
Egyptian hieroglyphics, 51, 141, 154, 166
eight witnesses, 6
elder, 20, 27, 31, 53, 59, 83, 95, 107, 115, 120, 121, 135, 149,
    166, 193
endowments, 80, 102, 115, 149, 150, 156, 157, 178, 179, 180,
    181, 182, 186, 188, 195, 196, 214,
Elder's Journal, 62, 161, 220
Ensign of Liberty, The, 80, 98
Evening and Morning Star, 66, 133, 176, 220
Exaltation (godhood), 138, 148, 153, 178, 211

F Fancher Wagon Train, (Mountain Meadows Massacre), 111,
    112
Far West, Missouri, 25, 31, 63, 67, 68, 70, 71, 72, 98, 109, 157,

JJack-Mormon, 196
Jackson County, Missouri, 64, 65, 66
Jaredites, 130, 212
Jennings, Colonel William O., 72
Jessee, Dean C., 168
Jesus Christ, polygamist, 106, 201
John the Baptist,27, 39, 52, 215
Johnson, John, 31, 59
Johnson, Luke, 63

KKelly brothers, 32, 33
Kimball, Heber C., 14, 61, 154
    Kimball, Spencer W., 13, 134, 146, 179
Kinderhook plates, 83
King Follett funeral sermon, 145, 173, 200
King James Version, 58, 122, 128, 204
Kirtland, Ohio, 6, 8, 10, 22, 30, 31, 32, 54, 55, 56, 57, 59, 60, 61,
        62, 63, 64, 65, 67, 68, 69, 80, 98, 123, 133, 134, 139,
        140, 141, 156, 178, 214, 216, 220
Kirtland Safety Society Bank, 63, 166, 216, 217
Kirtland Temple, 8, 180, 216, 219
Knight, Joseph, Sr., 134
Kolob, planet near throne of God, 144

LLamanites, (American Indians), 55, 130, 131
Lane, Reverend George, 39
    Law, William, 85, 98, 175, 217, 220
"Lectures on Faith", 24, 135, 219
Lee, Ann, 7
Lee, John D., 70, 109, 112, 113
Lehi, Book of Mormon character, 17, 130, 131
Liberty, Missouri, 72, 136
liquor, 9, 31, 54
Lost Tribes, 15, 125, 127

Lucifer, 146, 147, 186, 201

M Mack, John, great-grandfather of Joseph Smith, 4
Mack, Solomon, grandfather of Joseph Smith, 3, 4
Mahoning Baptist Association, 22, 55
Maid of Iowa, Mormon steamboat, 17
Manchester, New York, 3, 5, 53
Manifesto, 66, 108, 176
Manuscript Found, 122, 123, 124, 126
Manuscript Story, 123, 124
Marquardt, H. Michael, 53
Marsh, Thomas B., 70, 72, 134
Marshall, Elihu F., 52, 86
Masonry, 13, 115, 153, 155, 156, 170, 180, 181, 182, 217
Matheny, Raymond T., 129
Mather, Cotton, 127
McBride, Thomas, 72
McConkie, Bruce R., 143, 144, 146, 158, 160, 177, 201
McKay, David O., 38
McLellin, William E., 80, 81, 98
Melchizedek priesthood, 24, 28, 39, 52, 95, 121, 147, 158, 178, 180, 210
Mentor Baptist Church, 22, 55
Messenger and Advocate, 173, 220
Messenger and Advocate of the Church of Christ (Rigdon), 94
Methodist, 5, 12, 21, 39, 40, 43, 59, 61, 81
Metropolitan Museum of Art, (New York), 141
migration to Utah, 12, 218
millennialism, 30, 55
Millennial Star, 145, 168, 220
Miller, William, 10
money-digging, 12, 32, 43
Morgan, Dale, 5
Morgan, William, 153, 154
Moroni, the angel, 44, 46, 131, 215

Mountain Meadows Massacre, 111, 114, 218
Mother in heaven, 144, 201
mummies sold to Joseph Smith, 140, 141
Murray, Eli, 107

N Nauvoo, Illinois, 6, 14, 17, 25, 31, 35, 67, 69, 70, 76, 77, 79, 81, 82, 85, 86, 87, 88, 89, 90, 91, 94, 95, 96, 97, 99, 102, 103, 109, 119, 120, 134, 137, 140, 146, 153, 155, 156, 167, 169, 170, 175, 178, 180, 181, 217, 220
Nauvoo Expositor, 86, 175, 217, 220
Nauvoo Legion, 19, 79, 86, 87, 88, 155
Nauvoo Neighbor, 101, 220
Neely, Albert, 12
Nephi, *Book of Mormon* character, 45, 46, 130
Nephites, 15, 129, 131, 206
New Jerusalem, 10, 20

O occult, 11, 12, 13, 14, 19, 30, 33, 43, 44
organization of church, 6, 28, 93

P Page, Hiram, 14, 20, 55, 202
Page, John, 96
papyri, Egyptian, 19, 140, 141, 142, 216
Paine, Tom, 7
Painesville Telegraph, (Ohio), 51, 123
Palmyra, New York, 3, 4, 5, 6, 7, 8, 10, 11, 16, 21, 32, 37, 38, 39, 40, 41, 43, 49, 50, 52, 122, 153, 215, 216, 219
Parrish, Warren, 62, 64, 166
Partridge, Edward, 56, 67, 133, 134
Patriarch, Office of, 6, 31, 97, 121, 122, 155
Patten, David W., prophecy of, 71, 202
Patterson, Robert, 122, 123, 124

Pearl of Great Price, The, 46, 59, 122, 139, 140, 141, 143, 144, 150, 172, 179, 194, 203, 204, 216, 219

Pearsall, Emily, 12

Peck, Reed, 159

Penn, William, 127

Peterson, Ziba, 55

Phelps, W.W., 8, 66, 72, 133, 134, 154, 176

pillar of fire, 38

plates, golden, 6, 13, 14, 19, 24, 44, 45, 46, 49, 50, 52, 131, 154, 155

plurality of gods, 42, 133, 144, 145

polygamy, (plural marriages), 6, 24, 29, 69, 77, 78, 79, 80, 85, 86, 95, 96, 98, 106, 107, 108, 121, 134, 135, 139, 158, 167, 175, 176, 196, 201, 202, 212, 217, 218

polytheism, 173, 200

Pratt, Orson, 20, 97, 106, 134, 183, 201, 206

Pratt, Parley Parker, 23

prevarication, 4, 49

Priest, Josiah, 127

priesthood, 23, 24, 27, 28, 39, 52, 95, 115, 121, 134, 147, 150, 151, 153, 156, 158, 177, 178, 179, 180, 203, 204, 209, 210, 211, 212, 213, 216

prophecy, 53, 54, 55, 58, 120, 137, 140, 170, 171, 202, 206, 207

Prophet/President, 120

Purple, W.D., 12

Q Quincy, Illinois, 14, 72, 75
Quincy, Josiah, 140

R *Reflector, The Palmyra*, 10, 11
reform, 42, 86, 93, 196

Reformed Egyptian, 50

Reorganized Church of Jesus Christ of Latter-Day Saints, (RLDS), 28, 32, 58, 78, 79, 98, 137, 167, 213

Robinson, George W., 168
Rockwell, Orrin Porter, 31, 70, 86, 109
Royalton, Vermont, 5
Ryder, Simonds, 59, 60

S *Saints' Herald*, 31
Salt Lake City, Utah, 81, 95, 104, 105, 106, 112, 134, 150,
    167, 178, 182, 189, 210, 218
Scott, Walter, 21, 22
sea gulls, 104, 105, 218
sealings, 180
second vision, 42, 45
secret/sacred temple rituals, 175, 181
seer stone, 11, 12, 13, 14, 43, 50, 55, 123, 137
Seventh Day Adventists, 9
Shakers, 7, 8, 9
Sharon, Vermont, 3, 215
Sharp, Thomas C., 85
Shook, Charles A., 123
Shumway, Charles, 102
Smith, Asahel, grandfather of Joseph Smith, 3
Smith, Don Carlos, brother of Joseph Smith, 5, 6, 69, 76
Smith, Emma Hale, wife of Joseph Smith, 13, 31, 43, 44, 49, 50,
    55, 58, 59, 77, 80, 86, 87, 91, 94, 140, 215
Smith, Ethan, author of *View of the Hebrews*, 16, 122, 124, 125,
    126
Smith, George Albert, cousin to Joseph Smith, 94, 103, 167
Smith, George D., 77
Smith, Hyrum, brother of Joseph Smith, 5, 6, 23, 25, 77, 86, 88,
    90, 91, 101, 122, 134, 153, 155, 176, 181, 217
Smith, Jason, 9
Smith, Joseph Fielding, son of Hyrum, sixth president of LDS
    Church, 1, 38, 127, 134, 144, 148, 149, 186, 187, 188
Smith, Joseph, Jr.

Y